RADIO

**Recent Titles in
American Popular Culture**

RADIO

A REFERENCE GUIDE

THOMAS ALLEN GREENFIELD

AMERICAN POPULAR CULTURE
Series Editor: M. Thomas Inge

Greenwood Press

New York • Westport, Connecticut • London

Library of Congress Cataloging-in-Publication Data

Greenfield, Thomas Allen, 1948-
 Radio : a reference guide / Thomas Allen Greenfield.
  p.   cm.—(American popular culture, ISSN 0193-6859)
 Bibliography: p.
 Includes index.
 ISBN 0-313-22276-2 (lib. bdg. : alk. paper)
 1. Radio broadcasting—United States—Bibliography. I. Title.
II. Series.
Z7224.U6G74   1989
[PN1991.3.U6)
016.38454—dc19   88-24647

British Library Cataloguing in Publication Data is available.

Library of Congress Catalog Card Number: 88-24647
ISBN: 0-313-22276-2
ISSN: 0193-6859

First published in 1989

Greenwood Press, Inc.
88 Post Road West, Westport, Connecticut 06881

Printed in the United States of America

The paper used in this book complies with the
Permanent Paper Standard issued by the National
Information Standards Organization (Z39.48-1984).

10 9 8 7 6 5 4 3 2 1

To my parents,
Ellis and Harriet Greenfield

CONTENTS

ACKNOWLEDGMENTS

I am grateful for the tireless efforts, endless patience, and generous encouragement of Dr. Thomas Inge, the general editor of the series in which this volume
appears. His support and kindness are matched by those of the editors at
Greenwood Press, particularly Cynthia Harris.

I owe a special debt to my friend and colleague Dr. Nicholas Sharp of Virginia
Commonwealth University, who introduced me both to the field of radio and to
this particular project. His historical perspective on the radio field was
invaluable to the overall shaping of the manuscript. His influence is most clearly
evident in the chapters on the historical background and on networks and
stations. I, of course, assume full responsibility for their content.

My research efforts were aided immeasurably by several people. Catharine
Heinz and the staff at the Broadcast Pioneers Library in Washington, D.C.,
were an extraordinary source of assistance and encouragement throughout the
years in which the research was performed. I share with others in the field the
sentiment that working with BPL is one of the genuine pleasures of doing
research in broadcasting.

No less helpful and patient was the staff of the Bellarmine College library,
especially its two superior resource sleuths, Rosalind Parnes and Marquita Breit.
Without their prompt and efficient negotiation of countless interlibrary loan
transactions, the cost and duration of my research could easily have doubled.
Susan Hill of the National Association of Broadcasters Library in Washington
was also helpful on several occasions, as were the staffs of the Library of
Congress and the Virginia State Library. Gloria Thomas of the Federal
Communications Commission provided invaluable assistance in the tricky
business of tracking down government documents.

Financial assistance for this research was provided by a Bellarmine College Summer Stipend, Bellarmine College faculty travel funds, and a Southern Research Education Board travel grant. I am very grateful for this invaluable support.

That a complete manuscript ever rises out of the ash heap of note cards, legal pads, and xeroxed pages is something of a miracle, usually performed by the magic of a superior typist and secretary. Patricia Allen of Bellarmine College has worked more than a few miracles on this manuscript as typist, proofreader, and interrogator.

I am especially grateful to my wife, Moine, for her loving support throughout the duration of this project and for taking the kids to McDonald's when I needed some evenings alone.

PREFACE

The purpose of this text is to provide the scholar or student of popular culture with an evaluative survey of available research materials in the field of radio. As a reference book for the study of popular culture, it focuses upon popular radio programming as its principal (but by no means only) area of concern. As a bibliographic study, the book follows the many paths laid down by the writers who have produced the several hundred sources cited within its pages: paths that have led to conventional works of scholarship, best-sellers and would-be best-sellers, fan literature and fan history, popular and scholarly articles, and sources that simply defy categorization.

The eclectic nature of the written material available on radio will come as no surprise to anyone familiar with the development of radio and radio programming. Unlike television, whose popular programming history is rooted in the New York-based corporations, radio owes much of its programming heritage to early garage experimenters and small local stations (often one-, two-, or three-person operations). Thus Schenectady, New York, becomes in the early 1920s a center of radio drama, a Detroit-based adman becomes the nation's leading creator of action serials, and country music is nurtured in Southern radio stations for half a century before it becomes a staple of nationwide programming. In that respect, the pioneer period of radio probably has a closer kinship with the early history of the personal computer than it does with the history of television, for beneath the highly visible mainstream initiatives of the corporate leaders there flowed a furious undercurrent of populist experimentation that often influenced and at times even confounded the giants of the industry. *Radio: A Reference Guide* attempts to provide recognition, if not to do justice, to both the mainstream and undercurrent literatures that make up the body of information available on radio.

All bibliographies are "selected" bibliographies, including those that cover a substantial amount of material, and this book is no exception. The preparation of this bibliographical study required the same kinds of choices that one would confront in the preparation of a selected bibliography for a book of criticism, a dissertation, or even an article. Decisions regarding how to organize the material, what to exclude, and what to emphasize do not diminish in number simply because one chooses to take on a large number of sources. If anything, the larger number of sources intensifies the need for selectivity.

Some of the bases for inclusion and exclusion were made early in the preparation of the manuscript. For the most part, college textbooks on broadcasting and communications are not included in what is principally a discussion of research sources (there are exceptions when such books contain material that is particularly distinctive or useful). The period between 1920 and 1940 saw the publication of dozens of "how-to" books on radio (how to write a radio play, how to break into the radio business, and so on); these books, along with similar books of more recent vintage, have also been largely excluded.

As noted throughout the book, the published material on many aspects of radio is often scant and scarce. As a result, frequent citations of doctoral dissertations are made. Although dissertations are maligned as research sources in some areas of study, in the radio field they often hold some of the best available information on certain subjects (such as the history and development of National Public Radio). Moreover, the fact that copies of dissertations can be obtained at reasonable prices through University Microfilms Incorporated of Ann Arbor, Michigan, and university libraries makes these highly valuable and generally underutilized sources of research information in radio easily accessible.

Decisions of inclusion and exclusion by type of material are simple in comparison to decisions of inclusion and exclusion by quality. Almost every resource cited in this work is viewed as having at least some value to the field of radio and popular culture. The material considered to be of no substantive value has been excluded so that the bibliographic lists at the end of each chapter can function effectively as suggested bibliographies. In general, harsher criticisms and faint praise are saved for two types of sources: works that pale in comparison to similar works cited in this book and relatively well known sources in the field that are overrated or at least overcited. (An example in this last category is Eric Sevareid's mid-life autobiography *Not So Wild a Dream,* a long-standing staple of broadcasting bibliographies. It is interesting reading, but just what it contributes to the knowledge of radio or broadcasting history escapes me.)

In addition to matters of selection of material, the issue of how the material would be organized and for whose purposes was also important to the fashioning of this guide. It is assumed that this book, like any reference book, is not likely to be read cover to cover for anything other than reviewing purposes. Users will be looking for familiar categories and topics. As a result, except in the opening historical overview, chapter and section headings are generally conventional rather than innovative (music, sports, drama, and so on). These are very common areas of research in popular culture, both within and beyond the circle of broadcasting interests, and are designed to reflect subject matters of interest to a large number of researchers.

Readers should note that works discussed in the chapter essays appear with full citations in the appended chapter bibliographies. A list of published and unpublished radio station histories is included as an appendix to chapter 1.

It is anticipated that the book will also be useful to researchers who do not have a specific interest in radio history per se but may have an interest in the content field of individual chapters, such as music or news. Since these readers may wish to consult only one or two chapters of the book, key reference works have repeat citations on a very limited basis (such as Erik Barnouw's pivotal three-volume *History of Broadcasting in the United States*) in more than one chapter when it was believed that their centrality warranted multiple citations. There are only a few works whose quality and scope merit this treatment, but the reader consulting only one or two chapters may appreciate not having to hunt through other chapters for the first and solitary citation of an indispensable source.

Finally, a conscious effort has been made to distinguish between material that is specific to radio and material that is relevant to broadcasting, giving clear preference to the former. The giant shadow that television cast over radio in the 1940s and 1950s had its parallel in the production of copy on radio. One of the sobering lessons I was to learn in the preparation of this book is that sources on broadcasting written after 1950 tend to focus upon television at the considerable expense of radio. I chose to include here broadcasting sources that showed at least a reasonable balance in their treatment of the two media. This occurred far less frequently than I might have wished.

RADIO

INTRODUCTION: A HISTORICAL OVERVIEW OF THE MEDIUM

The history of American broadcast radio, both as a communications system and as the content or programming of that system, falls into four periods. First, there was the "pioneer" era. This began when Guglielmo Marconi first acquired British capital for the commercial production of wireless telegraphy and ended in 1926 with the formation of the first American broadcasting network.

Second, the network era began in November 1926 when the National Broadcasting Company (NBC) broadcast its first gala program over a dozen stations. It ended in 1948, the first year that network television's advertising revenues exceeded those of network radio. It is this period that is referred to as radio's "golden age" and during which the bulk of radio's growth occurred. It is also the period that has drawn the greatest attention of writers, critics, and historians of radio, as the following pages will reflect.

The third period, more or less equivalent to the decade of the 1950s, was a time of disorientation. Radio, confused about its place in American culture, tried to compete with television and floundered badly as it experimented with ways to attract and hold listeners.

The fourth period, beginning in the early 1960s and continuing to the present, can be called the era of "narrowcasting." Having clarified to itself that radio could not compete with television, the industry embraced the format approach to broadcasting and began a period of new prosperity as it sought to narrowcast programming designed for tightly identified elements in the market or audience.

THE PIONEER ERA TO 1926: COMMERCIAL AND TECHNICAL ADVANCES

During the first quarter of the twentieth century, the most important radio developments came from scientists, engineers, and the heavily capitalized industrial corporations that financed them. During the 1890s, Guglielmo Marconi's British and American corporations developed wireless telegraphy. They profited immensely by equipping His Majesty's fleet (and other naval powers) with history's first truly effective system of ship-to-shore and ship-to-ship communications. Much of that profit was plowed back into research and development, rapidly improving the range and power of the wireless.

Others wanted part of this highly lucrative business. In America the Westinghouse Corporation, General Electric, AT&T, Columbia Fruit (due to its heavy Latin American involvements), and others invested heavily in wireless. On a smaller scale, hundreds of lesser firms and amateur inventors did the same.

During the early decades of the twentieth century, primarily with the backing of the financial giants of the electrical and the telephone/telegraph industries, engineers and inventors made huge technological advances. Lee De Forest invented the microphone. Reginald Fessenden created the vacuum tube. Improvements were made in transmission power and controls, and receivers continually grew better and cheaper.

By the early 1920s hundreds of companies and individuals were transmitting on their own equipment, and thousands of people had receivers. Newspapers and retail stores set up transmitters to gain publicity and began broadcasting sporting events, dance bands, news, and recordings to entertain listeners. AT&T developed the idea of "toll broadcasting." For a fee, companies or individuals could use the telephone company's powerful New York transmitter to read commercial messages to listeners. Meanwhile, hundreds of amateurs set up transmitters in their basements and garages, where they would play records or sing songs to amuse all who cared to tune in.

Surprisingly, perhaps, people listened. After convoluted negotiations among various patent holders, the early industrial giants of wireless had pooled their resources to form the Radio Corporation of America. RCA led the way in marketing reasonably priced receivers, and people brought them. By the early twenties it was a rare American who did not have some kind of access to a radio receiver. Broadcasts of political speeches and sports events had audiences in the millions.

The result of this huge growth was mayhem. Under the early radio legislation of 1910 and 1912, the Department of Commerce had very limited powers to control point-to-point communication by wireless telegraphy, and the courts held that it had virtually no control over broadcasting. Stations interfered with each other's signals, and no one had the power to require that broadcasters stay on their proper frequencies or meet other technical standards.

Secretary of Commerce Herbert Hoover could not abide this disorganization. During the middle 1920s, he held several National Radio Conferences designed to bring order to the airwaves. The result of these conferences was a legislative package to set up a National Radio Commission within the Commerce Department. That commission would assign frequencies, set minimum technical standards for broadcast licenses, and generally take charge of broadcasting. It would be bipartisan and, except for limiting obscenity and guaranteeing that stations operated in the public interest, would have virtually no control over the content of broadcasting. Due to intense bureaucratic battling with the Navy, the Post Office, and the Department of the Interior—each of which wanted to control radio for its purposes—Hoover failed to get his bill through Congress until 1927. American broadcasting then came, for the first time, under effective governmental regulation.

THE NETWORK ERA: CONSTRUCTING THE GOLDEN AGE OF RADIO, 1926–1949

Because the Radio Corporation of America was initially meant to be a marketing division for the radio equipment and services of its parent corporations (Westinghouse, General Electric, and AT&T), it always had a serious interest in broadcasting. If good programs were on the air, listeners would buy receivers.

Under the vigorous leadership of David Sarnoff, therefore, RCA realized that a national system of stations linked together to broadcast the same programs could improve program quality. Using AT&T's telephone lines to link themselves together, stations had already experimented with broadcasting the same program simultaneously over separate transmitters. The technology was there, waiting to be organized. By such linkages, high-quality, popular programs originating in one location could be sent all over the country, not broadcast to a single limited area.

In 1926 RCA announced the formation of a new, wholly owned subsidiary corporation, the National Broadcasting Company. Its whole purpose would be to get separately owned stations across the country to link themselves together via telephone lines to broadcast programs simultaneously. Thus the first permanent national radio network was born.

NBC had little trouble finding stations to affiliate with it. In fact, NBC soon had two separate groups of affiliates, the Red Network and the Blue, each carrying different programs. By 1927, after considerable initial difficulties with financing and organization, another network was also successfully gathering affiliated stations, the Columbia Broadcasting System (CBS). During the 1930s, yet another national network, the Mutual Broadcasting System, began gathering affiliates across the country.

Sponsors loved the networks. Initially, at least, the system worked almost exclusively the way they wanted. A large company (Proctor and Gamble, American Tobacco, or the like) would go to an advertising agency such as J. Walter Thompson's in New York. The agency (not the network) would develop a program that, in their estimation, would draw listeners to hear, along with entertainment, commercial messages designed to sell the sponsor's product. The agency would then negotiate with the various networks to broadcast the show over all or some of the affiliated stations. When a deal had been struck, the advertising agency would use the network's facilities to broadcast its program. The big sponsors got something they wanted, a national audience for their commercials. Local sponsors also got something they wanted in the form of time on the local stations while large audiences were listening, basically, to programs developed with much more quality than any local small business could possibly afford. Local stations were delighted to get programs far superior to anything they could develop themselves, and thus to get higher revenues. Audiences in Biloxi and Omaha were enchanted to hear the live voices of stars they might otherwise have never come within a hundred miles of seeing.

The radio networks gained their first huge audiences with situation comedies and variety shows. "Amos 'n Andy," first a local program in Chicago, enthralled the whole country when it went onto NBC's national network. Vaudeville comedians such as Eddie Cantor and Ed Wynn also attracted large audiences. By the later 1930s dramatic programs such as Cecil B. DeMille's "Lux Radio Theater" drew huge followings. Music of all kinds, from the Grand Ole Opry to Arturo Toscanini's NBC Symphony Orchestra, was always popular, especially dance bands featuring "crooners" such as Bing Crosby and Vic Colombo.

After some turbulent conflicts with the newspapers and wire services in the 1920s and 1930s, the networks' national news programs became very powerful and popular too. With the coming of World War II, news correspondents and especially news commentators (that is, editorialists) such as H. V. Kaltenborn, Boake Carter, Elmer Davis, and Edward R. Murrow gained immense followings and influence.

The growing dominance of the networks did not escape the attention of Roosevent's New Deal Congresses. In 1934 Congress passed the Federal Communications Act, consolidating control of telephone, telegraph, and radio in the hands of a seven-member bipartisan Federal Communications Commission (FCC). The FCC commissioners were appointed by the president for six-year terms and were bound by legislation passed by Congress and decisions made in federal appellate courts. Beyond that, however, they answered to no one on decisions concerning licensing, frequency assignments, and all other matters regarding the technical (as opposed to the content) aspects of broadcasting.

Under the Communications Act of 1934, the people responsible for American broadcasting were the individual licensees who operated the country's radio stations. The FCC was disturbed by the growing dominance of the networks because they were effectively beyond the commission's control; networks were not required to be licensed, only stations. In a landmark 1941 decision the FCC set strict limits on the kinds of contracts that stations could sign with networks. In essence the FCC precluded the networks from forcing local stations to carry programs and required local stations to take responsibility for everything transmitted over their frequencies. At the same time, they decided that no single company could operate more than one network and thus forced NBC to sell its Blue Network, which later became the American Broadcasting Corporation (ABC).

During this same period, the FCC had to deal with two other problems—FM radio and television. By the early 1940s, the commissioners had allotted frequency space to FM stations and had started issuing licenses to FM broadcasters. During the same time, the commission assigned frequencies for television stations and generally did its part to prepare the country for the large-scale development of commercial TV that both RCA/NBC and CBS assured it was imminent.

World War II delayed the development of both television and FM radio, putting standard AM radio into a more or less static phase until well after the war. By 1948, however, most major cities had at least one operating commercial television station broadcasting on very high frequency (VHF), and most cities had one or two FM radio stations operating (usually) as an adjunct to established AM stations. From 1948 to 1952 the FCC froze the issuance of new VHF television licenses while it worked out a decision regarding technical requirements; CBS and RCA/NBC had competing and incompatible systems, each with distinct advantages, and the FCC agonized for years before setting standards favorable to the RCA television system. By then, however, network radio was already losing substantial advertising dollars to TV, and in 1949 the radio networks, despite television's initial technical problems, began a long period of declining importance in broadcasting.

THE ASCENDENCY OF TELEVISION, 1949-1960

In 1949 network radio's advertising revenues declined for the first time ever. In November 1960 the last network radio programs—CBS's daytime soap operas "Ma Perkins," "Young Dr. Malone," and "The Second Mrs. Burton"—left the air. During the intervening years, network radio revenues had fallen from $203 million to $43 million, although total radio advertising had grown slightly from $571 million to $692 million. Obviously it was a decade of change for radio, especially for networks and for the stations.

Basically what happened was that network radio's best talent moved to television, taking audiences and advertisers with them. At the station level, the same thing happened. The best and most experienced station managers, program directors, announcers, and engineers went over to TV.

Ever since the late 1930s the whole industry had been waiting for the change. Radio finally got the visual element that it had always wanted and expected. In a nutshell, the problem was that during its golden age, radio had come to think of itself as an entertainment medium, a part of show business closely linked to Hollywood and Broadway, *Variety* and *Billboard*. When television added the visual component, audiences naturally preferred to see the entertainers. Radio simply could not compete with television as a medium for entertainment aimed at mass audiences.

It tried, however. During the early and middle 1950s, radio networks devised some of the best, most creative entertainment programs they ever had. One example illustrates the kind of creativity they could come up with. Recognizing that science fiction had tremendous popularity (in the mid-1950s more than twenty pulp magazines were publishing science fiction and fantasy) and that at the time decent special effects were almost impossible for TV, NBC worked with *Galaxy* magazine (one of the best science fiction pulps) to produce *X-Minus-1*. The resulting shows were excellent dramatizations of first-rate science fiction stories and novellas. They were fine entertainment, but they did not attract a large audience. Audiences wanted to see, not just hear, their entertainers. Even with deep cuts in advertising rates, sponsors were not interested in network radio shows, so radio as an entertainment medium simply withered away.

With declining revenues from the networks, stations needed more freedom to aim at local audiences. For the most part, especially at the old, established stations that had profited most from long-standing network affiliations, station managers simply continued a scaled-down, lower-budget version of their old programming. Relying heavily on recorded music, they tried to appeal to a broad audience by "blocking in" various kinds of programs. They might play three hours of classical music on a Wednesday night, then on Thursday feature three hours of jazz, with an announcer offering commentary and live or recorded interviews. By doing so, they cut costs and increased local advertising income, but they continued to lose audiences.

Recognizing that conventional programming was, at best, unsatisfactory, three young midwesterners decided to try some different approaches. Starting in Milwaukee, Dallas, Omaha, and other secondary markets, Gordon McLendon, Robert "Todd" Storz, and Gerald Bartell began separate experiments that would, by the sixties, completely revolutionize the nature of radio programming.

Each of them focused stations on limited parts of the audiences. McLendon, for instance, believed that radio should concentrate on music and news, especially local news. By playing popular music and keeping the air filled with news bulletins, profiles, weather reports, and live coverage of local events, McLendon could attract and hold people who wanted to know what was happening in Dallas. He could not keep them away from their TV sets during prime time, but during the mornings and afternoons, he could keep Dallas listeners tuned to KLIF so that they would know what was happening in their own home town. He abandoned the idea of radio as broadcast entertainment, focusing instead on its power as an information medium, and quit thinking of it as a national mass medium, defining it instead as a local phenomenon.

Todd Storz learned to focus on a single buying group. He set up stations that played Top 40 records, those early rock and roll 45s so dear to teenagers of the 1950s. He converted announcers into disc jockeys and tried to make audiences loyal not to any particular program but to a particular station. At KOWH in Omaha he showed advertisers that teenagers had money to spend, and he taught teenagers that KOWH was the only station they wanted to listen to.

Gerald Bartell, beginning with his WOKY in Milwaukee, helped bring the idea of objective programming into radio. By closely examining the findings of the various pollsters and rating services, he figured out what listeners wanted.

Then he put it on the air, whether he liked it or not. His goal was to make people listen by giving them the things they liked, no matter what his subjective feelings about them might be.

McLendon, Storz, and Bartell each regarded network affiliations as relatively useless. For them, radio was a local medium for information and music. Networks, with their emphasis on national news and entertainment, were a hindrance.

Two major technological developments helped McLendon, Storz, Bartell, and their increasingly large number of imitators. One was the automobile radio. By the early 1950s half the new cars coming out of Detroit had radios. As more and more Americans spent more and more time in their cars, especially during the morning and evening rush hours, radio found a new audience. In addition, as increasing numbers of teenagers gained access to cars in the 1950s, the market for Top 40 music expanded rapidly.

The other major change was the inexpensive portable radio, especially the small transistor radio that any teenager could afford to buy and carry around. The small portable radio could go places a TV could not—to the beach, to the office, and into the bathroom or the basement. To watch television, people had to sit around a large, immobile console, much as they had sat around a console radio in the thirties and forties. But radio could go with them to work, school, or play. Local broadcasters, led by McLendon, Storz, and Bartell, began to see that their audience was, in fact, using radio at different times and in different ways than it had in the past. Slowly they began recognizing that their future was in the commuter's drive to and from work, in the teenager's after-school hours, and in the mechanic's working days, not the traditional prime time when people sought entertainment rather than information and companionship.

By the end of the 1950s network radio amounted to almost nothing but hourly national news, some sports, and special events such as presidential speeches and national elections. Radio had become truly a local medium controlled by individual stations, and the stations had come to see clearly that their future lay not in the broadcasting of entertainment to a mass audience, but in the transmission of information and music to particular segments of the total audience in a particular community.

NARROWCASTING: 1960 TO THE PRESENT

Beginning in 1960, contemporary radio took its current shape. Three major developments explain its evolution. First, the art of broadcast formats became the key to success. Second, the science of public opinion analysis created new statistical and computerized methodologies and achieved remarkable sophistication. Third, FM radio finally began to develop as a major part of broadcasting.

Today's radio programming is ruled in large measure by the concept of a programming format designed to attract and hold a particular kind of listener in a specific area. Although the term is chiefly identified with music programming, "formatting" is also a general term for designing a station's entire programming content. Building on Todd Storz's ideas, today's radio program director tries to get a particular kind of listener to set his or her dial on one station and leave it there. Just as Storz tried to get Omaha's teenagers to listen to KOWH exclusively, today's programming decisions aim to get males eighteen to thirty-four years old, or white females forty-five to fifty-six years old, or black females, or some other particular kind of listener, to tune to a single station exclusively. Knowing that most people can and will listen to radio only at certain times of the day, programmers by and large do not try to attract listeners away from other activities such as TV viewing, work, and so on. Rather, they try to schedule programming such that when a listener has time to listen, he or she always turns to a particular station for music, news, or talk that he or she will like. To attract a heavy following within a certain kind of people, programmers develop formats that offer more or less the same kind of programs throughout the station's entire broadcasting period.

Thus a station may develop a country and western format whereby its entire broadcasting day is devoted to playing country-style music. It may have special time slots for bluegrass or for outlaw music, but the overall pattern, the format, will devote itself exclusively to country music. If things work properly, that portion of the local audience that likes country music will turn to that station every time it turns on the radio. The program director does not try to get his or her audience to give up TV's "Monday Night Football" in order to sit by the radio. But when people get in their cars to go to work on Tuesday morning, he or she wants a certain percentage of them to tune to his station.

This kind of programming is often called narrowcasting because in contrast to broadcasting it aims not at an amorphous mass audience but at a tightly defined, narrow audience. A station manager who knows that his format consistently attracts, say, 40 percent of the males eighteen to thirty-four years old who have their radios on at any given time is in an excellent position to bargain with record stores, beer distributors, motorcycle dealers, and other potential advertisers wishing to sell goods that appeal heavily to males eighteen to thirty-four years old. A station that consistently has 60 percent of the black female listeners in a large city will be able to get good advertising revenues from the distributors of cosmetics, publications, or clothing designed for black women's needs and interests.

Thus, since the early sixties, the creative part of radio has been the designing of formats that will attract major segments within a given market. In 1960 the Top 40 format was the hottest thing in radio because it could demand high advertising rates from the sellers of soft drinks, acne nostrums, casual clothing, records, and other products aimed at youthful consumers. Since then, many new formats have been designed. Among the many formats that broadcasters have tried, three seem particularly illustrative of the way format programming has influenced the development of radio narrowcasting.

The development of album-oriented rock (AOR) formats was a late 1960s phenomenon. It grew from two roots. First, the teenagers who were listening to Top 40 stations in the late 1950s grew up. They still liked rock and roll, but their interests turned to lp albums by successful rock bands; they matured, and their taste became too sophisticated for the pastiche of 45-rpm hit singles of their teen years. Second, progressive radio or underground radio developed as part of the late 1960s counterculture of drugs, pacifism, and revolutionary rhetoric. Rarely successful commercially, underground radio stations played lots of rock and roll albums by groups associated with the antiwar movement, the drug culture, and antiestablishment political protests. To no one's surprise, they had a hard time getting advertisers, but they did have listeners, most of whom were emphatically not hippies but young adults who liked the sophisticated kind of rock music they could hear on such stations. Eventually, the underground stations parted company with their revolutionary disc jockeys, went after sponsors interested in white consumers eighteen to thirty-four years old, and kept on playing albums by the Rolling Stones, Led Zeppelin, Jefferson Airplane, and other successful rock bands. Thus the AOR format was born. It capitalized on the loyalty and interest that many young, white adults felt for particular bands (as opposed to teenagers' interest in particular songs), and by the mid-seventies it had become one of the most widespread and commercially successful radio formats in the country.

Middle-of-the-road (MOR) formats are the direct heirs of the old radio broadcasting programs. Aimed at basically middle-class white consumers thirty-four to sixty years old, they specialize in inoffensive popular music ranging from soft rock and roll such as the Beatles' quieter records to pop singers such as Diana Ross and Barbra Streisand and the more sophisticated kinds of country music. To this, they add a strong dose of local information programming (helicopter traffic reports, detailed local sport reports, local election coverage, local talk shows featuring telephone conversations between the host announcer, audience, and locally prominent guests, and so on). They are the nearest thing left in radio to the old mass audience programming, yet even they are basically narrowcasting to a single segment of the community, namely, the middle-class listener with an active, personal involvement in the economic, social, and political life of the local community. The MOR station typically places an emphasis on having personable, amusing announcers and is generally a 50,000-watt clear-channel station that serves a comparatively large geographic area.

In the early 1980s the "music of your life" format enjoyed remarkable success among middle-aged and older listeners, mostly white. Featuring nonrock popular music from the 1930s, 1940s, 1950s, and 1960s, it carved out a substantial listenership among older people who were becoming a more significant consumer segment and who used radio more for companionship and nostalgic amusement than for information or real musical interest.

Numerous other formats, including nonmusic formats, have been tried with varying degrees of success. In the nation's largest cities, all-news and all-talk (that is, interviews, phone-in shows, and so on) formats can hold enough listeners to get adequate advertising revenues. Ethnic formats for black Americans, Spanish-speaking Americans, and other minorities thrive wherever their listenership represents a significant economic element in the community. In New York during the late 1970s, an all-disco music format made WKTU the most listened-to station in the city. Country and western, classical, religious, and other formats are commonplace throughout the country, and at any given moment dozens of stations will be trying out new variations on standard formats or entirely new concepts.

In all cases, however, the key to success is the format's ability to attract and hold a significant segment of the community. A station that can identify a substantial group of people in its area and then develop a format to keep them listening should survive and prosper. A station that fails to do so will perforce either develop a new format for a different group or go bankrupt. Even noncommercial stations must have a format attractive enough to draw listener contributions or citizens' tax dollars. Contemporary radio functions by narrowcasting to specific subgroups within a community. Formats are the programming designs that attract those subgroups, and a station's success or failure depends on the effectiveness with which the program director manages his or her format.

The whole concept of narrowcasting however, would be impossible without effective means of determining who and how many listen to what. For radio, the Arbitron Company determines the success or failure of a station's format. By subscription, radio stations pay Arbitron and other companies to measure and analyze the radio audience by age group, sex, ethnicity, listening times, and so on. With their periodic reports from Arbitron, radio stations can decide who to seek for advertisers, how much to charge, and how well their format is succeeding. Without Arbitron and its competitors in the field of public opinion research, narrowcasting simply could not work.

As early as the 1930s the Cooperative Association of Broadcasters (CAB, later the Crossley service) and the Hooper ratings determined how many people listened to various radio broadcasts. During the 1960s, the American Research Bureau (ARB) devised a system of listener diaries that yielded better information about radio listeners than any previous method. After merging with Control Data Corporation (a computer firm) and renaming itself the Arbitron Company in the early 1970s it could produce extraordinarily detailed and reliable analyses of listener patterns, and these soon became the crucial determiners of radio's programming efforts and advertising revenues. Shortly after a bad set of Arbitrons arrived in the station manager's office, an entire station's personnel might be fired and an entirely new format brought in. In some cases such wholesale and rapid changes might continue for a year or more until the Arbitron report showed that a format had been found that could bring in a decent share (percentage of the market listening within any demographic division or geographic area) or rating (percentage of the market population for any demographic division). With good Arbitrons in hand, a station's time salesman could approach advertisers aggressively and with confidence; without them, he had trouble even getting in to see people.

Perhaps the most important thing to happen in contemporary radio, however, was the FCC's 1964 decision to open up FM radio. FM radio had been around since the early 1930s. Edwin H. Armstrong, originally backed by RCA, developed a system for transmitting radio based on modulation in the frequency (hence FM, frequency modulation) instead of the amplitude (AM, amplitude modulation) of the radio wave. FM had real technical advantages: by its nature it was immune to static interference, and it could reproduce sounds with a range and clarity far greater than those of AM. Standard or AM broadcasts cannot transmit sounds within the full range of the human ear; thus AM always sounds somewhat muted or tinny because it simply cannot reproduce many of the sounds our ears are used to hearing. FM can transmit anything the human ear can hear and more. AM has the advantage that it can transmit farther than FM, but that is its only advantage.

By the late 1930s, however, when Armstrong was ready to begin commercial development of FM, RCA had lost interest. CBS tried to work with Armstrong, but the FCC did not really know what to do with FM, especially since some of the frequencies originally assigned to FM were also being claimed for television. After years of indecisive and ineffectual treatment by both the FCC and the industry, FM entered the 1950s in terrible shape. In 1947 more than 900 licenses had been issued for FM. By 1956 the total number had dropped to 534. In 1950 more than 2 million people had bought FM receivers; in 1956 less than 230,000 were sold. Virtually no commercial FM stations could show a profit, and only the noncommercial FM stations could claim to be building an audience of classical-music and jazz fans who could hear the superiority of FM.

Recognizing that something should be done, the FCC decided in the mid-1950s that it would encourage the public to explore FM by allowing simulcasting. Under this arrangement, AM stations could use FM transmitters to broadcast simultaneously (simulcast) programs over AM and FM. Their idea was that once people heard their regular AM programs on FM, the superiority of FM's sound would convince them to buy FM receivers. With the development of high-fidelity recordings, people were getting used to better sound quality, and the FCC's idea worked. By 1962 FM radio sales had climbed above 2.5 million.

Also, by the early sixties AM frequency space was getting crowded. With the narrowcasting formats proving that local stations could make money, lots of people wanted into radio. The problem was that there are only a limited number of frequencies within the AM band, and they were virtually all taken.

So, in the public interest the FCC in 1964 decided to encourage more diversity of programming by disallowing AM-FM simulcasting. If an AM station could not develop separate programming for its FM station, then it had to give up its FM license to a competitor. At the same time, the commission steered many of its applicants for AM licenses toward FM. The result was a boom in FM. As more programming became available on FM, more people bought receivers. As more people became FM listeners, nore advertisers went to FM stations. As more advertising dollars went to FM licenses, more investors took an interest in owning FM stations. They were still not as profitable as their older brothers in the AM or standard band, but they were gaining. In today's market it is not unusual for an FM station to lead the Arbitrons in any given market, and most FM stations yield at least a reasonable return on investment for their owners.

By opening up the FM spectrum in 1964, the FCC effectively encouraged the development of a greater variety in programming and inadvertently increased the competition for formats that would narrowcast to better-defined subgroups within the mass market of any given area. This was a crucial decision in making radio into the diversified, multifaceted business that it has become, and it was critical in fostering the wide range of programming choices that are available even in relatively small markets to listeners today.

All of these changes—the development of format narrowcasting, the improvements in public opinion analysis, and the growth in FM broadcasting— made the 1970s and the 1980s an era of extraordinary growth and improvement in the radio industry. In 1960 there were slightly more than 4,100 commercial radio stations on the air, fewer than 700 of which were FM. By 1977 nearly 7,500 commercial broadcasters were in business, and almost 3,000 of them were transmitting FM signals. Listeners had far greater variety to choose from, and fierce competition for various market segments, especially for the heavy-spending group of those eighteen to thirty-four years old, meant that program directors continually sought ways to improve programs or at least to make listeners happier.

By the 1980s, therefore, a number of new things were happening in radio, all of them the result of radio's having found its real niche in the structure of American mass communications. For one thing, networks were coming back strong. No longer did they try to provide the mass audience programming of the 1930s and 1940s; the individual stations remained firmly in charge of their own formats for programming. But new networks had arisen to provide different styles of news and special-events programming for stations serving different types of people. In the late sixties the Mutual Black Network began offering hourly national news broadcasts stressing minority interests. In 1973 the National Black Network began competing service. In 1977 ABC Radio split itself into four networks: the ABC Contemporary, ABC Entertainment, ABC-FM, and ABC Information networks. Each aimed at different kinds of news services for affiliated stations with different kinds of listeners. The Contemporary Network, for instance, aimed at Top 40 listeners, while the FM network was primarily for AOR (album-oriented rock) formats. Reversing its 1941 ruling against a single company's operation of more than one network, the FCC approved the quadruple network setup. By the late 1970s CBS and NBC were following ABC's lead, and other networks were also springing up.

A potentially ominous development was the arrival of computerized broadcasting in the late 1970s and early 1980s. By programming a computer properly, a licensee could eliminate virtually all personnel except the sales and engineering staff of his station. In fact, however, most of the fully computerized stations were profitable but not really popular. A computer could lower operating costs and thus keep advertising rates low, making for a nice return on an investor's dollar. But such stations rarely drew especially large audiences (another reason why their advertising rates were so cheap), and their real importance lay in paving the way for broadcasters to start using computers as tools to improve, not replace, the performance of programming personnel.

Perhaps the most important development from radio's success, however, was the movement to deregulate. Arguing that radio was so competitive that the marketplace itself (that is, competition among broadcasters) was the best possible way to guarantee that broadcasting served the public interest, a number of economists and lawyers persuaded the FCC to loosen its requirements for public service broadcasting. The FCC, therefore, began to pull back on many of its former requirements and restrictions because it was convinced that radio was so keenly responsive to audience interests that it would provide exactly as much public service programming as the public was willing to listen to. The FCC, in other words, felt that radio would serve the public best by being left to make its own decisions without government interference. Such a move was in itself an indication of just how successful the industry had become in providing the American people with the kind of programming it wanted.

CONCLUSION

The history of radio can be viewed as a four-step process of (1) early development as a local medium; (2) a twenty-year period of diversion away from its originally local nature while the national networks used radio as a sort of portable television for the establishment of a national, mass audience that was the proper sphere for television; (3) a decade of confusion as radio, responding to the phenomenon of television, groped its way back toward an essentially local identity; and (4) a final period in which radio established itself as a local, specialized medium serving not only a geographically limited population but a variety of different groups and subgroups within any given region. Radio's history, in other words, is basically a history of growth as a local, specialized medium with the individual station as the key element in broadcasting. Its history included a twenty-five-year period when it was diverted away from its properly local functions as the networks used the stations to prepare for the advent of TV, but it found its right and proper place in the structure of American society after TV had become a reality and the individual stations were able to get back to their proper jobs of serving the local groups and populations within their own broadcast areas.

1 RADIO NETWORKS AND STATION HISTORIES

Networks no longer dominate radio. It is true that during the 1970s and 1980s several new networks came into being. It is also true that the older radio organizations—the Mutual, American, Columbia, and National broadcasting systems—have recently pumped some new life into their network programming. For the most part, however, modern radio stations are independent entities, developing the vast majority of their programming for themselves and relying on their own sales forces for their revenue.

This was not always the case, of course. During the 1930s and 1940s, the networks controlled radio, and the most successful local stations were those affiliated with one of the major networks. During the formative years, the decades from 1920 to 1950 when our national system of broadcasting assumed its present form, local licensees were delighted to rely on the networks for the bulk of their programs and the major part of their income. To understand American radio, therefore, it is necessary to pay close attention to the development of the four major radio networks—the National Broadcasting Company, the Columbia Broadcasting System, the Mutual Broadcasting System, and the American Broadcasting Company (which, prior to 1943, was that part of NBC known as the Blue Network).

GENERAL HISTORIES

A good starting point for any consideration of broadcasting is Walter B. Emery's *National and International Systems of Broadcasting: Their History, Operation, and Control.* Arranged by continent, region, and country, this large book gives a brief background and description for the broadcast system of every country on the globe as of the late 1960s. Of course, changes have occurred since then, most notably in Africa and Southeast Asia. Emery's explanation of American broadcasting, however, is clear and succinct, and it makes interesting comparisons to the systems prevailing elsewhere. Emery gives a good sense of how truly unique the American system is.

Perhaps the best single history of American broadcasting is Erik Barnouw's three-volume *A History of Broadcasting in the United States.* Volume 2, *The Golden Web,* covering the period between 1933 and 1953, deals largely with the networks' David Sarnoff, William Paley, Frank Stanton, and others; it covers the growth of the network system, its various conflicts with the FCC and other entertainment industries, and the eventual switch from radio to television.

In *Stay Tuned: A Concise History of American Broadcasting,* Christopher H. Sterling and John M. Kittross devote much attention to the rise of the networks. They give less heed to programming and personalities than does Barnouw, and they give more scrutiny to organizational detail. They make far more careful analyses of various court decisions and spend more time on technology, legislation, and administration. Less readable than Barnouw's, theirs is yet an excellent history.

Laurence Bergreen's *Look Now, Pay Later: The Rise of Network Broadcasting* is a fine history of the networks. Bergreen writes well, with a real sense of how to turn a phrase, and he has a true historian's skepticism about the mythic and legendary lore so thoroughly integrated into the folkways of broadcasting's subculture. For instance, he continually points out the lack of evidence to support both David Sarnoff's supposedly critical role in informing the world about the disaster of the SS *Titanic* and William Paley's carefully crafted image of himself as a purveyor of quality programming. No one who reads Barnouw or Sterling and Kittross should fail to read Bergreen. His book provides an important element of critical skepticism to the more or less credulous and at times hero-worshipping histories of the other major writers on the topic.

A number of the standard survey textbooks for introductory college courses on broadcasting include good historical background on the radio networks. Giraud Chester, Garnet R. Garrison, and Edgar E. Willis intersperse virtually every chapter of *Television and Radio* with a dosage of historical background. Sydney W. Head's *Broadcasting in America: A Survey of Television and Radio* includes several chapters outlining the history of the networks. Eugene S. Foster's *Understanding Broadcasting* takes an explicitly chronological and developmental approach to the broadcasting system; Foster spends a good deal of time examining the early history of the networks as a way of explaining how our current system began.

Over the years, a number of relatively popular histories of network radio have also appeared. Lowell Thomas's *Magic Dials: The Story of Radio and Television* came out in 1939. Decorated with many pretty photographs, this big book sings the praises of American commercial broadcasting and yet manages to get a fair amount of historical fact into the text. Irving Settel's *A Pictorial History of Radio* is oriented heavily toward programming; it is a nostalgia piece intended for the coffee tables of folks who want to reminisce about the good old days of "The Chase and Sanborn Hour" by glancing at publicity photographs of Edgar Bergen and Charlie McCarthy. Still, the text presents a fairly solid brief history of network radio. Curtis Mitchell's *Cavalcade of Broadcasting* is a work in a similar vein, though the proportion of text to photographs is higher than in Settel's book.

The best popular history of radio yet published, however, appeared as a series of articles in 1980-1981 called "The First Fifty Years of Broadcasting" in *Broadcasting,* published by Broadcasting Publishing in Washington, D.C. Slickly written and embellished with good photographs, the series covered one year each week. It summarized the main events in about 2,000 words, and thus reviewed the period from 1930 to 1980 in fifty weeks. Without going into great depth on any issue, it still treated the most important points both thoroughly and interestingly. In 1982 the editors of *Broadcasting* published the series in book form entitled *The First Fifty Years of Broadcasting: The Running Story of the Fifth Estate.*

PREHISTORIES

In 1926 NBC became the first permanent radio broadcasting network. A wholly owned subsidiary of the Radio Corporation of America, the National Broadcasting Company was created by a deal between RCA (and its parent corporations, General Electric and Westinghouse) and the American Telephone and Telegraph Company. NBC bought AT&T's New York broadcasting station WEAF, unquestionably the best equipped and most commercially successful station in the country at that time, for $1 million. AT&T, in turn, agreed to provide NBC with exclusive service on its long-distance telephone cables to link stations together. Thus permanent radio network broadcasting became possible.

From this original deal all other American network broadcasting has sprung. CBS, for instance, began when Arthur Judson failed to receive NBC's permission to become its exclusive booking agent; in a fit of pique he decided instead to form a network of his own. ABC came into existence when, at the FCC's insistence, NBC had to sell one of the two networks it had begun operating in 1926. Even MBS, the Mutual Broadcasting System, came into existence as a way of enabling essentially independent radio stations to compete effectively against NBC and CBS affiliates.

Something of the milieu within which permanent networks were born can be caught in a pair of delightful articles from *American Heritage.* The August 1955 issue carried "Music in the Air and Voices on the Crystal Set," a selection of transcripts from fifteen broadcast pioneers' contributions to Columbia University's Oral History Project. In these selections people like William Hedges, for many years head of the National Association of Broadcasters, and H. V. Kaltenborn reminisce about the context within which the idea of permanent network broadcasting was generated. In August 1965 Robert Saudek contributed "Program Coming In Fine. Please Play 'Japanese Sandman.'" In brief, vivid phrases Saudek, a long-time executive and later the head of the Museum of Broadcasting in New York City, described the transition from the amateur enthusiasm of Dr. Frank Conrad's Westinghouse station KDKA to the big-business atmosphere of NBC.

Erik Barnouw's first volume of *A History of Broadcasting in the United States,* entitled *A Tower in Babel,* covers early broadcasting through 1933 including the first wireless telegraphy and the early networks, NBC and CBS. With real gusto Barnouw tells of the careers of David Sarnoff, William Paley, Edward Klauber, and the other men and women who created the network system. As some more recent historians, notably Laurence Bergreen, could point out, Barnouw's enthusiastic admiration for the network pioneers led him into an uncritical acceptance of some dubious "facts"; he retells, for instance, the legendary episode of David Sarnoff's reception of the SS *Titanic*'s distress calls without a shadow of doubt as to its total reliability. Still, his recounting of the basic process by which AT&T led the experiments with toll broadcasting and early commercially sponsored programs is certainly very interesting.

Much of Barnouw's material, of course, came from earlier sources such as *The Radio Industry: The Story of Its Development* and Gleason L. Archer's *History of Radio to 1926,* which are enthusiastic accounts of the technological and organizational experiments that preceded the formation of permanent networks. An admirably terse, accurate recounting of early network experiments is to be found in the FCC's 1941 *Report on Chain Broadcasting;* Lawrence W. Lichty and Malachi C. Topping include the section of the report called "Early History of Network Broadcasting" in their *American Broadcasting: A Source Book on the History of Radio and Television.*

Two books of corporation history also include important information for the understanding of the early experimental networking that preceded RCA's decision to found NBC. N. R. Danielian's *A.T.&T.: The Story of Industrial Conquest* helps explain how important the Bell system was in both the whole development of commercial broadcasting as a concept and in the provision of crucial technical support services for the establishment of permanent affiliations between stations and NBC. W. J. Baker's *History of the Marconi Company* helps explain how important Marconi's original organization was in all early broadcasting, even after the post–World War I patent pooling by American governmental and corporate leaders managed to ease the American division of the Marconi Company out of the competition.

David Sarnoff's role in the development of American radio was certainly less critical than many of his legendary tales would seem to indicate, but the man was unquestionably the single most influential person in the development of network broadcasting. Two of his early writings, the "Letter to E. W. Rice, Jr., Honorary Chairman of the Board, General Electric Company" of June 17, 1922 (in *Looking Ahead: The Papers of David Sarnoff*), and the "Memorandum to E. J. Nally 1915-1916," (reprinted in various places, most notably in Frank J.

Kahn's *Documents of American Broadcasting*), prove just how early it was that the leadership of RCA began to realize the potential of broadcasting, especially of network broadcasting.

Although it is not a work of radio history per se, Marshall McLuhan's 1965 classic *Understanding Media: The Extensions of Man* offers rich and provocative commentary on the impact of radio on cultural and social history, particularly its profound impact upon Asia and Africa and the irreversible changes it has made in the ways in which the East and the West view each other.

Plenty of governmental reports also supply information about the early phases of network experimentation. The first volume of John W. Kittross's *Documents in American Telecommunications Policy* includes all or most of the text of the following early documents: the U.S. Commissioner of Navigation's *Annual Report to the Secretary of Commerce* for the years 1921 to 1926; the "Recommendations of the National Radio Committee" as reported in *Radio Service Bulletin* (of the Department of Commerce) for April 1923; and the Commerce Department's *Recommendations for Regulation of Radio Adopted by the Third National Radio Conference* of 1924 and *Proceedings of the Fourth National Radio Conference and Recommendations for the Regulation of Radio* of 1926.

Two useful articles in the *Journal of Broadcasting* help to analyze and explain the importance of these and other early governmental efforts in the shaping of our network system of broadcasting. In 1956 C. M. Jansky published an article on "The Contribution of Herbert Hoover to Broadcasting" that helps explain the critical role Hoover played while he was secretary of commerce. Edward F. Sarno, Jr., published a useful analysis of "The National Radio Conference" in the Spring 1969 volume of the *Journal of Broadcasting*.

Today it is difficult for Americans to imagine that broadcasting networks could ever have been anything except commercial or, at least, profit-oriented enterprises. That fact was not nearly so obvious to the early broadcasters themselves, and Werner J. Severin published an interesting article on "Commercial vs. Non-Commercial Radio during Broadcasting's Early Years" in the 1978 volume of the *Journal of Broadcasting* that points out how close the country came to developing a British Broadcasting Corporation (BBC) type of noncommercial or public service–oriented broadcasting system, even after the beginnings of early network experimentation. Jennie Irene Mix's 1925 editorial from *Radio Broadcast* magazine, reprinted in Lichty and Topping's *American Broadcasting,* helps explain how American sentiment switched from an early abhorrence of the idea of broadcast advertising to an acceptance of the idea that somehow, someone was going to have to pay for national programming of good quality. It is a useful article for anyone who wants to understand how public acceptance of commercial networks came into being even before the permanent networks had been founded.

The importance of Herbert Hoover and Guglielmo Marconi during the formative years of broadcasting has already been indicated. A full appreciation of these two men and of their philosophies and ideas is a necessary part of a real comprehension of American radio's development during the years between the U. S. Navy's surrender of control over radio in 1919 and the formation of NBC in 1926. Several good biographies of Marconi are available in most libraries. Orrin E. Dunlap, Jr.'s 1937 *Marconi: The Man and His Wireless* emphasizes the technical genius of the man. Degna Marconi's *My Father, Marconi* offers an intimate portrait of the man's personal quirks, foibles, and strengths. W. P. Jolly's *Marconi* paints a fair, balanced portrait of the man, his ideas, his abilities, and his limitations.

There is only one really good biography of Herbert Hoover, David Burner's *Herbert Hoover: A Public Life,* and it pays scant attention to Hoover's involvement with radio. It does, however, explain much about Hoover's general philosophy of capitalism, free enterprise, and public service. It goes far in revealing how it was that a man so adamantly opposed as Hoover to the idea of commercial broadcasting yet became the granddaddy of America's advertising-oriented networks. Fortunately, we also have *The Memoirs of Herbert Hoover: The Cabinet and the Presidency, 1920-1933* to help discover some of Hoover's own thoughts and deeds in pulling together the hodgepodge system of broadcasting that existed when he took over the Commerce Department. Despite his limitations, Hoover was a man of principle and vision, and an understanding of his philosophy of Americanism is absolutely critical to a comprehension of how the scene was set during the early and mid-twenties for the development of network broadcasting during the 1930s. Without denying the importance of Sarnoff, Marconi, or anyone else, it certainly seems fair to say that Herbert Hoover, while serving as secretary of commerce, did more to develop the atmosphere within which American network broadcasting would eventually flourish than any other individual.

THE ERA OF NETWORK DOMINANCE

Once Herbert Hoover and the other participants in the various national radio conferences had established the basic patterns by which the government would regulate frequency assignments, licensure, and other technical matters of broadcasting, the stage was set for the networks to move into the spotlight. Numerous histories have been written about how the networks assumed center stage.

Though written in 1942, Francis Chase, Jr.'s *Sound and Fury: An Informal History of Broadcasting* is still one of the most entertaining and enjoyable accounts of how the networks took control during the 1930s. Chase believes that networks were able to fill a basic need for entertainment in the depression-ridden American soul. By providing enjoyable programs, the networks took control, so his book emphasizes the development of programs, and he offers many spicy anecdotes and laughable details. Robert Landry's *This Fascinating Radio Business* concentrates more on organizational and corporate matters, but it too provides entertaining reading about the history of radio up to the early 1940s.

Lloyd R. Morris's *Not So Long Ago* is a social history of American life in the first half of the twentieth century. It traces the impact of the automobile, the airplane, and other technological developments on the everyday life of American society. The last quarter of the book is devoted to radio, its history, and its impact on the way Americans lived. His basic assumption is that radio means network broadcasting. His book makes good reading and helps place the development of the networks in the proper context of other rapidly developing changes in American institutions and ways of life.

In stark contrast, a number of heavy-duty business histories cover the radio networks from a distinctly organizational and economic viewpoint. Gleason L. Archer's *Big Business and Radio* pontificates and overwrites itself through an extraordinarily revealing account of the corporate machinations behind the formation of NBC; the writing is pure torture, but the story it tells is critical to an understanding of how NBC came to be. Orrin E. Dunlap, Jr.'s *The Story of Radio* is well written; Dunlap was the radio columnist of the *New York Times,* so at least he knew how to construct good, clean paragraphs and sentences. Unfortunately, his book was written in 1935, four years before Archer revealed his findings about the corporate wheeling and dealing that preceded RCA's decision to form NBC, so Dunlap simply misses some important facts in telling his story. The FCC's 1941 *Report on Chain Broadcasting* covers the business histories of CBS, NBC, and MBS in terse, clear prose, but it keeps its story brief. It hits only the high spots, but it covers them well and understandably.

Thomas P. Robinson's *Radio Networks and the Federal Government* offers an expanded version of the story told by the FCC's report, giving more depth and detail of the organizational and economic development of the networks up to the early years of World War II. W. Rupert MacLaurin's *Invention and Innovation in the Radio Industry* is also an essentially business-oriented history of the networks up through the late 1940s, but his primary emphasis is on the influence of technological developments on the economic and organizational dynamics of the business.

Two good articles have been published on the history of the National Association of Broadcasters (NAB) and its peculiar relationship to the networks. Basically an organization made up of individual licensees, the NAB has always enjoyed a cozy relationship with the networks because many of the NAB's most affluent and influential members have also been major-market network affiliates. David Mackey's "The Development of the National Association of Broadcasters" appeared in the first volume (1956) of the *Journal of Broadcasting;* it helps portray the early role of the networks in pushing the NAB to become the extremely influential lobbying and mutual protection association that it eventually was to become. "Two Exciting Decades" is a long, self-serving bit of history that the NAB published about itself in the October 16, 1950, issue of *Broadcasting.* It sheds light on how the NAB and the four major networks cooperated and helped each other on any number of occasions during the 1930s and 1940s.

Surprisingly, no real history of NBC has yet been published. According to Laurence Bergreen's *Look Now, Pay Later: The Rise of Network Broadcasting,* the David Sarnoff Library of the David Sarnoff Research Center in Princeton, New Jersey, houses a fifty-six-volume history called "Radio and David Sarnoff" by RCA vice president E. E. Bucher. A decent proportion of this official corporate history, it can be reasonably assumed, deals with NBC and its early years. But only those who gain official approval to work in the "shrine [which] recalls Soviet museums dedicated to preserving the spirit of Lenin" (Bergreen, p. 10) have access to it.

Of course, there are some fluffy histories available. *The Golden Years of Broadcasting: A Celebration of the First 50 Years of Radio and TV on NBC* by Robert Campbell stands in the quarto section of most public libraries for anyone who wants to help NBC celebrate its self-satisfaction. *Sponsor* magazine published a substantial but hardly serious history called "NBC: A Documentary" in its issue of May 16, 1966. *Broadcasting* published one of its typically slick, well-written but uncritical articles called "The First Fifty Years of NBC" in its issue of June 21, 1976; not exactly fluffy, perhaps, the article still manages to ignore any potentially negative or unpleasant facts about NBC, RCA, and their grand panjandrum, General Sarnoff.

CBS, on the other hand, has had some fairly serious attention directed toward it, most notably Robert Metz's *CBS: Reflections in a Bloodshot Eye.* Metz is a journalist and free-lance writer, not a professional historian, so he keeps the reader's attention on the more sensational and controversial aspects of CBS's peculiar history. The result is probably not completely fair to CBS or its prime mover, William Paley, but at least it is interesting. It certainly is not uncritical. As companion pieces to their articles on NBC, both *Sponsor* and *Broadcasting* published long pieces on CBS in 1965 and 1977, respectively. The article in *Sponsor*'s issue of September 13, 1965, was called "CBS: Documenting 38 Years of Exciting History." The title reveals much about the spirit of the piece. "CBS: The First Five Decades" appeared in the September 19, 1977, issue of *Broadcasting.* Tightly written, well documented, and, as always, illustrated with truly interesting photographs, this long essay is as careful to avoid serious questioning of CBS and William Paley as the earlier essay was to avoid serious criticism of NBC and David Sarnoff.

Histories of MBS and ABC are even harder to come by. There is always the *Report on Chain Broadcasting* of 1941; the section on the Mutual Broadcasting System is reprinted in Lichty and Topping's *American Broadcasting,* but it only runs to about four pages of large print. No thesis is listed in John M. Kittross's *A Bibliography of Theses and Dissertations on Broadcasting, 1920-1973,* a very reliable source. Aside from that, not much has been written about MBS, despite its status for many years as the largest of the radio networks in numbers of affiliates.

As for ABC, most of its history as a pre–TV-era radio network is part of NBC's history. ABC was simply NBC's Blue Network until the mid-1940s. Sterling Quinlan's *Inside ABC: American Broadcasting Company's Rise to*

Power was published when Fred Silverman was shaking up the whole TV industry by bringing ABC from its traditional poor third in the Neilsen ratings to a temporarily unchallenged first by the development of "jiggle" or "T & A" programs such as "Charlie's Angels" and "Three's Company," mindless but prurient. Not at all surprisingly, therefore, the book concentrates on ABC as a television network, with only occasional backward glances toward the mid-1940s when ABC was still emerging from its RCA-built cocoon within the branches of NBC Radio.

There are several other short histories of radio networks available, but most of them focus on networks that have emerged since the rise of commercial television. They will be covered in a later portion of this chapter.

Networks are basically organizations, and the essence of all organization is people. Biographies, autobiographies, and memoirs, therefore, provide an invaluable source of information about the way the networks actually worked during the years of their dominance in the field of radio.

The place of honor must go to David Sarnoff. Three excellent biographies of the man have been published. Anyone who reads one should read the others as well; they complement each other nicely, and among them they probably paint a fairly accurate picture of a man who was surely a giant and a genius, but not a hero or a saint. Eugene Lyons was a cousin of Sarnoff, and his *David Sarnoff: A Biography* had both the official sanction of the Sarnoff Family and the full cooperation of Sarnoff's associates at RCA and NBC. It is a fine book, detailed and honest but cut in the pattern of that peculiarly American form of hagiography called the Horatio Alger story. Carl Dreher's *Sarnoff: An American Success* has the advantage of being able to use Lyons's material without having developed any obligations or attachments to the Sarnoff family or RCA. Far from being an attack on Sarnoff, it is still an essentially admiring portrait of the man, but a portrait painted with a willingness to include the warts and wrinkles that Lyons occasionally smoothed over or left out. Kenneth Bilby's *The General: David Sarnoff and the Rise of the Communications Industry* is more readable than the others. Bilby makes an intriguing connection between Sarnoff's lifelong interest in Hebrew prophetic literature and his uncanny ability to predict trends within his industry. Bilby suggests that Sarnoff's religious upbringing undergirded his ability to foresee his industry's future and work ceaselessly toward the fulfillment of that vision. Bilby occasionally hacks away at Lyons, whose familial and sycophantic relationship to Sarnoff troubles him. Yet Bilby himself is a former Sarnoff staffer, and *The General*, while neither lionizing nor "Lyonsizing" Sarnoff, flatters his former boss greatly.

A name far less familiar than Sarnoff's is Merlin Aylesworth. He was the first president of NBC, a man recruited from the top management of America's public utility companies to run NBC because David Sarnoff believed that broadcasting networks ought to be like power and light companies, that is, run with a primary commitment to serving the "public interest, convenience, and necessity" (in the words of the 1927 Radio Act and the 1934 Communications Act). In a series of four articles written with the journalist Ben Gross for

Collier's magazine during the weeks of April 17, April 25, May 1, and May 8, 1948, under the title "Men, Mikes, and Money," Aylesworth reminisced about the problems and difficulties of getting NBC off the ground. Undoubtedly less than fully candid, yet still very revealing, Aylesworth told Gross and the world about the process by which NBC gradually abandoned its early public service philosophy and replaced it with an increasingly commercial, profit-oriented approach. The article is light reading, sensationalized and flattering to Aylesworth, Sarnoff, NBC, and RCA. But for the person who will go back and dig out the yellowing pages of *Collier's*, adorned with advertisements for Packard automobiles and Lava soap, there is much to be read between the lines of Aylesworth's remarks.

For some reason, CBS has always seemed more glamorous, less bureaucratic, and less dull than NBC. Probably the reason is William Paley, a man who has worked hard to be both glamorous and respectable, one of the originals of that kind of American known a few years ago as "the beautiful people." In his overblown book on America's media personalities, *The Powers That Be,* David Halberstam pictures Paley very much the way that Paley projects himself—deft at the handling of power and people, instinctively smart about problems and personalities, and above all, innately tasteful, intelligent, and elegant. In short, Halberstam's Paley is olympian, perhaps not God, but surely a force somehow more than natural in his ability to create a multimillion-dollar empire from a pile of rubble while still living with elegance and style.

Halberstam's portrayal is much in the spirit of Paley's own *As It Happened: A Memoir.* Paley, of course, is less blatantly convinced of his own semidivinity. He does not hesitate, however, to remember his instinctive recognition that Bing Crosby would be one of the great personalities of American entertainment, and he makes his famous raid on NBC's comedy talent seem like a beneficent act done out of a kindly intention to rescue Jack Benny et al. from the unenlightened executives at NBC. If Halberstam makes Paley seem a sort of Zeus enthroned on the top of Olympus, Paley sees himself more as a kind of Prometheus bringing splendor into the lives of others less capable of illumination than himself.

Even Tony Schwartz, one of the smartest men ever to write about broadcasting, finds William Paley irresistibly engaging in an interview called "An Intimate Talk with William Paley" in the *New York Times Magazine* of December 28, 1980. Even as far back as 1935, in a *Fortune* article on CBS called "And All Because They're Smart," this basic William Paley image was thoroughly established.

The simple fact seems to be that Paley is smart, elegant, and extremely competent. That image places him somewhat beyond the range of ordinary mortals, but it has more than once made him a target of humor. E. J. Kahn, Jr.'s "At Home with the Paleys," originally published in the *New Yorker* and later reprinted in E. B. White and Katharine S. White's *A Subtreasury of American Humor*, underscores the vulnerability to satire of anyone whose image goes quite as far as Paley's. Peter C. Goldmark's autobiographical *Maverick Inventor: My Turbulent Years at CBS* certainly shows Paley's human frailties. But while Paley may not live up to other peoples' image, or even to his own, he is a remarkable man with a true sense both of how to work in the media and of how to live in the cosmos.

Some of the most useful information of golden age network broadcasting comes from documents published during the 1930s and 1940s. On the light side, for instance, two articles reprinted in Lichty and Topping's *American Broadcasting* give a nice sense of how the networks appeared to the general public as they were first starting out. John Wallace's "What We Thought of the First Columbia Broadcasting Program" appeared in *Radio Broadcast* magazine in December 1927. It is a wonderfully serious review of the first program, charmingly solemn in its evaluation of a broadcast that even a few years later could only have seemed quaint and naïve in its misunderstanding of the medium. Similarly, Charles Magee Adams's "What about the Future of Chain Broadcasting?" in *Radio News* for February 1928 pondered seriously the question of whether networks could survive in the face of increasingly sophisticated programming by local stations. He concluded that networks would probably stick around for awhile—they were not merely a flash in the pan—but that the local stations would develop so well that networks could never play a really serious role in broadcasting. He was right, of course, but he was thirty years early with his predictions.

Most of the articles and books about radio published during the 1930s and 1940s, however, were unequivocally optimistic about network programming and its future. In 1930 Martin Codel edited *Radio and Its Future*, a wonderful collection of essays forecasting glorious things for broadcasting. David Sarnoff, no less, contributed an article on "Art and Industry." William Paley, in a totally predictable counterpoint, wrote a few pages on "Radio and Entertainment." Other luminaries on the list of contributors included Merlin Aylesworth, William S. Hedges (defending the idea of broadcast advertising as a means of serving the "public interest, convenience, and necessity"), Senator James Couzens, and Lee De Forest. The whole thing has something of the flavor of George Babbitt extolling the virtues of Zenith to a meeting of one of Sinclair Lewis's Main Street booster clubs, yet it has a kind of appealing naïveté that makes the book wonderful reading. One gets the sense that these writers really believed that radio was going to save man from the blight of original sin.

In a similar vein, but much more obviously propagandistic in intent, the National Association of Broadcasters published *Broadcasting in the United States*. It is an apologia for network broadcasting at a time when the NAB feared potential ill from the congressional debates that eventually created the Communications Act of 1934. They need not have worried; no matter what their intent, Roosevelt's New Deal Congresses did far more to help the networks than to hurt them. Alfred N. Goldsmith and Austin C. Lescarboura's *This Thing Called Broadcasting* of 1937 was a similar sort of explanatory defense of the network system as it existed after the Communications Act of 1934, and *Fortune*'s May 1938 series of articles on various aspects of the radio industry was similarly laudatory. The collection of speeches, essays, and correspondence collected in *Looking Ahead: The Papers of David Sarnoff* reveals how thoroughly the General himself believed in the positive good being done by broadcast networks, and the respected social historian Frederick Lewis Allen, reviewing the 1930s in his *Since Yesterday,* published in 1940, attributes to network radio the extraordinary rise in serious musical interest by the American public during the 1930s. As disinterested and fair as any American could possibly have been in 1940, Allen unequivocally believed that the networks really were doing pretty much what Paley, Sarnoff, and Hedges claimed that they were, namely, enlightening the American people and entertaining them, almost without cost, at a time when the public desperately needed both.

Robert Landry's *Who, What, Why is Radio?* of 1942 is an expository explanation of how prewar broadcasting worked. Less interesting than his *This Fascinating Radio Business,* which was basically a history, Landry's description of American radio is a subtle apologia and takes on some of the inevitably tiresome qualities that apologetics always seem to assume. It is worth remembering that as Landry was writing, the FCC was conducting the studies that eventually led to the 1941 *Report on Chain Broadcasting.* It is fair to assume that the NAB supplied a free copy of Landry's book to each of the seven FCC commissioners and their staffs.

Not all commentary from the 1930s was favorable, however, not by any means. Lots of Americans, and not just leftists, either, thought that the country would be far better served by a broadcasting system such as Canada's CBC, Australia's ABC, or, especially, the United Kingdom's BBC. Ruth Brindze's *Not to Be Broadcast: The Truth about the Radio* of 1937 was just one of many mildly muckracking attacks on the American system of commercial networks. Robert West's *The Rape of Radio* in 1941, far more sensational in its title than in its substance, was another example of the same genre, as was Franklin Mering Reck's *Radio from Start to Finish* in 1942. Basically exposés of minor abuses and dubious practices, such works were more in the nature of journalistic investigative reporting than serious proposals for change.

Other works, however, revealed real dissatisfaction with the whole American approach. Charles A. Siepmann, for instance, a former employee of the BBC and a pure Rooseveltian New Dealer at heart, regarded commercial broadcasting as an unhappy relic of the predepression Republican mentality and proposed serious restructuring in his *Radio's Second Chance* of 1946. Lyman Bryson's *Time for Reason about Radio* played variations on the same theme when it appeared in 1948. Siepmann's *Radio, Television, and Society* of 1950, a virtual classic in its intelligent and balanced description of the history and structure of the total broadcasting system, was written as a serious plea to reorganize broadcasting as television supplanted radio. Siepmann's arguments may have been wrong and certainly did not have much effect on the course of broadcasting history, but a great deal of what he says still makes sense. His may be the best piece of social criticism ever written about American broadcasting; it is certainly among the sanest and most reasonable.

From the late 1920s broadcasting exerted such remarkable influence on society that the economists, sociologists, and political scientists could hardly ignore it. During the period from 1929 to 1941, the American Academy of Political and Social Science (AAPSS) devoted three special issues of its academically prestigious *Annals* to the subject of radio, and the Arno Press collected and reprinted all three of these special issues in its 1971 series on "The History of Broadcasting: Radio to Television" under the title *Radio: Selected A.A.P.S.S. Surveys, 1929-1941*. The first of these surveys was edited in 1929 by Irvin Stewart and issued as a special supplement to the AAPSS *Annals* (volume 107) for the year. It covered all aspects of radio, including point-to-point communications and amateur broadcasting, from the viewpoint of social and political scientists. In 1935 Herman S. Hettinger edited *Radio: The Fifth Estate* as volume 177 of the *Annals,* and again in 1941 he edited *New Horizons in Radio* as volume 213. All three volumes involved sober, academic investigations of radio as a political, economic, and social institution.

In 1942 Carroll Atkinson did an about-face within the ranks of educational broadcasters, most of whom formed a solid if ineffectual phalanx of resistance to network dominance, by publishing *Radio Network Contributions to Education.* He defended the positive influence of Walter Damrosch's "Music Appreciation Hour" and CBS's "Columbia Workshop" (which had aired radio plays by Archibald MacLeish and other literary luminaries of the day) and claimed that the networks had a substantial educational influence on Americans. It may be worth noting that the book appeared at a time when the FCC was investigating the networks with an apparently unfriendly intent, but it still mounts an interesting case for the positive educational benefits of commercial network broadcasting.

Other more or less disinterested studies of network broadcasting during the era of network dominance include Llewellyn White's 1947 *The American Radio: A Report on the Broadcasting Industry in the United States from the Commission on Freedom of the Press,* which was generally positive though hardly uncritical; Tsao Eoyang's *An Economic Study of the Radio Industry in the United States of America,* which has all the fire and passion that microeconomists usually bring to their topics (that is, none); the FCC Engineering Department's 1938 *Report on Social and Economic Data Pursuant to the Informal Hearing on Broadcasting,* which fired the opening salvo in the FCC's attack on the networks; the FCC's 1941 *Report on Chain Broadcasting,* which concluded that the networks had too tight a grip on the stations (even though the stations, as later became obvious, were simply delighted to put themselves in the networks' loving arms); and the FCC's 1947 follow-up report called *An Economic Study of Standard Broadcasting,* which could have greatly aided the development of FM, but did not.

Broadcasting was born during the boom years of the Coolidge era, but it went through its adolescence during the Great Depression. It only reached real maturity during World War II, and despite the many criticisms and questions that can be raised about the networks during their domination over radio, their performance during World War II was unequivocally magnificent. Without surrendering their autonomy, CBS, MBS, and the NBC Red and Blue networks contributed to the national morale, sacrificed manpower and technical expertise (not to mention profits), and generally contributed splendidly to the Allied effort to defeat fascism. Two early bits of propaganda—Sherman Harvard Dryer's *Radio in Wartime"* (1942) and Charles J. Rolo's *Radio Goes to War: The "Fourth Front"* (1942)—might be dismissed as simple jingoistic drumbeating except for one fact. The radio networks really did perform very much in the spirit in which Dryer and Rolo predicted they would.

MODERN RADIO NETWORKS

NBC, CBS, MBS, and ABC did not cease to be radio networks when TV arrived on the scene, but they did cease to be terribly important. A number of other networks arose in radio, and during the 1970s, some new approaches to radio networking enjoyed real success. No overview of these modern networks exists, but Peter Fornatale and Joshua E. Mills's *Radio in the Television Age* touches on most of the more interesting developments.

Certainly the most interesting of the post-TV radio networks was Gordon McLendon's short-lived but sensational Liberty Broadcasting System. Fornatale and Mills have much to say about McLendon in their book; while they do not exactly revere the man, they obviously regard him, along with Todd Storz, as the founder of contemporary radio. Frank X. Tolbert contributed "Man behind a Network," an interesting analysis of McLendon and the Liberty Broadcasting System (which was built on daily broadcasts of baseball to local stations) to *Nation's Business* in March 1952, shortly before the network's demise. David T. MacFarland wrote a brief history of the Liberty network for Lichty and Topping's *American Broadcasting.* The best single history of the network, however, is Edwin Glick's "The Life and Death of the Liberty Broadcasting System" in the *Journal of Broadcasting* (1979). As both MacFarland and Glick point out, the Liberty network was like most contemporary radio networks, a system of affiliations built around a single purpose—in Liberty's case, baseball broadcasting. Thus the whole fate of the network depended on the success of a single type of programming. This provides a sharp contrast to the older network approach to radio, and the Liberty system can be legitimately viewed as a case study in how contemporary radio networks function.

Sad to say, there is abundant information from the 1950s and early 1960s about how badly the commercial radio networks functioned. In 1958, for instance, the FCC did a report, *Network Broadcasting,* for the House of Representatives that documented how insignificant radio had become in network thinking. Pamela Johnson Sybert wrote a very interesting historical piece in the 1980 volume of the *Journal of Broadcasting* called "Mutual Admiration: MBS and the Dominican Republic" about the dreadful ethical standards during the year when TV was in the ascendant and Mutual, as the only one of the old "big four" that had failed to move from radio to television, was desperate. Desmond Smith, writing for the September 1964 issue of *Harper's*, commented on how low the standards of radio broadcasting had sunk and how unlikely the networks were to reassert positive leadership. Even *Broadcasting,* ever optimistic about the power of positive broadcasting, ran a May 14, 1962, article called "Radio at 40 Enters Its Critical Years." Not even the NAB could see how radio, especially the networks that had formerly been the medium's primary source of energy, could reestablish itself as a really significant medium.

Fifteen years later, however, things had changed. Alan Frank and Cary Bayer wrote "Network Radio Comes out of the Trenches" for the October 9, 1978, issue of *Broadcast Report.* Their main point was that the commercial radio networks, notably ABC's four separate services and the new black networks, were finally beginning to provide effective programming for their affiliates. *Forbes* magazine ran a piece called "The Return of Network Radio" later in the same year (October 30, 1978), which had much the same tone as Frank and Bayer's earlier article.

Undoubtedly, one impetus for the revitalization of network radio—not the only impetus, to be sure, but a major one—was the establishment of NPR, the National Public Radio network. The relative youth of National Public Radio as well as its historical struggle for recognition on a large scale may account for the paucity of published information about it. While articles abound on Garrison Keillor and "A Prairie Home Companion," the program that all but single-handedly brought NPR into popular culture, similar sources on NPR itself are relatively scarce. The archival information is contained largely in Corporation of Public Broadcasting publications and National Public Radio research publications (statistical reports on various aspects of broadcasting, programming content by category breakdowns, and various memoranda and letters from the myriad of pioneers in the public broadcasting venture).

NPR has had two incarnations. It first came into being in 1970 as an outgrowth of the Corporation for Public Broadcasting. Its primary function at this time was to provide a linkage among already established educational radio stations and begin the process of developing programming on a nationwide level. In 1977 NPR merged with the Association of Public Radio Stations (APRS), which had been formed in 1973 by station managers as an independent advocacy group for stations. The new organization took the name National Public Radio, and structurally that is the NPR we know today.

Public Broadcasting: The Role of the Federal Government, 1912-76 by George H. Gibson provides a comprehensive review of the whole involvement of the federal government in the broadcasting business and pays special attention to the establishment of the Public Broadcasting System (PBS) and National Public Radio. It is probably the best place to start any investigation of NPR, especially since it includes a thorough listing of sources.

A few narrative histories of the actual formation of NPR have been produced with some success in doctoral dissertations. Joseph Brady Kirkish's "A Descriptive History of America's First National Public Radio Network: National Public Radio, 1970–1974," is the first part of a two-dissertation, long-distance collaboration between Kirkish (University of Michigan, 1980) and Kenneth John Garry ("The History of National Public Radio, 1974–1977," Southern Illinois University, 1982). This unique if somewhat awkward partnership has produced a dry but well-researched history of how NPR came into being in 1970 and grew quickly in quality and prestige. Kirkish, covering more or less the three-year term of NPR's first president, Donald Quayle, received generous assistance from NPR and its founding fathers, most notably William Siemering, Richard (Dick) Estelle, and Al Hulsen. The material for a dramatic adventure is here, but the narrative skims away the energy and suspense of what must have been an absolutely thrilling sequence of events. Almost encyclopedic at times, the narrative does perk up during the long and very valuable discussion on "All Things Considered" as something of William Siemering's vision and passion for this radio magazine program comes through the layers of who, what, where, and when. The dissertation is also surprisingly brief in its discussion of pre-1970 public radio. But in general it does the job it set out to do.

Garry picks up the period from 1974 to 1977, the years in which Lee Frischknecht served as NPR's second president. Perhaps overly constrained by the structuring of the narrative by fiscal year and, in fairness, deprived of the pioneering spirit that informs the earlier years, Garry's work shows a disappointing emphasis (from a popular culture point of view) on the ebb and flow of finances and internal organization. The organizational tale ends with the merger of the old NPR and the APRS, a subject that forms the center of James Michael Haney's dissertation, "A History of the Merger of National Public Radio and the Association of Public Radio Stations" (University of Iowa, 1981). Haney charts the reorganization and the events leading up to the merger in admirable if turgid detail and analyzes the many, overlapping reasons for it: to unify the management and advocacy functions of public radio, to head off potential strife between the old NPR and APRS, and to allow for critical staffing and management changes in both organizations.

Under the Reagan administration, PBS and NPR suffered substantial cutbacks in their funding. And yet, all things considered, NPR emerged from its bureaucratic battles relatively whole and stable. The best popular source of information on this entire episode is the series of stories carried in the *New York Times* and accessible through its annual index for 1983.

As NPR's popularity has grown, so has the attention being paid to its stars and its audiences. "All Things Considered" former host Susan Stamberg wrote a book under a title that must have come out of several staff meetings and a small corporate shake-up—*Every Night at Five: Susan Stamberg's "All Things Considered" Book*. It is coffee-table collage, arranged (or disarranged) much like the show itself: a mixture of the profound and the whimsical held together improbably by the writer's uncommon good sense. The press has also discovered "Morning Edition" 's Bob Edwards and profiled him in a *New Yorker* piece ("Reporting," August 13, 1984). But the major celebrity to come out of NPR is, of course, Garrison Keillor, enigmatic yet overexposed host of "A Prairie Home Companion." Between 1983 and 1986 puff and profiles appeared in *Saturday Evening Post* (Sutin 1986), *Christian Today* (Youngren 1985), *Mother Earth News* (Hemingson 1985), and many other publications, all readily accessible through the *Readers' Guide to Periodical Literature.*

There is a profusion of information available on the history of America's radio networks. That information is, however, diffuse and scattered—much as it is in many other aspects of radio history. Fortunately, Laurence Bergreen's book pulls together most of the information and presents it within a single cover. His *Look Now, Pay Later* was a major step forward in the scholarly understanding of how business, government, and the consumer interact within the limits of the American system of mass communication. At the same time, it seems almost amazing that his should be the only such book in the field. It is hard to understand why America's historians have paid so little attention to so extaordinary a story. Almost equally surprising is the dearth of information on men like Merlin Aylesworth and Frank Stanton, men admittedly overshadowed by their mythic employers, Sarnoff and Paley, and yet still individuals of extraordinary influence in the shaping of our modern communication system.

It is perhaps inevitable that broadcasting history should focus the majority of its attention on men and women who actually went on the air, whose voices and ideas have become familiar items to literally millions of Americans. At the same time, however, it seems strange that with the wealth of information available on Edward R. Murrow, Elmer Davis, and even on Eddie Cantor and Bob Hope, there should be so little in print about the men and women who created and operated the system that brought these stars to prominence.

STATION HISTORIES

While the rise of the networks forms a major part of the core of the general history of broadcasting, station histories dot the landscape as outposts of relatively isolated broadcasting information. Ranging from master's theses, doctoral dissertations, and serious-minded books to in-house, self-congratulatory puff pamphlets, relatively few are of value as material over and above sources of information on the particular station at hand. However, there are exceptions.

Perhaps the most widely known station history (and justifiably so) is William Peck Banning's *Commercial Broadcasting Pioneer: The WEAF Experiment, 1922–1926.* The book is valuable as broadcasting history because of WEAF's (New York) critical position as the first commercial radio station to become important, influential, and successful on a fairly large scale. This comprehensive, well-written book is as much a history of early corporate influence and technical development in commercial radio as it is a history of a single station.

Because of the station's place in broadcasting history, the far less satisfying material available on KDKA (Pittsburgh) is at least worthy of mention. Many years ago Westinghouse, KDKA's parent company, published an undated in-house pamphlet *It Started Hear: The History of KDKA Radio and Broadcasting*. In addition, Westinghouse produced an unpublished sixty-plus-page history of KDKA that is in the Broadcast Pioneers Library in Washington, D.C. To my knowledge, no full-length history of KDKA is extant, and one needs to be written.

It should be noted that Joseph E. Baudino and John M. Kittross defended KDKA's claim to being radio's oldest station against three challengers (WWJ [Detroit], WHA [Madison], and KQW [San Jose]—the forerunner to San Francisco's KCBS). Their article "Broadcasting's Oldest Stations: An Examination of Four Claimants" in *Journal of Broadcasting* (Winter 1977) sets up criteria and measures all claimants against it. KDKA emerges as the winner.

Many of the general histories of radio broadcasting, including those cited in this chapter and in other chapters of this book, contain useful information about stations. Archer's *Big Business and Radio* contains information on KDKA, WEAF, and WJZ (New York). Archer's *History of Radio to 1926* also contains historical information on these three stations. Erik Barnouw's *A Tower in Babel* incorporates into its narrative the founding of KDKA, WEAF, and WJZ and their role in the early chain-linking experiments that eventually led to the development of the networks. Jim Harmon's *The Great Radio Heroes* offers an informal programming history of WXYZ (Detroit), birthplace of "The Lone Ranger," "The Green Hornet," and other adventure serials. A wonderful but little-known source of station history is the research service Broadcast Pro-File, which operates out of Hollywood, California. Typically, Broadcast Pro-File is capable of producing a 2,000-word "biography" on a station, often with emphasis on its corporate and licensing history—a fact that suggests heavy reliance on public documents. The prices for individual histories are quite modest. Broadcast Pro-File warns that "accuracy is not guaranteed" but assures that "every professional research effort has been made to insure an accurate profile." *Radio Station Treasury: 1900-1946* by Tom Kneitel is a recently published and, as of this writing, not widely distributed history of radio stations. Although we have not yet examined it firsthand, early reviews from radio enthusiasts are very favorable.

A selected checklist of published and unpublished station histories follows. This list was compiled with the invaluable assistance of the Broadcast Pioneers Library in Washington, D.C. and is used by permission.

STATION HISTORIES BY STATION

1. KCBS. *See* KQW.
2. KDKA. Davis, H.P. "The History of Broadcasting in the United States: An Address Delivered before the Graduate School of Business Administration, Harvard University, April 21, 1928." 24 pages. Primarily about KDKA.
3. KDKA. "History of KDKA." 62+ pages.

4. KDKA. [Westinghouse Broadcasting Company.] "The History of KDKA Radio and Broadcasting." Pittsburgh: Westinghouse Broadcasting Company, n.d. 17 pages.

5. KDKA. "Radio's First 25 Years." *Bulletin Index: Pittsburgh's Weekly News-magazine,* November 3, 1945, 17–21+.

6. KDKA. [KDKA.] "Souvenir Program of the National Broadcasting Company and the Westinghouse Electric & Manufacturing Company upon the Occasion of the Fourteenth Anniversary of Radio Station KDKA and the Opening of Its New Studios in the Grant Building, Pittsburgh, November 2, 1934." Pittsburgh: KDKA, 1934. No pagination.
   Cover title: "KDKA Fourteenth Anniversary Program." Contains three pages of history.

7. KEX. "KEX Technical History." 12+ pages. Unpublished typed manuscript from Westinghouse Broadcasting Company.

8. KGCX. " The KGCX Story." August 1961. No pagination. Unpublished typed manuscript, gift of Suzanne Krebsbach Knudsvig, whose grandfather, E. E. Krebsbach, was cofounder of the station.

9. KGNC. KGNC. "The Way It All Began." Amarillo, Tex.: KGNC, [1952]. No pagination. Includes the story of stations KGRS and WDAG, which preceded KGNC.

10. KGRS. *See* KGNC.

11. KMA. Birkby, Robert. *KMA Radio: The First Sixty Years.* Shenandoah, Iowa: May Broadcasting Company, 1985. 248 pages.

12. KOB. Velia, Ann M. *KOB: Goddard's Magic Mast: Fifty Years of Pioneer Broadcasting.* Las Cruces: New Mexico State University, 1972. 195 pages.

13. KQV. "History of KQV—Pittsburgh, Pa." 2 pages. Unpublished typed manuscript.

14. KQW. [Baudino, Joseph E., and Gordon Greb, comps.] [Folder.] Voluminous unpublished documentation, including copies of early licenses, of KQW, San Jose, which became KCBS, San Francisco.

15. KRE. Schneider, John F. "The KRE Story." 1971. 16 pages. Unpublished manuscript prepared by the author for a book about San Francisco radio stations.

16. KSD. "KSD: 50 Years of Radio; KSD-TV: 25 Years of Television—And the Best Is Yet to Come." *St. Louis Post-Dispatch,* February 6, 1972, 1-16G.

17. KSD. KSD. "The First Forty." St. Louis: Pulitzer Publishing Company, 1962. No pagination.

18. KWG [KWG.] Hollywood, California, Broadcast Pro-File [1973?]. 3 pages. Published by a company that specializes in producing station histories.

19. KXOK. Hereford, Robert A. "From Tom-Tom to Hi-fi: A St. Louis Saga." St. Louis: KXOK Broadcasting, 1957. 30 pages. Some history. Most of text is promotion.

20. KYW. "History of KYW." 30+ pages. Unpublished typed manuscript from Westinghouse Broadcasting Company of KYW in its various locations.

21. KYW. "KYW History, November 11, 1921-December 3, 1934." n.d. Various paginations. Unpublished typed manuscript from Westinghouse Broadcasting Company, including a wealth of documentation of the Chicago station.

22. KYW. Baudino, Joseph E. "The Story of KYW: A Talk . . ." given at the meeting

of the Delaware Valley Chapter of the Broadcast Pioneers on September 24, 1975. 7 pages. History of the travels of the "peripatetic call letters" of KYW from Chicago to Philadelphia to Cleveland to Philadelphia.

23. KYW. McCluer, Paul, comp. "Westinghouse Radiophone Station KYW, Chicago Pioneers [1921-1934]." 1970. 2 vols. Scrapbooks of KYW Chicago history.

24. WBZ. "History of WBZ." 45+ pages. Unpublished typed manuscript from Westinghouse Broadcasting Company.

25. WCAU. WCAU. "WCAU Celebrates 25th Anniverary . . . . Commemorating a Quarter Century of Community Service." Philadelphia: WCAU, 1947. No pagination.

26. WCCO. Sarjeant, Charles F., ed. *The First Forty: The Story of WCCO Radio.* Minneapolis: T. S. Denison, 1964. 124 pages.

27. WCCO. Haeg, Larry, Jr. "Sixty Years Strong: The Story of One of America's Great Radio Stations, 1924-1984." Minneapolis-St. Paul: WCCO Radio, 1984. 132 pages.

28. WCSH. WCSH. "The First 40 Years: Recorded . . . and Transcribed." Portland, Maine: WCSH, [1964?]. No pagination. Also contains brief histories of WRDO, Augusta, and WLBZ, Bangor, all part of the Maine Broadcasting System.

29. WDAG. *See* KGNC.

30. WEAF. Banning, William Peck. *Commercial Broadcasting Pioneer: The WEAF Experiment, 1922-1926.* Cambridge, Mass.: Harvard University Press, 1946. 308 pages.

31. WEAF. *Weather Vein* 7, no. 3; (1927). 56 pages. Quarterly periodical.

32. WENR. McCluer, Paul. "Radio Station WENR: The Voice of Service, Chicago." 2 vols. Scrapbooks of WENR history.

33. WFAA. [WFAA.] "Counting Start and Kilocycles: 25th Anniversary, WFAA, Dallas." Dallas: WFAA, [1947]. 44 pages.

34. WFBM. The WFBM Stations. "From Crystal to Color: WFBM." 1st ed. Indianapolis: The WFBM Stations, 1964. 189 pages.

35. WFIL. [Clipp, Roger W.] "History of WFIL and Triangle Radio and Television Stations." 9 pages. Unpublished typed manuscript.

36. WGAR. WGAR. "Exhibits of the WGAR Broadcasting Company. Cleveland: WGAR, [1949]. 2 vols. Exhibits before the FCC. Section 1 devoted to history. Other sections contain history.

37. WGAY. Brechner, Joseph L. "You, Too, Can Own a Radio Station." *Saturday Evening Post* 219, (January 25, 1947): 26-27+.

38. WGBF. WGBF. "Our First 30 years." Evansville, Ind.: WGBF, 1953. 36 pages.

39. WGN. "WGN: A Pictorial History." Chicago: WGN, 1961. [111] pages.

40. WGY. WGY. "40th Anniversary, 1922-1962." Schenectady, N.Y.: WGY, [1962]. No pagination.

41. WGY. WGY. "A Message from WGY." Schenectady, N.Y.: WGY, 1930. 12 pages.

42. WGY. WGY. "Silver Anniversary of Farm Broadcasting over WGY," Schenectady, N.Y.: WGY, 1951. 16 pages.

43. WGY. "WGY—Technical Pioneer (Historical Background)." Schenectady, N.Y.: WGY, 1964. 8 pages. News release, December 15, 1964.

44. WGY. WGY. "This is WGY Schenectady, Radio 81." Schenectady, N.Y.: WGY, [1979]. No pagination.

45. WHA. WHA. "The First 50 Years of University of Wisconsin Broadcasting: WHA, 1919-1969, and a Look Ahead to the Next 50 Years." Madison, Wis.: WHA, [1969]. No pagination.

46. WHA. Smith, R. Franklin. "'Oldest Station in the Nation'?" *Journal of Broadcasting* 4 (Winter 1959-60): 40-55. Cites other articles referring to KQW, KDKA, and WWJ as candidates for the oldest station.

47. WIBW. WIBW. "The WIBW Years: 50, 1927-1977." Topeka, Kans.: WIBW, [1977]. No pagination.

48. WIP. Lee, Robert E. "WIP Is the Story of Radio: [Address before the] Greater Philadelphia Chamber of Commerce Luncheon, Philadelphia, Pennsylvania, April 26, 1957." 8 pages. A portion of the speech is devoted to WIP history.

49. WJR. WJR. "50 Years of Unique Radio." Detroit: WJR, 1972. No pagination.

50. WKZO. WKZO. "50th Fetzer Anniversary." Kalamazoo, Mich.: The Fetzer Stations, 1981. No pagination. Also refers briefly to other Fetzer stations.

51. WLBZ. *See* WCSH.

52. WLS. WLS. "Stand by: 25th Anniversary Issue, April 12, 1949." Chicago: WLS, 1949. 16 pages.

53. WLW. Lichty, Lawrence W. "'The Nation's Station': A History of Radio Station WLW." 1964. Various paginations. Draft of doctoral dissertation, Ohio State University (?).

54. WMAQ. Caton, Chester F. "Radio Station WMAQ: A History of Its Independent Years (1922-1931)." Ph.D. diss., School of Speech, Northwestern University, 1951. 407 pages.

55. WMAQ. WMAQ. "The Story of WMAQ: The Personality of a Broadcasting Station." Chicago: WMAQ, 1931. 40 pages.

56. WMC. Memphis Commercial Appeal. "WMC Memphis, 'DOWN IN DIXIE.'" Memphis: Memphis Commercial Appeal, [1932]. No pagination.

57. WMT. WMT. "The WMT Radio Story: 40th Anniversary, 1922-1962." Cedar Rapids, Iowa: WMT, 1962. No pagination. The serious version.

58. WOI. Curtis, Alberta. "Listeners Appraise a College Station: Station WOI, Iowa State College, Ames, Iowa." Washington, D.C.: Federal Radio Education Committee, 1940. 70 pages. Includes some history.

59. WOR. WOR. "'. . . A Few Bright Candles on the Cake.'" New York: WOR, 1967. 24 pages.

60. WOR. WOR. "WOR Radio, 1922-1982: The First Sixty Years." New York: WOR, 1982. No pagination.

61. [K]WOS. Willets, Gilson. Letter to Missouri Broadcasters Association, August 14, 1975. 2 pages. About history of WOS, later KWOS, which the author founded.

62. WQXR. Sanger, Elliott M. *Rebel in Radio: The Story of WQXR*. New York: Hastings House, 1973. 190 pages.

63. WRC. National Broadcasting Company. "Progress Through the Years: WRC Television and Radio." Washington, D.C.: National Broadcasting Company, n.d. No pagination. Very brief discussion of WRC Radio history.

64. WRDO. *See* WCSH.

65. WRR. Smith Detective Agency and Nightwatch Service, Inc. "WRR." Dallas: Smith Detective Agency and Nightwatch Service, 1959. No pagination.

66. WSB. WSB. "Welcome South, Brother: Fifty Years of Broadcasting at WSB, Atlanta, Georgia." Atlanta: WSB: 1974. 112 pages.

67. WTAR. Lott, George Edward, Jr. "The History of Radio Station WTAR: The Pioneer Years, 1923-1934." Ph.D. diss., College of Communication Arts, Michigan State University, 1970. 258 pages.

68. WTIC. WTIC. "WTIC: Radio to Remember." Hartford, Conn.: WTIC AM and FM, 1958. No pagination.

69. WTMJ. WTMJ. "WTMJ, WTMJ-TV, WTMJ-FM, 1927-1969." Milwaukee: WTMJ, 1969. 38 pages.

70. WUOM. University of Michigan Broadcasting Service. "WUOM-FM." Ann Arbor: University of Michigan Broadcasting Service, [1950?]. No pagination.

71. WVOX. Collins, Michael. "Our Ratings Book. WVOX and WRTN: A Retrospective and History." New Rochelle, N.Y.: WVOX, WRTN [1984]. No pagination.

72. WWJ. Rimes, Robert P. "The Night Radio Was Born." *Detroit News,* August 21, 1960, 1-E+.

73. WWJ. WWJ. "The Story of WWJ Radio One: Where It all Began." Detroit: WWJ, 1970. No pagination.

74. WWL. Pusateri, C. Joseph. *Enterprise in Radio: WWL and the Business of Broadcasting in America.* Washington, D.C.: University Press of America, 1980. 366 pages.

75. WWL. Loyola University. "WWL AM-FM-TV: The Second Campus of Loyola University, New Orleans." New Orleans: Loyola University, 1969. 24 pages.

76. WXYZ. Osgood, Dick. *WYXIE WONDERLAND: An Unauthorized 50-Year Diary of WXYZ Detroit.* Bowling Green, Ohio: Bowling Green University Popular Press, 1981. 537 pages.

BIBLIOGRAPHY FOR RADIO NETWORKS AND STATION HISTORIES

Adams, Charles Magee. "What about the Future of Chain Broadcasting?" *Radio News* (February 1928): 869-71. In *American Broadcasting: A Source on the History of Radio and Television,* edited by Lawrence W. Lichty and Malachi C. Topping, 181-85. New York: Hastings House, 1975.

Allen, Frederick Lewis. *Since Yesterday.* New York: Harpers, 1940.

"And All Because They're Smart." *Fortune* (June 1935): 80-83.

Archer, Gleason L. *History of Radio to 1926.* 1938. Reprint New York; Arno Press, 1971.

———. *Big Business and Radio.* 1939. Reprint. New York: Arno Press, 1971.

Atkinson, Carroll. *Radio Network Contributions to Education.* Boston: Meador, 1942.

Aylesworth, Merlin H., and Ben Gross. "Men, Miles, and Money." *Collier's* 121 (April 17, 1948): 13-15, 65-68; (April 25, 1948): 26-27, 97-98; (May 1, 1948): 68-72; May 8, 1948: 30-39.

Baker, W. J. *A History of the Marconi Company.* New York: St. Martin's, 1972.

Banning, William Peck. *Commercial Broadcasting Pioneer: The WEAF Experiment, 1922-1926.* Cambridge, Mass.: Harvard University Press, 1946.

Barnouw, Erik. *A Tower in Babel.* Vol. 1 of *A History of Broadcasting in the United States.* New York: Oxford University Press, 1966.

_____. *The Golden Web.* Vol. 2 of *A History of Broadcasting in the United States.* New York: Oxford University Press, 1968.

Baudino, Joseph E., and John M. Kittross. "Broadcasting's Oldest Stations: An Examination of Four Claimants." *Journal of Broadcasting* 21 (1977): 61-83.

Bergreen, Laurence. *Look Now, Pay Later: The Rise of Network Broadcasting.* Garden City, N.Y.: Doubleday, 1980.

Bilby, Kenneth. *The General: David Sarnoff and the Rise of the Communications Industry.* New York: Harper and Row, 1986.

Brindze, Ruth. *Not to be Broadcast: The Truth about the Radio.* 1937. Reprint. New York: Da Capo, 1974.

Bryson, Lyman. *Time for Reason about Radio.* New York: George Stewart, 1948.

Bucher, E. E. "Radio and David Sarnoff." 56 vols. Unpublished manuscript at the David Sarnoff Research Center, David Sarnoff Library, Princeton, New Jersey (cited in Bergreen, *Look Now, Pay Later*).

Burner, David. *Herbert Hoover: A Public Life.* New York: Knopf, 1978.

Campbell, Robert. *The Golden Years of Broadcasting: A Celebration of the First 50 Years of Radio and TV on NBC.* New York: Scribner, 1976.

"CBS: Documenting 38 Years of Exciting History." *Sponsor* 19 (September 13, 1965): 92-127.

"CBS: The First Five Decades." *Broadcasting* (September 19, 1977): 45-116.

Chase, Francis, Jr. *Sound and Fury: An Informal History of Broadcasting.* New York: Harper and Bros., 1942.

Chester, Giraud, Garnet R. Garrison, and Edgar E. Willis. *Television and Radio.* 5th ed. Englewood Cliffs, N.J.: Prentice-Hall, 1978.

Codel, Martin, ed. *Radio and Its Future.* 1930. Reprint. New York: Arno Press, 1971.

Danielian, N. R. *A.T.&T.: The Story of Industrial Conquest.* 1939. Reprint. New York: Arno Press, 1974.

Dreher, Carl. *Sarnoff: An American Success.* New York: Quadrangle, 1977.

Dryer, Sherman Harvard. *Radio in Wartime.* New York: Greenberg, 1942.

Dunlap, Orrin E., Jr. *Marconi: The Man and His Wireless.* 1937. Reprint. New York: Arno Press, 1971.

_____. *The Story of Radio.* New York: Dial, 1935.

Emery, Walter B. *National and International Systems of Broadcasting: Their History, Operation, and Control.* East Lansing, Mich.: Michigan State University Press, 1969.

Eoyang, Tsao. *An Economic Study of the Radio Industry in the United States of America.* 1936. Reprint. New York: Arno Press, 1974.

"The First Fifty Years of Broadcasting." *Broadcasting.* Weekly series of articles, October 13, 1980-September 28, 1981.

The First Fifty Years of Broadcasting: The Running Story of the Fifth Estate. Washington, D.C.: Broadcasting Publishing Company, 1982.

"The First Fifty Years of NBC." *Broadcasting* (June 21, 1976): 44-100.

Fornatale, Peter, and Joshua E. Mills. *Radio in the Television Age.* Woodstock, N.Y.: Overlook Press, 1980.

Foster, Eugene S. *Understanding Broadcasting.* Reading, Mass.: Addison-Wesley, 1978.

Frank, Alan, and Cary Bayer. "Network Radio Comes out of the Trenches." *Broadcast Report* (October 9, 1978): 38-41.

Garry, Kenneth John. "The History of National Public Radio, 1974-1977." Ph.D. diss., Southern Illinois University, 1982.

Gibson, George H. *Public Broadcasting: The Role of the Federal Government 1912-76.* New York: Praeger, 1977.

Glick, Edwin. "The Life and Death of the Liberty Broadcasting System." *Journal of Broadcasting* 23 (1979): 117-38.

Goldmark, Peter C. *Maverick Inventor: My Turbulent Years at CBS.* New York: Dutton, 1973.

Goldsmith, Alfred N., and Austin C. Lescarboura. *This Thing Called Broadcasting.* New York: Holt, 1937.

Halberstam, David. *The Powers That Be.* New York: Alfred Knopf, 1979.

Haney, James Michael. "A History of the Merger of National Public Radio and the Association of Public Radio Stations." Ph.D. diss., University of Iowa, 1981.

Harmon, Jim. *The Great Radio Heroes.* Garden City, N.Y.: Doubleday, 1967.

Head, Sydney W. *Broadcasting in America: A Survey of Television and Radio.* 3rd ed. Boston: Houghton Mifflin, 1976.

Hemingson, Peter. "The Plowboy Interview: Garrison Keillor, the Voice of Lake Woebegon." *Mother Earth News,* no. 93 (May/June 1985): 16-20+.

Hettinger, Herman S., ed. *Radio: The Fifth Estate.* Annals of the American Academy of Political and Social Science, vol. 177. 1935. Reprinted in *Radio: Selected A.A.P.S.S. Surveys.* New York: Arno Press, 1971.

_____. *New Horizons in Radio.* Annals of the American Academy of Political and Social Science, vol. 213. 1941. Reprinted in *Radio: Selected A.A.P.S.S. Surveys.* New York: Arno Press, 1971.

Hoover, Herbert. *The Memoirs of Herbert Hoover: The Cabinet and the Presidency, 1920-1933.* New York: Macmillan, 1952.

Jansky, C. M. "The Contribution of Herbert Hoover to Broadcasting." *Journal of Broadcasting* 1 (1956): 241-49.

Jolly, W. P. *Marconi.* New York: Stein and Day, 1972.

Kahn, E. J., Jr. "At Home with the Paleys." In *A Subtreasury of American Humor,* edited by E. B. White and Katharine S. White, 624-27. New York: Coward-McCann, 1941.

Kahn, Frank J., ed. *Documents of American Broadcasting.* 3rd ed. Englewood Cliffs, N.J.: Prentice-Hall, 1978.

Kirkish, Joseph Brady. "A Descriptive History of America's First National Public Radio Network: National Public Radio, 1970-1974." Ph.D. diss., University of Michigan, 1980.

Kittross, John M. *Documents in American Telecommunications Policy.* New York: Arno Press, 1977.

_____. *A Bibliography of Theses and Dissertations in Broadcasting, 1920-1973.* Washington, D.C.: Broadcast Education Association, 1978.

Kneitel, Tom. *Radio Station Treasury 1900-1946.* Commock, N.Y.: CRB Research, 1988.

Lackmann, Ron. *Remember Radio.* New York: G. P. Putnam's Sons, 1970.

Landry, Robert. *Who, What, Why is Radio?* New York: George Stewart, 1942.

_____. *This Fascinating Radio Business.* Indianapolis, Ind.: Bobbs-Merrill, 1946.

Lichty, Lawrence W., and Malachi C. Topping, eds. *American Broadcasting: A Source Book on the History of Radio and Television.* New York: Hastings House, 1976.

Lyons, Eugene. *David Sarnoff: A Biography.* New York: Harper and Row, 1966.

MacFarland, David T. "The Liberty Broadcasting System." In *American Broadcasting: A Source Book on the History of Radio and Television,* edited by Lawrence W. Lichty and Malachi C. Topping, 188-90. New York: Hastings House, 1976.

Mackey, David. "The Development of the National Association of Broadcasters." *Journal of Broadcasting* 1 (1956): 305-25.

MacLaurin, W. Rupert. *Invention and Innovation in the Radio Industry.* 1949. Reprint. New York: Arno Press, 1971.

McLuhan, Marshall. *Understanding Media: The Extensions of Man.* New York: McGraw-Hill, 1965.

Marconi, Degna. *My Father, Marconi.* New York: McGraw-Hill, 1962.

Metz, Robert. *CBS: Reflections in a Bloodshot Eye.* Chicago: Playboy Press, 1975.

Mitchell, Curtis. *Cavalcade of Broadcasting.* Chicago: Follett, 1970.

Mix, Jennie Irene. "Good National Programs Prove 'What the Public Wants.'" *Radio Broadcast* (May 1925): 62-65. Reprinted in *American Broadcasting: A Source Book on the History of Radio and Television,* edited by Lawrence W. Lichty and Malachi C. Topping, 164-66. New York: Hastings House, 1976.

Morris, Lloyd R. *Not So Long Ago.* New York: Random House, 1949.

"Music in the Air and Voices on the Crystal Set." *American Heritage* 6 (August 1955): 64-88.

National Association of Broadcasters. *Broadcasting in the United States.* Washington, D.C.: National Association of Broadcasters, 1933.

"NBC: A Documentary." *Sponsor* 20 (May 16, 1966).

Paley, William. *As It Happened: A Memoir.* Garden City, N.Y.: Doubleday, 1979.

Quinlan, Sterling. *Inside ABC: American Broadcasting Company's Rise to Power.* New York: Hastings House, 1979.

"Radio at 40 Enters Its Critical Years." *Broadcasting* 62 (May 14, 1962): 75-80.

"Radio." *Fortune* 17 (May 1938): 47-52+, 53-57+, 60-62+.

The Radio Industry: The Story of Its Development. 1928. Reprint. New York: Arno Press, 1974.

Reck, Franklin Mering. *Radio from Start to Finish.* New York: Thomas Y. Crowell, 1942.

"Recommendations of the National Radio Committee." *Radio Service Bulletin* (April 1923): 9-13. In *Documents in American Telecommunications Policy,* edited by John M. Kittross. vol. 1. New York: Arno Press, 1977. Various pagnations.

"Reporting" (profile of Bob Edwards). *New Yorker* 60 (August 13, 1984): 21-23.

"The Return of Network Radio." *Forbes* 122 (October 30, 1978): 152.

Robinson, Thomas P. *Radio Networks and the Federal Government.* New York: Columbia University Press, 1943.

Rolo, Charles J. *Radio Goes to War: The "Fourth Front."* New York: Putnam, 1942.

Sarno, Edward F., Jr. "The National Radio Conferences." *Journal of Broadcasting* 13 (Spring 1969): 189-202.

Sarnoff, David. *Looking Ahead: The Papers of David Sarnoff.* New York: McGraw-Hill, 1968.

———. "Memorandum to E. J. Nally." In *Documents of American Broadcasting,* edited by Frank J. Kahn, 3rd ed., 15-17. Englewood Cliffs, N.J.: Prentice-Hall, 1978.

Saudek, Robert. "Program Coming in Fine. Please Play 'Japanese Sandman.'" *American Heritage* (August 1965): 24-27.

Schwartz, Tony. "An Intimate Talk with William Paley." *New York Times Magazine,* December 28, 1980, 15-18+.

Settel, Irving. *A Pictorial History of Radio.* 2nd ed. New York: Grosset and Dunlap, 1967.

Severin, Werner J. "Commercial vs. Non-Commercial Radio during Broadcasting's Early Years." *Journal of Broadcasting* 22 (1978): 491-504.

Siepmann, Charles A. *Radio's Second Chance.* Boston: Little, Brown, 1946.

———. *Radio, Television, and Society.* New York; Oxford University Press, 1950.

Smith, Desmond. "American Radio Today." *Harper's* 229 (September 1964): 58-63.

Stamberg, Susan, and National Public Radio. *Every Night at Five: Susan Stamberg's "All Things Considered" Book.* New York: Pantheon, 1982.

Sterling, Christopher H., and John M. Kittross. *Stay Tuned: A Concise History of American Broadcasting.* Belmont, Calif.: Wadsworth, 1978.

Stewart, Irvin, ed. *Radio.* Supplement to Annals of the American Academy of Political and Social Science, vol. 142. 1929. Reprinted in *Radio: Selected A.A.P.S.S. Surveys.* New York: Arno Press, 1971.

Sutin, L. "Lake Woebegon, the Little Town That Time Forgot." *Saturday Evening Post* 258 (September 1986): 42-45.

Sybert, Pamela Johnson. "Mutual Admiration: MBS and the Dominican Republic." *Journal of Broadcasting* 24 (1980): 189-99.

Thomas, Lowell. *Magic Dials: The Story of Radio and Television.* New York: Lee Furman, 1939.

Tolbert, Frank X. "Man behind a Network." *Nation's Business* 42 (March 1952): 52-60.

U.S. Commissioner of Navigation. *Annual Report to the Secretary of Commerce.* 1921-1926. Selections reprinted in *Documents in American Telecommunications Policy,* edited by John M. Kittross, vol. 1. New York: Arno Press, 1977.

U.S. Congress. House. Federal Communications Commission Office of Network Study. *Network Broadcasting.* 85th Cong. 2nd sess. H. Rep. 1297. Washington, D.C.: Government Printing Office, 1958.

U.S. Department of Commerce. *Recommendations for Regulation of Radio Adopted by the Third National Radio Conference.* 1924. In *Documents in American Telecommunications Policy,* edited by John M. Kittross, vol. 1. New York: Arno Press, 1977.

———. *Proceedings of the Fourth National Radio Conference and Recommendations for the Regulation of Radio.* 1926. In *Documents in American Telecommunications Policy,* edited by John M. Kittross, vol 1. New York: Arno Press, 1977.

U.S. Federal Communications Commission. *Report on Chain Broadcasting.* 1941. Reprint. New York: Arno Press, 1974.

———. *An Economic Study of Standard Broadcasting.* 1974. Reprint. New York: Arno Press, 1974.

———, Engineering Department. *Report on Social and Economic Data Pursuant to the Informal Hearing on Broadcasting.* 1938. Reprint. New York: Arno Press, 1974.

Wallace, John. "What We Thought of the First Columbia Broadcasting Program."
    Radio Broadcast (December 1927): 140-41. In *American Broadcasting: A Source
    Book on the History of Radio and Television,* edited by Lawrance W. Lichty and
    Malachi C. Topping, 175-78. New York: Hastings House, 1976.
West, Robert. *The Rape of Radio.* New York: Rodin Publishing Co., 1941.
White, Llewellyn. *The American Radio: A Report on the Broadcasting Industry in the
    United States from the Commission on Freedom of the Press.* Chicago: University
    of Chicago Press, 1947.
Youngren, J. A. "The News from Lake Woebegon." *Christian Today* 29 (November
    22, 1985): 33-36.

2   RADIO DRAMA

The British playwright Richard Hughes claims with complete confidence that the birth of radio drama occurred on January 15, 1924, when his script, *A Comedy of Danger,* was aired on the BBC. Equally confident is E. P. J. Shurick, who fixes the date as August 3, 1922, in Schenectady, New York (WGY), with the production of *The Wolf* by Eugene Walters. There is no shyness in Barnouw's claim that radio drama begins in 1923 with the production of a play called *The Queen's Messenger.* A good case can be made that radio drama really began on various local radio stations around 1920 or 1921 when song and chatter performers created fictional characters like Bryon Harlen's rube humorist and front-porch sage, Uncle Josh, who spoke to the radio audience sometimes from script, sometimes ad libbing, and sometimes doing both in the same program—or even in the same minute. An equally meritorious claim is the one made by radio historian J. Fred MacDonald—namely, that radio drama does not really begin ''in earnest'' until the 1930s.

That we have a great deal more difficulty in fixing the date of the first radio drama than we do in fixing the date of the fall of the Roman Empire is only partly the fault of chaotic scholarship in the field of radio drama; it is really a problem with the term ''radio drama'' itself. Depending upon whom one consults, that term can be so broad as to mean anything that is said or sung on the air by a fictional character or persona. It can also be so narrow as to include only those scripts written specifically for broadcast production, excluding the adaptations of novels, plays, and movies. Some believe that the radio play is so different from the stage play that the stage playwright must virtually relearn his or her craft in order to write for the radio. Others believe that a play is a play no matter where it is presented, and that the salient differences between stage drama and radio drama lie in the production and not in the writing of the drama.

In recognition of the various modes of presentation, the wide variety of content, and the diversity of purposes that programs calling themselves radio drama embrace, Harrison B. Summers in his standard reference work, *A Thirty-Year History of Programs Carried on National Radio Networks in the United States, 1926-1956,* devised about a dozen subcategories of radio drama, including informative drama, daytime informative drama, thriller drama, comedy drama, prestige drama, daytime prestige drama, daytime light drama, light-homey-love interest drama, women's drama, daytime women's serial drama, daytime comedy drama, daytime thriller drama, and so on. (As extensive as Summers's breakdown is, one can argue for the addition of more categories, such as religious drama.) But fortunately for scholars in the field, the scholarship and criticism of radio drama has not evolved nearly so elaborate a system of classification as the one developed by Summers. Most of the relevant material on radio drama, whether it is found in books, literary and scholarly periodicals, or popular and fan magazines, acknowledges two very broad categories of radio drama that, for the purposes of organizing such material, we will adopt as the framework of this chapter: prestige or serious drama and popular serial drama.

No term works better than Summers's "prestige drama" to describe those programs and individual broadcasts that sought to create an aesthetically and artistically superior broadcast drama. Shows like "The Mercury Theater on the Air," "Lux Radio Theater," and "The March of Time" fall under this category. Admittedly, the term "prestige" or "serious" when applied to these programs and not to such programs as "Vic and Sade" or "The Rise of the Goldbergs" can invite a misleading critical prejudice. As John Houseman admitted in a *Harper's* article, "The Men from Mars," "The Mercury Theater on the Air" was capable of putting on some dreadfully dull stuff. Moreover, at their best, Gertrude Berg ("The Rise of the Goldbergs") and Paul Rhymer ("Vic and Sade") were as skilled in storytelling as anyone who ever wrote for the medium. We also recognize that programs such as "Against the Storm" or Arch Oboler's "Lights Out" can reasonably be classified as prestige or serious drama as well as popular serial drama. Yet for all its potential drawbacks, the classification of prestige drama as something separate from the various forms of popular serial plays accommodates well the literature on radio drama.

What makes prestige drama a distinct subgenre (and, certainly, what has attracted the interest of scholars, critics, and reviewers far beyond what either the number of these programs or their ratings would otherwise warrant) is the conscious effort on the part of its creators to find in the radio drama an outlet for high culture on a massive scale. The following discussion of prestige radio drama will open with a survey of a virtually unresearched area of study in the field: radio drama's poetics. In the 1930s and 1940s various magazines, including *Theatre Arts Monthly, Saturday Review of Literature, Radio Digest,* and even *Wireless Age* carried many articles and review essays on the essence of the radio drama as an art form: how it should be written, how the listener responds, what its inherent aesthetic characteristics are, and what its artistic potential is. These articles are a fascinating legacy to an art form that never found the greatness that some of the most creative artists in the medium believed it could have achieved.

The other major category is the serial or the series, which dominated radio drama in the golden age. This category embraces eleven out of Summers's twelve drama programming subcategories. In the 1943-1944 season, popular serial programming accounted for thirty-six hours per week of network airtime (prestige dramas accounted for only four hours of network programming per week). These serials include soap operas, comedy series, mysteries and thrillers, and action programs. These subcategories will be addressed in the larger discussion of serial drama. Among their common characteristics is the repertory nature of the programs: usually a familiar cast of characters or a familiar hero returns daily or weekly. (In the case of some of the thriller series, such as "Crime Club" or "True Detective Mysteries," there would be a repeating format, often with a permanent host or narrator.) The serial built its audience on familiarity and repetition; for most radio listeners, this was the essence of radio drama. The content should be as familiar as the piece of furniture through which it was broadcast.

GENERAL WORKS

There are relatively few book-length studies that address the whole of radio drama. More often than not, information on radio drama is found as a smaller portion of larger discussions on radio programming. Oddly enough, book-length discussions of individual dramas ("War of the Worlds," "Vic and Sade," "Easy Aces") are far more common than book-length works on drama as a whole. However, there are some important standard works that address the broad topic of radio drama and serve as references for the entire field.

Scholars familiar with Erik Barnouw's three-volume history of broadcasting know that Barnouw covers succinctly, yet clearly, almost every event that is important to any phase of radio, and radio drama proves to be no exception. In volume 1 of the history, *A Tower in Babel,* he traces the earliest, prenetwork experiments with original radio drama, particularly the work done by WGY in Schenectady and WLW in Cincinnati in the early 1920s. He notes the wide range of activity across the country in the broadcasting of adaptations of stage drama—from Shakespeare to contemporary one-acts—as early as 1923. He also notes the development of "hayseed drama" in early network drama productions, and in doing so helps broaden the critical definition of radio drama very early in the history of radio scholarship.

In volume 2, *The Golden Web,* which covers the period from 1933 to 1953, Barnouw runs through the development of drama in the golden age of radio. Paying little attention to adventures, mysteries, and thrillers, Barnouw's discussion of serial drama focuses on the general area of women's dramas, with special attention paid to the Hummerts, the most prolific soap opera writers in history. He devotes considerable time to the prestige dramas (again, more than either their numbers or their ratings would warrant), with special mention of "The Columbia Workshop" in the 1930s and "The War of the Worlds" broadcast in 1938. The usually terse Barnouw devotes some five pages of discussion (a remarkably large amount of time for any one topic in his history) to Norman Corwin's career with CBS. Barnouw's marvelous historical sweep places small events into nearly perfect perspective. As a result, his short discussions tend to loom very large.

Other histories that at least touch on radio drama in some useful manner include Sam J. Slate and Joe Cook's *It Sounds Impossible*, which is a topical, firsthand account of radio history, including chapters on soap opera and comedy. Lloyd R. Morris's *Not So Long Ago* and Robert Campbell's *The Golden Years of Broadcasting: A Celebration of the First 50 Years of Radio and Television on NBC* are both useful. Morris's book is a general history of the 1930s, and Campbell's is a frothy but detailed picture story of the rise of NBC. There is a full-length dissertation available on the early history of radio drama, Donald W. Riley's "A History of American Radio Drama, 1914-1944," written in 1944. This informative, narrative recounting of early drama experiments was a major source for Lawrence W. Lichty's more widely known essay "Radio Drama: The Early Years" in Lichty and Malachi C. Topping's anthology *American Broadcasting*.

The closest thing in existence to a one-volume encyclopedia of radio drama is John Dunning's comprehensive *Tune In Yesterday: The Ultimate Encyclopedia of Old-Time Radio, 1925-1976*. (The self-serving subtitle is not undeserved.) Dunning gives background, histories, and reviews of every network show on the air for the fifty seasons from 1925 to 1976. Although all shows are covered, Dunning's particular fondness and interest in drama—both the serials and the prestige shows—come through in the rich, well-researched, and energetically written essays on dramatic programs. These essays, which range from 150-word thumbnail sketches to the equivalent of short chapters, contain full information on show history, cast, producers, directors, sponsor, and the kind of backstage anecdotes that so effectively take the better popular culture studies out of the realm of dry academics without sacrificing the quality and quantity of the information. Among the most useful and most thorough essays in the book are Dunning's pieces on "Columbia Presents Corwin," "One Man's Family," "Vic and Sade," "The Mercury Theater on the Air," and "The Lone Ranger."

Dunning's book has clear and clearly acknowledged debts to an earlier encyclopedic work, Frank Buxton and Bill Owen's *The Big Broadcast, 1920-1950*. (This volume was an updated and expanded version of their earlier book, *Radio's Golden Age*.) Buxton and Owen's book features outlines one inch to one column in length of every network program from the 1920s to 1950. The information is sketchy: first broadcast date, last broadcast date, network, cast, director, and producer. Analysis or discussions are rare and cursory. There are many photographs and some recreational fan material in the book, but as a scholarly reference work it has been eclipsed by Dunning. Vincent Terrace's *Radio's Golden Years: The Encyclopedia of Radio Programs, 1930-1960* claims to be "the most complete reference work ever published" on the subject. Actually, its debt in format and content to Buxton and Owen is apparent, and it offers less information than does Dunning. Its value is doubtful. The standard reference work for programming history (what show was playing on what network at what time) is the aforementioned Harrison B. Summers's *A Thirty-Year History of Programs Carried on National Radio Networks in the United States, 1926-1956.* A season-by-season listing of every show on the radio networks, grouped by genre and subgenre, and accompanied by the sponsor and the seasonal ratings, the book is a major reference work in any field of radio programming history. Treating drama as he does—breaking it down into more subcategories than anyone studying the field before or since—Summers provides a clear indication why the term "radio drama" is so hard to define. A more contemporary programming index is the *Radio Programming Profile,* published quarterly by BF Communications since 1967. It offers an analysis of programming, audience, and policies for the top 100 stations in the country. For drama scholars, the Summers book will be more useful because of the near void of radio drama programming in the last twenty-five years.

There are a few works that are very useful for locating available scripts and recordings of radio programs. Michael R. Pitts's *Radio Soundtracks: A Reference Guide* is an extensive but not complete listing of available tapes and records of radio shows, with a particularly strong listing in drama. Marietta Chicorel's three-volume set (7, 7a, and 7b of the Chicorel Index Series), *Chicorel Index to the Spoken Arts on Discs, Tapes, and Cassettes,* is very helpful for radio drama enthusiasts, even though Chicorel's emphasis is on "legitimate" drama and oratory. Used in conjunction with Pitts's work, an admittedly awkward pairing in some respects, it will provide scholars with as nearly complete a listing of available recorded work in drama as they are likely to find anywhere. For locating scripts, G. Howard Poteet's *Published Radio, Television, and Film Scripts* devotes 125 pages to radio dramas available in print. Poteet is thorough in his listings and annotates his entries skillfully. There are several thousand program tapes available for listening at the Museum of Broadcasting in New York and the Museum of Broadcast Communications in Chicago, the two largest public collections.

There are a few critical studies of radio that are so generous in their treatment of radio drama that they deserve mention as general works in the field. One very comprehensive study of radio that includes several fine chapters on radio drama is J. Fred MacDonald's *Don't Touch That Dial! Radio Programming in American Life, 1920-1960.* MacDonald is indebted to Barnouw's historical approach but, writing ten years later than Barnouw, has access to additional information. He also uses popular radio magazines for sources (something that Barnouw did not do), and when he chooses to expand his discussion of a particular area, he does so in a highly scholarly manner. Raymond William Stedman's original study, *The Serials,* which is a comprehensive examination of the serial in film, radio drama, and television, contains three excellent chapters on radio. His book, although useful as a reference work, is a highly cohesive and factual narrative. Unlike the scholarly works of MacDonald and Stedman, Jim Harmon's *The Great Radio Heroes* is the product of the fan/researcher. This particular breed of author helps make the study of popular culture unique among academic disciplines. Their lighter styles and sometimes whimsical methods of organizing materials fall in the category of popular writing. But when their research is solid, and Harmon's is, they offer creative and refreshing contributions to the field. Individual chapters from MacDonald, Harmon, and Stedman will be cited further in appropriate sections of this chapter. Richard Kostelanetz's "The American Horspiel" in the December 1985 issue of *North American Review* discusses the radio drama in the context of the acoustical artistic development of the radio medium, from "acoustic jokes" to sonoral techniques for character development. (It should be noted that Kostelanetz's approach is historical and not theoretical. Theoretical treatments of the aesthetics of radio drama are discussed later.)

Book-length studies of radio drama or, for that matter, radio programming in general are sufficiently rare that, up to a point, every book in existence makes some level of contribution to the scholarship. Certainly a weak link in that very short chain is Ron Lackmann's *Remember Radio.* Seemingly intended for fans only, the book is a disorganized, nonhistorical, and noncritical goulash of still photographs and fan-club chatter. Other than the fact that Lackmann notes that "One Man's Family" was the longest-running serial in radio history (1932-1958), there is little that the historian or scholar can expect to take from this book.

PRESTIGE DRAMA: THE POETICS

With the broadcasting of serious stage drama as early as 1923, it became apparent to many that the radio play itself could possibly become a serious art form: that it might conceivably take its place with the stage opera or the legitimate theater as an integral part of American high culture. When original drama began to appear regularly on radio in the 1930s, creators and critics of radio drama began to speculate that a body of fine literature "equal to that of the stage" might evolve eventually. Yet by the 1930s a frustratingly uneven record in the writing and production of high-quality drama raised a serious theoretical question: was high-quality radio drama possible? Did the radio play itself have sufficient range as a genre to allow for a body of quality literature to grow? One college textbook, David Mackey's *Drama on the Air,* attempted to analyze the component theoretical parts of radio drama, from comparisons with the stage and theoretical definitions of plot, action, exposition, and compression to a lengthy analysis of a single drama. But despite its pretensions to Aristotelian thoroughness and clarity, the book is far more descriptive than it is analytical or theoretical, and it does not handle the central problems of the issue nearly as well as do many magazine articles written on the subject. The best work on this question can be found in several articles appearing in various magazines between 1931 and 1945.

Perhaps the first serious discussion of the theoretical dimensions of the radio play is British author Gordon Lea's 1926 book, *Radio Drama.* In this book Lea defends the theoretical potential of the radio drama in light of the limitations of modern stage drama. His point of departure is that the radio drama, like the Renaissance drama, is all but devoid of set and other modern theatrical devices and thus compensates with a stronger, more complete text. Lea also makes a key distinction between the radio drama adaptation (for which he advocates a narrator) and the original stage drama (for which he insists that a self-contained script [that is, no narrative devices] be developed). Among the earlier applications of theoretical issues in the debate over programming is drama critic Merrill Dennison's article "The Broadcast Play" in the December 1931 issue of *Theatre Arts Monthly.* Dennison's article is a stirring defense of the genre in the wake of the derision and scorn radio drama tended to receive at the hands of reviewers of early radio plays. Arguing, as all defenders of radio drama must, that the radio play has yet to reach its full growth, Dennison asserts that the radio drama is able to convey a greater sense of reality than any other form of dramatic medium because the "blind" audience's inner eye can visualize scenes beyond the "physical powers of designers to build or the camera to photograph." His most compelling point is that radio drama can compress time and can suspend action out of real time more successfully than can the stage drama. Perhaps because so few successful productions were available to him, Dennison's case is weakened by his failure to provide examples of the theoretical dimensions of the radio play in action. But in his discussions of how the "blind" audience responds to drama and how flexible the radio drama can be when compared to other dramatic or literary forms, he set the agenda for the theoretical discussions that followed.

One year later, Craig Rice wrote a two-part article in the May and June issues of *Radio Digest* entitled "What Is Wrong with Radio Drama?" Rice, a producer and columnist, is somewhat self-pitying in her complaint, but she adds several new dimensions to the discussion of broadcast drama, many of which are still heard in the debates over the quality of contemporary television writing. Notably, Rice will not forgive the genre its youth ("Surely we ought to be getting somewhere by now"). She is aware of the fact that the audience for radio drama is a willing victim to distractions around the house and that this has a profound effect upon what the medium can do. Moreover, she may be the first to have articulated publicly the now-clichéd considerations of mass productions' encroachments upon the creative process: low pay to writers, no time to work on the production, and unrealistic limitations placed upon creative people by the medium itself. Although the piece ends with a vague, optimistic expression of hope for drama (possibly in deference to the editors, who may not have wanted a wholly downbeat article in what is essentially a fan magazine), Rice's article is probably the first to suggest that the quality of drama in the mass commercial media may simply be limited by definition and necessity. The June issue of *Radio Digest,* in addition to carrying the second part of Rice's article, also included an interview with radio producer Dana Noyes conducted by Douglas D. Connah. In the course of that interview, entitled ''Action is the Soul of the Radio Play,'' Noyes made a stunning comparison between the radio drama and the silent movie: both art forms make an appeal to one sense but create the illusion of appeals to the other senses. Noyes concluded that as a consequence, the limiting of the direct appeal to one sense expanded the possiblities of illusions in the genre and thus expanded the potential of the appeal and quality of radio drama.

Of the earliest defenses of radio drama, the most important is certainly Rudolf Arnheim's *Radio: An Art of Sound,* which first appeared in 1936. (Da Capo published a new edition in 1972.) This landmark work on the technical aesthetics of radio sound production relies heavily on radio drama for its examples and illustrations. It is so technical at times that it seems to anticipate the fine sound distinctions that appear in relatively recent discussions of stereo sound equipment. Among Arnheim's more significant discussions are those on the importance of sonoral themes to a radio play (and how an author and producer go about creating them), the necessity and technique of vocal contrasts within a play, microphone distancing, and creating ''the sound character'' of a setting within a radio play.

Other committed defenders of the faith include CBS's venerable Norman Corwin, who discusses the playwright's theoretical problems in ''The Sovereign Word'' in *Theatre Arts Monthly* (February 1940). Here Corwin makes a significant, subtle point that has been taken up in later theoretical scholarship about radio: radio drama owes less to its roots in legitimate theater than it does to oral/aural traditions such as storytelling. As a result, radio plays require simplicity, not because the audience lacks intelligence but because the playwright, like the storyteller, must recognize the ''physical limitations'' of the ear. One major practical consequence of that characteristic of the radio drama is that the radio play cannot evolve gradually, as can the stage play; it must be direct (''I don't suggest that all radio plays must begin like a bat out of hell, but it helps.'') Another major radio playwright, Arch Oboler, took up theoretical issues in an article for *New Republic* (September 1, 1947). Entitled ''Oboler on Reading,'' the article is a plea for intelligent reading of radio plays by audiences and critics. Claiming that radio drama engages the ''personal participation'' of the reader more thoroughly than does any other form of literature, he notes that critics of prestige or quality radio drama have placed upon radio drama aesthetic criteria that were developed for other forms of literature. Specifically, Oboler believes that critical praise for broadcast verse dramas reflects an inappropriate prejudice on the part of critics against prose dramas. He goes on to try to cultivate in his reader a better understanding of the prose of radio drama.

Perhaps the single most intriguing (and energetic) defense of the medium is Frederick Morton's "Radio Propaganda: New Style" in the February 1943 issue of *Theatre Arts Monthly*. Morton begins with two astonishing assumptions: first, that America's lack of a national propaganda at the start of World War II was nearly as detrimental to the war effort as would have been a comparable deficiency in the building of airplanes, and second, that good propaganda plays represent radio drama at its best. Morton asserts that literature fails on radio because "there are too many words, too many long words, too many inactive phrases." He points to the style of propaganda plays like those of Norman Corwin as being the most appropriate for radio drama.

Despite the energy, enthusiasm, and thoughtfulness of many of radio drama's defenders, the uneven (to put it generously) quality of "quality drama" gave rise to detractors who believed that the fault lies in the stars. They argued that except in the rarest of instances, the medium was simply not equipped to accommodate the artistic pretensions of its defenders. Leading the assault was Jerrold Lapham, whose article "What Hope Radio Drama?" (*Theatre Arts Monthly*, January 1934) accused Dennison and other defenders of artistic radio drama of participating in "idealistic speculation." Expanding upon Rice's observations that the commercial considerations of the radio drama so heavily encroach upon the art form that it no longer becomes an art form, Lapham contended that the quality radio drama is doomed because no one wants to produce quality radio drama and not enough people want to hear it. A far more damaging attack comes from Bernard DeVoto's *Harper's* review of the production of Norman Corwin's celebration of America's victory in World War II, "On a Note of Triumph." Although DeVoto's essay ostensibly is a review of only one production, its implications are very broad, for within that essay DeVoto attacks savagely the very element of radio scriptwriting that Corwin and others claim to be the source of the genre's power: its directness and seeming simplicity. "It is bad writing." Aware of the fact that he is attacking the genre—or the best of the genre—DeVoto slams critics who have developed a fondness "for this bastard form of speech which has neither the discipline of verse nor the structural strength of prose."

The debate over radio drama all but died out by 1950. As radio drama was replaced by television drama, the debate shifted to the potential of television drama. The tension between the two mediums is the subject of scores of publications, the most important of which are probably Gilbert Seldes's *The Public Arts* and J. Robert Burrull's article "Radio's Challenge" in the *Journal of Broadcasting* (Summer 1967).

PRESTIGE DRAMA: PROGRAMS

Only a small handful of programs comprise the significant quality of prestige drama productions that were broadcast on network radio in the 1930s and 1940s. Among those discussed to some degree in the critical, popular, and scholarly literature in the field are "The Columbia Workshop," "The Mercury Theater on the Air," "The Radio Guild," "Lux Radio Theater," "The March of Time," and "Against the Storm."

"The Columbia Workshop" has attracted a fair amount of critical attention, largely because it was one of the first attempts on the part of a network to explore the radio play and the radio production in order to find its artistic potential. This effort was bolstered substantially by a landmark production in 1937 of Archibald MacLeish's verse play *The Fall of the City*. Barnouw in *The Golden Web* gives some very brief background on the program. Far more generous attention is paid in John Dunning's *Tune in Yesterday*. In Robert Lewis Shayon's "Along the Sustaining Culture Circuit," a 1957 review of NBC's "The New Theater" program, the author cites "The Columbia Workshop" as the last authentic and meritorious drama on the air while accusing "Lux Radio Theater" and other generally highly regarded drama programs of "selling Hollywood" and other betrayals of quality. Among the more valuable reviews of "The Columbia Workshop"'s *Fall of the City* productions are Gilbert Seldes's "People and the Arts: The Production of 'Fall of the City'" in *Scribner's* (June 1937) and E. V. Wyatt's "Post-war Poets and the Theater: 'Fall of the City'" in the August 1937 *Catholic World*.

In its prime "The Lux Radio Theater" was the most popular prestige drama show on the air. (Those who may have thought that this honor would have gone to "The Mercury Theater on the Air" need only to be advised that "Mercury Theater" was on against the remarkably popular "Chase and Sanborn Hour" with Edgar Bergen and Charlie McCarthy.) "Lux Radio Theater" initially offered hour-long radio versions of Broadway stage plays and later offered adaptations of Hollywood films. Although the program is generally associated with its most famous host, Cecil B. DeMille, it did run for two years prior to his arrival and ten years after his departure. Dunning, in *Tune In Yesterday,* gives this program special attention. His treatment is particularly good in that it encapsulates nicely the pre- and post-DeMille history of the program while re-creating in some detail the flamboyance and resulting success that DeMille brought to the show. In *The Autobiography of Cecil B. DeMille*, DeMille does little more than recount his successes: the parade of film stars he brought to the program, his dramatic broadcast one evening from his own hospital bed, and a union dispute with the American Federation of Radio Artists (AFR)—a dispute that caused him to be removed from the show in 1945 because of his refusal to pay to the union a one-dollar political fee. Considering that he called the show the single event in his career that brought him closer to the American people than anything else he had ever done, his treatment of his nine-year stint on the program is surprisingly short, a fact that may well reflect his widely alleged "in name only" status as producer. The background discussion of "The Lux Radio Theater" in Gene Ringgold and DeWitt Bodeen's *The Films of Cecil B. DeMille* is disappointing, but the book offers some pleasant photographs of some of the stars at work on the show and, more significantly, a week-by-week listing complete with date, title, and major casting roles of every production that was broadcast during DeMille's tenure as host.

"THE WAR OF THE WORLDS"

It is fair to say that more writing is available on this one evening's program than on any other hour in radio—possibly even all broadcasting. Everyone is in on it: scholars, fans, sociologists, psychologists, journalists, and broadcast historians. "The Mercury Theater on the Air"'s weekly broadcast of serious drama had been critically well received since its debut on July 11, 1938. But coming up against the staples of Sunday evening radio, Edgar Bergen and Charlie McCarthy, it was, to use accurately an overly used media phrase, "getting killed" in the ratings. It is reasonable to speculate that, with Hollywood beckoning, Orson Welles would likely have abandoned his duties as producer, host, and overseer of the program shortly after its debut, and the program might well have slipped into obscurity. But it did not. The 1938 Holloween evening broadcast of H. G. Wells's "The War of the Worlds" managed to convince many people (the number is believed to be in the millions) that the earth was being invaded by Martians. "Mercury Theater"'s place in broadcasting history was secured.

Anyone going through the literature on "The War of the Worlds" should be aware that the field—and in the area of prestige drama it is the one subject that can reasonably qualify as a field in and of itself—has its standard works. The single most useful book-length work is Howard Koch's *The Panic Broadcast*. Koch, who was the scriptwriter for "Mercury Theater on the Air" and who wrote the script for the "War of the Worlds" broadcast, put together a fascinating remembrance of the "Mercury Theater" program, including a minute-by-minute, behind-the-scenes diary of the production. At times Koch gets carried away with himself and his memories (the book contains an embarrassing chapter on the planet Mars itself). But the inclusion of the script, Koch's survey of the press response, and the behind-the-scenes look at "The Mercury Theater on the Air" make the work invaluable. A somewhat more objective, although shorter, insider's look at the broadcast is John Houseman's article in the December 1948 *Harper's* entitled "The Men from Mars." Houseman notes the fateful appearance that night of a dreadful singer on the Bergen program, with the consequence that many people turned off Bergen and tuned in late to the "Mercury Theater," only to catch "the crisis" unfolding. The article also contains a marvelous narrative and description of the young Orson Welles at work. In Peter Noble's excellent biography of Orson Welles, *The Fabulous Orson Welles,* the chapter "Orson Scares America" contains no new or unique information on the production itself. But the first-person recollections of the somewhat bemused young Welles, who had no idea what he had wrought until hours after the panic was under way, makes this a valuable volume, especially since Welles granted Noble a generous amount of interview time for the preparation of the book. Not surprisingly, this most unusual broadcast generated what must be regarded as the most peculiar single volume in the field of radio scholarship: Hadley Cantril's *The Invasion from Mars.* The first project undertaken by the highly regarded Princeton University Office of Radio Research, *The Invasion from Mars* is a formal (sometimes to the point of mind-boggling tedium) sociopsychological study of the panic that ensued during the broadcast of "War of the Worlds." Despite data collection that, by today's standards, is rather primitive, and despite the amount of attention that is paid to matters that are as obvious as they are insignificant (people with advanced education tended to be less convinced of the broadcast's "authenticity" than people with elementary education), the book still offers some valuable information. Its most important conclusion is one that it makes, ultimately, on speculation rather than on the basis of research—namely, that a full year of emergency broadcasts of the crisis in Europe coupled with the attendant miseries of the depression had "primed" the American public for bad news and made it particularly vulnerable to believing in a catastrophe. Furthermore, Cantril did a general overview of press concern, finding that the program was still drawing significant press attention three weeks after the incident. Taking up where Cantril left off in his survey of the press reaction to "The War of the Worlds," G. Joseph Woolf, in his article "'War of the Worlds' and the Editors" (*Journalism Quarterly,* Spring 1980), surveyed the specific content of press reaction in eighteen major newspapers. Woolf places press reaction to the broadcast (which, in general, castigated the public for its gullibility and chastised radio itself for its irresponsible breach of public trust) in the context of the war between newspapers and radio. According to Woolf, the fierce competition between the two, which saw newspapers lose readership and advertisers to radio, laid groundwork for the press to use an opportunity to blast away at radio and the people who listen to it. Woolf's interpretation is sensible, and the article implicitly raises the question of how much press reaction contributed to what is now the historical phenomenon of the broadcast, and how much of that reaction was prompted by self-motivations that were not relevant to the program or the reaction of its listeners.

OTHER WORKS ON PRESTIGE DRAMA

Radio actor Joseph Julian's autobiography, *This Was Radio,* is an intriguing and intelligent account of the radio trade in the 1930s, 1940s, and 1950s. There is a very useful discussion of sound effects as a central part of the creativity in radio drama production. Even more significant are Julian's recollections of working with Norman Corwin (on Corwin's "An American in Europe" program). Julian is among the most convincing of Corwin's many admirers in his argument for the man's genius. Only slightly self-promotional is Julian's handling of his own imbroglio with other radio people when he wrote a letter to *Variety* complaining that radio drama was produced so haphazardly that no one who rightly called himself an actor could get any serious work done. Such luminaries as Bing Crosby saw fit to take Julian on in print. Julian's is probably the best radio actor's memoir, but Mary Jane Higby's *Tune In Tomorrow* is quite useful and, as are so many nicely crafted show-biz biographies, very pleasurable reading.

In 1986 R. Leroy Bannerman published *Norman Corwin and Radio: The Golden Years,* a solid, long-overdue scholarly biography of Norman Corwin, CBS's acoustic drama genius. The book chronicles Corwin's achievements in playwriting, production, and technical innovation while narrating in great detail his long and illustrious career with CBS.

Magazine articles on individual programs' prestige as well as popularity flourished in the popular periodical literature from 1930 to 1950. One article that is a little bit above the average in this area is the unsigned "Theatre of the Air" in the January 1933 *Radio Digest.* A rare instance of a fan magazine taking on serious historical analysis, the article is worthy for its not entirely unfounded claim that the "Lucky Strike Theater" was responsible for precipitating a push for serious, quality drama during network prime time in the early 1930s. An article taking an unusual point of view with serious radio drama is Belle Becker's "The Radio Play as the Editor's Problem Child." Writing in *Publishers Weekly* (October 5, 1940), Becker, an editor at Random House assigned to edit Arch Oboler's *Fourteen Radio Plays* collection, discusses lucidly the textual problems inherent in a work that was not designed to be read or seen. She is particularly insightful in her discussion of the unique effect that music brings to radio drama and music's close relationship to text in radio drama.

There is an abundance of anthologies of radio plays in the stacks of public libraries. Several collections by Arch Oboler (*Fourteen Radio Plays, New Radio Plays, Oboler Omnibus*) and Norman Corwin (*Thirteen by Corwin, More by Corwin: 16 Radio Dramas*), although long out of print, are still available through the standard interlibrary loan systems and still circulate in many large city libraries. For war propaganda plays, the most famous anthology is Stephen Vincent Benet's 1945 *We Stand United and Other Radio Scripts,* a collection of World War II plays that aired on networks between 1941 and 1945.

POPULAR DRAMA: THE SOAP OPERAS

Without question the soap opera is the lightning rod for the entire genre of radio drama. It has attracted more writers, critics, and scholars, and certainly more fans, than any other form of radio drama—and probably more than all other forms of radio drama combined. It is one of the most widely studied areas in all of popular culture, often attracting authors who would rarely, if ever, write on any other aspect of the medium: feminists concerned about the status of women, psychiatrists in search of otherwise inexplicable disorders in their patients, English professors in search of a highly popular course and so on.

The amount of information is so formidable that the selection for discussion here has been limited to works that are either fundamental to the field (a surprisingly small number of works) and those works that are of considerable value and might otherwise go unnoticed. For sheer quantity, one can always turn to the *Readers' Guide to Periodical Literature* between 1930 and 1950 and find sixty articles pertaining to the genre. Additional material can be found in the standard radio magazines of that period—*Radio Digest, Radio Daily,* and so on—for some aspect of soap operas and their stars was standard fare in almost every issue of these magazines.

Probably the best piece of writing on soap operas available is James Thurber's five-part series that appeared in *New Yorker* in 1947. The following year, the five articles were combined as a section of Thurber's book *The Beast in Me and Other Animals.* Most famous as the source of Thurber's derisive definition of soap operas ("a kind of a sandwich . . . between thick slices of advertising spread twelve minutes of dialogue, add predicament, villainy, and female suffering"), the series is a thoroughly researched study of the genre, its history, its creators, and—the part that seems to intrigue Thurber the most—its audience. Thurber's portraits of the critical pioneers in the field (Frank and Anne Hummert, Irna Phillips, Eileen Carrington, and Robert Andrews) are, despite their brevity, vivid and human. The section on Andrews, a writer who produced over 100,000 words per week for the better part of a decade, is splendid. In an entire chapter Thurber singles out writers who tried to inject some quality and originality into a genre that thrived on the lack of both (Edward Wolf ["Hilltop House"], the Michaels ["Against the Storm"]). His description of the setting of soap operas is nothing short of brilliant theater analysis, and his essay on the depiction of men and women in soap operas has all of the insight of the best serious-minded essays on the subject along with Thurber's stock-in-trade—humor that celebrates life's gentle incongruities. Thurber even goes the scholars one better by assigning to the city of Chicago its proper role in the development of daytime drama and soap operas in particular; this is an area that media historians have not fleshed out well at all. The entire piece is quietly sarcastic, but primarily it is one listener's discovery of the radio soap opera and consequent awe at the size of the thing.

The most comprehensive discussion of the soap opera is Madeleine Edmondson and David Rounds's *From Mary Noble to Mary Hartman: The Complete Soap Opera Book,* a revised edition of their earlier work *The Soaps.* (Inasmuch as virtually all the revisions from the earlier book are concerned with television soap operas, scholars in radio drama can use either edition.) The book offers the ritualistic defense of the soap opera genre that admirers of the form make against their critics, namely that it is not as simple or as predictable as its harshest critics claim. The authors argue convincingly that the radio soap opera is far less formulaic than it is generally considered to be, even by its admirers. Their refusal to pin down the exact date of the first soap opera shows a sensitivity to the amorphous nature of early radio drama and the inadequacy of labels in the classification of such diverse and decentralized activity. Although these authors give a humorous, personal portrait of the Hummerts, they do not seem to capture the spirit of the major pioneers (the Hummerts, Carrington, and Phillips) as well as Thurber does despite the fact that they devote considerably more time to them in their discussions. A more factual single narrative on soap operas does not exist anywhere, but this is not by any means a remarkable piece of analytical work.

MacDonald's discussions of soap operas in *Don't Touch That Dial!* are quite original and thought-provoking, if occasionally overly analytical. His intriguing chapter on soap operas and World War II documents the extent to which soap operas gladly lent their resources to promoting the war effort, either by working prowar propaganda into story lines or by permitting government personnel to appear on the program and deliver a prowar service message as part of the script itself. In his discussion of themes in soap operas (besides those pertaining to war during the war years) MacDonald synthesizes well and enlarges upon what has been discussed in other works (including Thurber and Edmondson/Rounds), but his list of soap opera subgenres (for example, "the Cinderella story") is the result of an unsuccessful attempt to find generic distinctions among programs where there exist only dramatic distinctions. MacDonald is far more successful when he makes these distinctions in adventure/mystery programs.

One of the finer compressed overviews of the genre is Merrill Dennison's "Soap Opera" (*Harper's*, April 1940). It is critical yet balanced. It neatly traces the audience for soap operas back to movie serials, turn-of-the-century melodrama, and nineteenth-century "dreadfuls" and offers a stirring defense of "Vic and Sade" as the best written of the soaps. Apart from the fact that it touches on every issue related to the soaps—from derivation and economics to criticism—without seeming to rush the discussion, Gilbert Seldes's concise treatment of soap operas in *Great Audiences* is perhaps the most enthusiastic and persuasive defense of the artistic potential of the genre available. Edmondson and Rounds notwithstanding, Seldes details the formulaic nature of the soap opera yet argues with some skill that there is potential for considerable artistic achievement within that formula. One wishes that he had not chosen "*The Rise of the Goldbergs*" and "*Against the Storm*" as two of his examples of achievement, for it can be argued that these programs succeeded artistically at least partially because they broke certain formulaic rules. Nonetheless, this short section is impressively done. Thomas Meehan's "Twilight of the Soaps" in Poyntz Tyler's *Television and Radio* is particularly valuable because it analyzes key changes (or, more accurately, evolutions) in the soap opera genre as the soap moved from radio to television. Not only did the change force soap operas (and all dramas that made the switch) to speed up their action time (on television a customer could not spend four days in a barber's chair getting a shave as one once did on the radio soap "Just Plain Bill"), but the sophistication of the newer medium forced soap operas out of their sexual prudery. Meehan speculates that the emergence of such figures as the adulteress in daytime television soap operas helped break down prudishness on nightime television, which, as late as the

1960s, practiced self-censorship on a level similar to that of the 1940s radio dramas. As in the case of all categories of radio dramas, Dunning's *Tune In Yesterday* is the best single collection of individual program descriptions.

Since the defenders of the soap opera often publicly plead their cases against the severest critics of the genre, some mention should be made of the individuals who have, quite paradoxically, made the defense of the soap opera a necessity. *New York Herald* radio critic John Crosby had terrible things to say about the soap opera and said them often. Half tongue in cheek he accused soap operas of conspiring to keep women in a constant state of depression. In derision he wonders constantly about the state of the women who listen to these shows. His collection of columns, *Out of the Blue,* contains a generous dose of his cleverly articulated prejudice against soap operas. In *The Beast in Me and Other Animals,* Thurber tells of one critic who was not expressing tongue-in-cheek concern for the health of soap opera audiences: physician Louis Berg, who wrote that soap operas were a menace to women; accused the soaps of deliberately inducing anxiety among women through perverse appeals to their emotions. "Sadism," he is alleged to have called it. Berg's writing, which appeared in a widely discussed but hard-to-find pamphlet in 1942, anticipated contemporary antimedia criticism and the now common studies of the physiological effects of radio and television programs on members of the audience.

"AMOS 'N' ANDY"

More than any other radio dramatic series, "Amos 'n' Andy" has transcended its own medium and become a significant artifact of twentieth-century American culture. Its enormous success, its highly controversial portrayal of blacks, the marvelous genius of its two highly idiosyncratic creators, and its seminal role in opening up mass media to ethnic drama and humor make "Amos 'n' Andy" a subtopic in and of itself in the area of popular drama. Ironically, the one book by the creators of the program, Freeman Gosden and Charles Correll, was written two years before "Amos 'n' Andy" became a nationwide network success on NBC. In 1929, when Gosden and Correll wrote *All about Amos 'n' Andy,* the program was a highly popular syndicated show originating from WMAQ in Chicago. In this book the two authors tell the story of their meeting and the evolution of the program. There is much charming braggadoccio standing in the way of solid information, but as the two men's only book-length statement about their work, the book is valuable because it lacks competition. One marvelously unprophetic paragraph in the book states that the success of the show is based upon Gosden and Correll's "thorough understanding of the Negro race." Two years later, when the show went on the network, that claim was to be challenged soundly.

Bart Andrews and Ahrgus Juilliard's *Holy Mackerel: The Amos 'N' Andy Story,* a well-intended narrative chronology of the program and its history, derives some real benefit from interviews with former actors on the show as well as the recollections of Charles Correll's son. But much of the information here is already well established in other sources. The book attempts to frame the narrative within the race and race-consciousness issues that surrounded the show from the earliest days of its network radio run in the 1930s to the hue and cry over the televised version in the 1950s. But in their laudable attempts to balance the longstanding racial debate (the damage of sustained racial stereotyping versus the program's innocent intentions and astonishing popularity among both blacks and whites) the authors seem unable to resolve their own ambivalence over this subject, and the book suffers from a noticable uneasiness precipitated by the authors' fence-straddling.

Two articles discussing the racial conflict that arose when the National Association for the Advancement of Colored People (NAACP) led the nationwide protest against the airing of "Amos 'n' Andy" offer very different views of the origination of that movement. Norman Kagan's "Amos 'n' Andy: Twenty Years Late or Two Decades Early" (*Journal of Popular Culture,* Summer 1972) asserts that the controversy was an uncontrived, spontaneous outpouring of concern on the part of many blacks and their sympathizers over the ridiculous and demeaning manner in which the program portrayed black people. However, Arnold Shankman, writing in the *Journal of Popular Culture* six years later ("Black Pride and Protest: The Amos 'n' Andy Crusade") offers a persuasive conspiracy theory. According to Shankman, Robert C. Vann, editor of the second-largest black newspaper in America (the *Pittsburgh Courier*), contrived the protest as a means of generating circulation in the hopes that his paper would eventually surpass the circulation of the number one black newspaper in the country, the *Cleveland Plain Dealer*. Relying heavily on a biography of Robert C. Vann, Shankman asserts that the nationwide controversy—although filled with sincere people voicing seriously held convictions—has suspect origins indeed.

Although it scarcely even mentions the controversies stirred up over the show's portrayal of blacks, the best single piece of work on "*Amos 'n' Andy*" is Max Wylie's "Amos 'n' Andy: A Loving Remembrance" (*Television Quarterly,* Summer 1963). Wylie suggests that the show's genuineness and inexhaustible freshness relied heavily on the chemistry that existed between the idiosyncratic, oddball geniuses that created it. Wylie's portrait of Gosden and Correll is a masterful character study. Gosden, the brilliant, introverted hypochondriac, and Correll, the loud gregarious Irishman who talked too much and spoke too quickly, seemed to live out a white, prosperous version of the characters they created. Wylie also does a fine job of documenting the extensive and sometimes overlooked show-business credentials that both men had prior to teaming up to become radio performers.

Arthur Wertheim, writing in the *Journal of Popular Culture* (Winter 1976), credits the show with having some serious social consequences even if it had relatively little serious content. In an article entitled "Relieving Social Tensions: Radio Comedy and the Great Depression," he claims that "Amos 'n' Andy,"

"The Rise of the Goldbergs," and various radio comedians were partly responsible for nursing a demoralized nation back to emotional health. While he does not prove empirically that these shows had any genuine therapeutic value, Wertheim does offer a thought-provoking and useful thematic analysis of the show, noting that "Amos 'n' Andy" frequently engaged in social commentary at the expense of current economic conditions and reinforced traditional values of work and family in its programs. The 1976 article formed the basis of Wertheim's excellent "Amos 'n' Andy" chapter of his superb book *Radio Comedy*, which serves as first-rate social and broadcast history on the subject of the great and minor radio comedy programs. Wertheim's interest in the intrinsic social values of the "Amos 'n' Andy" scripts was anticipated by Dale Ross, who wrote a doctoral dissertation on "Amos 'n' Andy" in 1974 ("The 'Amos 'n' Andy' Radio Program, 1928-1937: It's History, Content, and Social Significance"). His treatment is a studious and original examination of more than 2,000 scripts. As with soap operas, "Amos 'n' Andy" was so popular in the 1930s that the standard radio magazines and fan magazines all but forced stories about the show into their pages. In 1932 *Radio Digest* even ran an "Amos 'n' Andy" scriptwriting contest, urging readers to write an "Amos 'n' Andy" episode. Names of winners were published, but Gosden and Correll, who were nothing if nòt prolific (and who were sufficiently popular to be immune to give-away promotions), passed up the opportunity to use fanwritten material on their program.

MYSTERY AND ACTION SERIALS

The progenitor of the early prime-time television action and drama program, the action serial (westerns, mysteries, thrillers, science fiction) became a staple on radio by the late 1920s. Taking its inspiration from the Saturday-morning serials in movie houses and adventure serials in boys' and men's magazines, the action programs usually tailored themselves to one of two available formats: the cliff-hanger, in which each of the installments ended with a hero or heroine dangling in seemingly hopeless peril, or the episode, in which a hero took on and solved a single case, problem, or crisis in thirty minutes or an hour. (It is interesting to note that when prime-time television developed its action drama, it was wedded so tightly to the episodic format that when various programs began experimenting with the old cliff-hanger form ["Peyton Place" in the 1960s and "Hill Street Blues" in the 1980s], they were looked upon as boldly experimental.)

One of the very few book-length discussions on adventure and action programs is Jim Harmon's *The Great Radio Heroes*. Three superior chapters on WXYZ (Detroit) and local adman George Trendle's contribution to action drama ("The Lone Ranger," "Sargeant Preston of the Yukon") are among the most useful and most readable essays on early station history available. Harmon brilliantly narrates how one man put together, piece by piece, an entire independent, high-quality operation after deciding to reject network programming in favor of his own instincts. Although there is an undistinguished discussion of superheroes, a chapter on "Tom Mix" reveals Harmon's perfect touch in handling the informal chronicle that is so appropriate for program histories. Harmon's book can be frustrating in that it lacks what academics seem to crave by instinct—a clear organizational or theoretical framework and a consistent point of view. But Harmon, a fan/scholar who combines the academic's ability to do research with the fan's penchant for whimsical arrangements of information, is in a real sense true to the evolution of radio drama; radio drama is genuinely a crazy-quilt of creative artists, commercial hacks, improbable dreamers, and casual experimenters. Scholars prepared to tolerate *The Great Radio Heroes'* occasional lapses into mindless fan-club chatter, gross exaggerations, and pointless plot summaries will reap the benefits of a bold, imaginative, well-researched discussion.

A highly original history of the serial (in magazine, movie, radio, and television) is Raymond Stedman's *The Serials*. Stedman's approach is clear, academic, and historical, but he writes with a fan's enthusiasm. In his three chapters on radio he gives no new information but synthesizes beautifully the radio serial into the whole history of the serial form. As he did with the soap opera, J. Fred MacDonald *(Don't Touch That Dial!)* offers a conventional academic analysis of the western and the mystery, although in this area his approach meets with considerably more success. In his chapter "Detective Programming and the Search for Law and Order" MacDonald breaks down the detective show into three types: realistic (the ploddingly rational approach to solving crimes, such as "Emo Crime Club" and "Sherlock Holmes"), glamorous (the fanciful embellishment of the detective's personality, in "The Thin Man," "The Shadow," or "The Green Hornet"), and the neo-realistic ("ugly crimes, brutalized detectives, and grim environments"). MacDonald also sees two types of western dramas in the history of radio serials: the juvenile western that exhibited and taught moral virtues such as self-sacrifice and independence ("Rin Tin Tin," "The Lone Ranger," and "Tom Mix") and the later adult western that included themes of sex and violence ("Gunsmoke"). In his discussions of the detective serials and the westerns, MacDonald's classifications do exactly what academic classifications should do: they give us new ways of looking at familiar material and provide us with new insights into that material.

In addition to the encyclopedic works mentioned earlier (Dunning's *Tune In Yesterday* and Buxton and Owen's *The Big Broadcast*), articles and sketches on individual shows are scattered around the literature. In the 1930s *Radio Digest* did several sketches of actors and writers of various serial programs. While many of these were simply fan-club chatter, two by radio writer Tom Curtin deserve special attention because they are analytical in their approach to the programs and because, as the creator of the shows about which he writes, Curtin gives some marvelous insights into how the programs came into being ("Police Thrillers: Action," *Radio Digest,* Summer 1932, and "Charlie Chan," *Radio Digest,* March 1933).

OTHER WORKS ON POPULAR DRAMA

Gertrude Berg's autobiography *Molly and Me* details both her immigrant history in East Harlem and her life with "The Rise of the Goldbergs." Unfortunately from our perspective, the personal history is written with more power and more detail than is the smaller section on the program, but as the one memoir by a very important writer of radio drama, the book has importance and stature. (In 1931 Berg authored a spin-off book based on "The Rise of the Goldbergs" and entitled, not surprisingly, *The Rise of the Goldbergs.*) During her tenure on radio and television, Berg was the subject of several profiles in popular magazines. William Birnie's "Molly Goes Marching On" in the November 1941 issue of *American Magazine* is typical of these articles.

Two books on "Vic and Sade" deserve special attention as well. Mary Frances Rhymer's *The Small House Halfway up in the Next Block* contains not only thirty scripts from the program that her husband created but also a very useful introduction describing the work routine, point of view, and value system of author Paul Rhymer. Perhaps chafing over the immortality of Frank and Anne Hummert, Mary Rhymer pointedly notes that her husband wrote every word of every script—an implied slap at the Hummert style of employing stables of anonymous writers who produced scripts under their bylines. Fred E. H. Schroeder's intriguing article "Radio's Home Folks, Vic and Sade: A Study in Aural History" (*Journal of Popular Culture,* Fall 1978) uses "Vic and Sade" as a test case for his convincing thesis that radio drama has its aesthetic and theatrical roots in folk drama and oral tradition. In the same issue of the *Journal of Popular Culture*, John E. DiMeglio's article "Radio's Debt to Vaudeville" suggests other nondramatic sources of radio drama, although his article is more concerned with the live comedians than it is with dramatic productions. Charles Stumpf's book *Ma Perkins, Little Orphan Annie, and High-Ho Silver* is an annotated listing in praise of dramatic comedy and music shows. It is enthusiastic, but other works cited here are far more helpful and thorough.

Although concerns about violence in the media are usually confined to visual media, Marilyn Sue Lawrence in a 1980 doctoral dissertation, "Violence on the Air: An Analysis of Radio Drama," presented grounds for similar concerns about radio audiences listening to violent radio drama shows in the 1930s and 1940s. The dissertation formed the foundation of her article "An Analysis of the Violence Content of Radio Thriller Dramas—and Some Comparisons with Television" in *Journal of Broadcasting* (Summer 1984). The author (appearing here as Marilyn Lawrence Boemer) discusses the possibility that popular violent radio programs such as "Gangbusters" stimulated young viewers to imitate the action. She further observes that a less complex society in the 1930s and 1940s was reflected in the optimistic outlook and the "bad guy"/"good guy" distinctions to be found in radio drama as opposed to the relative cynicism and sometimes blurred moral distinctions more prevalent in recent television drama.

Publishers Weekly (July 4, 1942) ran a delightful, unsigned article "Radio Program Builds Audience for 'Inner Sanctum' Mysteries." From a contemporary perspective, the article reveals how naïve publishers and broad-casters once were about the tie-in between book sales and broadcasts even remotely based upon those books (much less books based upon broadcasts). When the program "Inner Sanctum Mysteries" began airing in January 1941, the only tie-in that it had with the Simon and Schuster mystery series from which it took its name was a one-sentence plug for the latest Simon and Schuster book. Much to its surprise, Simon and Schuster was inundated with inquiries about the books from listeners of the program. Simon and Schuster went to work strengthening the tie in promotions, an act that gave birth to the now-commonplace bookstore display exploiting broadly any connection between a broadcast program and a book.

Although American radio drama may appear to have been pronounced dead in the 1950s, there has been something of a revival of interest in radio drama programming in the last few years. (This has been hailed as a "Renaissance" by one unbridled enthusiast and as "scattered pockets of interest" in the view of realists.) As a result, some relatively recent literature has emerged on the subject. Paul K. Jackson's dissertation, "Investigation into Earplay, National Public Radio's Drama Production Unit, 1971-1981: Towards an Aural Aesthetic in Drama." (University of Wisconsin, 1983) examines NPR's recent foray into radio drama production and adds some fuel to the smoldering fires of the debates over radio drama's poetics. Eli Segal, writing in the fall 1978 *Journal of Popular Culture* ("Radio Drama: No Need for Nostalgia in Kalamazoo") boasts of a very successful community-based series of original entertainment, serial drama productions that were broadcast in the 1970s over Western Michigan University's WMUK. These ventures notwithstanding, it is unlikely that drama will ever thrive as a nonvisual, aural medium in the United States—a fact generally recognized and accepted even by those with genuine admiration and awe for the beleaguered radio play.

BIBLIOGRAPHY FOR RADIO DRAMA

Ace, Goodman. *Ladies and Gentlemen—Easy Aces.* Garden City, N.Y.: Doubleday, 1970.

Andrews, Bart, and Ahrgus Julliard. *Holy Mackeral: The Amos and Andy Story.* New York: Dutton, 1986.

Arnheim, Rudolf. *Radio: An Art of Sound.* Rev. ed. New York: Da Capo, 1972.

Bannerman, R. LeRoy. *Norman Corwin and Radio: The Golden Years.* University, Ala.: University of Alabama Press, 1986.

Barnouw, Erik. *A Tower In Babel.* Vol. 1 of *A History of Broadcasting in the United States.* New York: Oxford University Press, 1966.

_____. *The Golden Web*. Vol. 2 of *A History of Broadcasting in the United States*. New York: Oxford University Press, 1968.

Becker, Belle. "The Radio Play as the Editor's Problem Child." *Publishers Weekly* 138, no. 14 (October 5, 1940): 1404-5.

Benét, Stephen Vincent. *We Stand United and Other Radio Scripts*. New York: Farrar and Rinehart, 1945.

Berg, Gertrude. *The Rise of the Goldbergs*. New York: Barse and Co., 1931.

_____. *Molly and Me*. New York: McGraw Hill, 1961.

Birnie, William. "Molly Goes Marching On." *American Magazine* 131 (November, 1941): 24-25.

Boemer, Marilyn Lawrence. "An Analysis of the Violent Content of the Radio Thriller Dramas—and Some Comparisons with Television." *Journal of Broadcasting* 28 (Summer 1984): 338-49.

Burrull, J. Robert. "Radio's Challenge." *Journal of Broadcasting* 11 (Summer 1967): 209-16.

Buxton, Frank, and Bill Owen. *Radio's Golden Age: The Programs and the Personalities*. New York: Easton Valley Press, 1966.

_____. *The Big Broadcast, 1920-1950*. New York: Avon, 1973.

Campbell, Robert. *The Golden Years of Broadcasting: A Celebration of the First 50 Years of Radio and TV on NBC*. New York: Scribner, 1976.

Cantril, Hadley, with Hazel Gaudet and Herta Herzog. *The Invasion from Mars*. Princeton: Princeton University Press, 1940.

Chicorel, Marietta, ed. *Chicorel Index to the Spoken Arts on Discs, Tapes, and Cassettes*. 3 vols. Chicorel Index Series, vols. 7, 7a, and 7b. New York: Chicorel Library Publishing Corporation, 1973-1974.

Connah, Douglas D. "Action is the Soul of the Radio Play." *Radio Digest* 26-27 (June 1932): 24.

Correll, Charles J., and Freeman Gosden. *All about Amos 'n' Andy*. New York: Rand McNally, 1929.

Corwin, Norman. "The Sovereign Word." *Theatre Arts Monthly* 24 (February 1940): 130-36.

_____. *Thirteen by Corwin*. New York: Holt, 1942.

_____. *More by Corwin: 16 Radio Dramas*. New York: H. Holt & Co., 1944.

Crosby, John. *Out of the Blue*. New York: Simon and Schuster, 1952.

Curtin, Tom. "Police Thrillers: Action." *Radio Digest* 27-28 (Summer 1932): 31.

_____. "Charlie Chan." *Radio Digest* 29-30 (March 1933): 11+.

DeMille, Cecil B. *The Autobiography of Cecil B. DeMille*. Englewood Cliffs, N.J.: Prentice-Hall, 1959.

Dennison, Merrill. "The Broadcast Play." *Theatre Arts Monthly* 15 (December 1931): 1008-11.

_____. "Soap Opera." *Harper's* 180 (April 1940): 498-505.

DiMeglio, John E. "Radio's Debt to Vaudeville." *Journal of Popular Culture* 12, no. 2 (Fall 1978): 228-35.

DeVoto, Bernard. "The Easy Chair." *Harper's* 191 (July 1945): 33-36.

Dunning, John. *Tune In Yesterday: The Ultimate Encyclopedia of Old-Time Radio, 1925-1976*. Englewood Cliffs, N.J.: Prentice Hall, 1976.

Edmondson, Madelaine, and David Rounds. *The Soaps*. New York: Stein and Day, 1973.

———. *From Mary Noble to Mary Hartman: The Complete Soap Opera Book.* New York: Stein and Day, 1976.

Goldman, Golda. "How Bertha Brainard Broadcasts Broadway." *Radio News* 5, no. 2 (August 1923): 134+.

Harmon, Jim. *The Great Radio Heroes.* Garden City, N.Y.: Doubleday, 1967.

Higby, Mary Jane. *Tune in Tomorrow.* New York: Cowles, 1968.

Houseman, John. "The Men from Mars." *Harper's* 197 (December 1948): 74-82.

Hughes, Richard. "The Birth of Radio Drama." *Atlantic Monthly* 200 (December 1957): 145-46.

Jackson, Paul K. "Investigation into Earplay, The National Public Radio Drama Production Unit, 1971-1981: Towards an Aural Aesthetic in Drama." Ph.D. diss., University of Wisconsin, 1983.

Julian, Joseph. *This Was Radio.* New York: Viking, 1975.

Kagan, Norman. "Amos 'n' Andy: Twenty Years Late or Two Decades Early." *Journal of Popular Culture* 6, no. 1 (Summer 1972): 71-75.

Koch, Howard. *The Panic Broadcast.* Boston: Little, Brown, 1970.

Kostelanetz, Richard. "The American Horspiel." *North American Review* 270, no. 4 (December 1985): 64-70.

Lapham, Jerrold. "What Hope Radio Drama?" *Theatre Arts Monthly* 18 (January 1934): 44-50.

Lawrence, Marilyn Sue. "Violence on the Air: An Analysis of Radio Drama." Ph.D. diss., University of Southern California, 1980.

Lea, Gordon. *Radio Drama.* London: Unum Bros., 1926.

Lichty, Lawrence. "Radio Drama." In *American Broadcasting, A Source Book on the History of Radio and Television,* edited by Lawrence W. Lichty and Malachi C. Topping. New York: Hastings House, 1976.

Lackmann, Ron. *Remember Radio.* New York: G. P. Putnam's Sons, 1970.

MacDonald, J. Fred. *Don't Touch That Dial! Radio Programming in American Life, 1920-1960.* Chicago: Nelson-Hall, 1979.

Mackey, David. *Drama on the Air.* New York: Prentice-Hall, 1951.

Meehan, Thomas. "Twilight of the Soaps." In *Television and Radio,* edited by Poyntz Tyler, 13-18. New York: Wilson, 1961.

Morris, Lloyd R. *Not So Long Ago.* New York: Random House, 1949.

Morton, Frederick. "Radio Propaganda: New Style." *Theatre Arts Monthly* 27 (February 1943): 95-102.

Noble, Peter. *The Fabulous Orson Welles.* London: Hutchinson, 1956.

Oboler, Arch. *Fourteen Radio Plays.* New York: Random House, 1940.

———. *Radio Plays.* New York: Random House, 1940.

———. *Oboler Omnibus: Radio Plays and Personalities.* New York: Duell, Sloan and Pearce, 1945.

———. "Oboler on Reading." *New Republic* 117 (September 1, 1947): 36-37.

Pitts, Michael R. *Radio Soundtracks: A Reference Guide.* 2nd ed. Metuchen, N.J.: Scarecrow Press, 1986.

Poteet, G. Howard. *Published Radio, Television, and Film Scripts.* Troy, N.Y.: Whitston, 1975.

"Radio Program Builds Audience for 'Inner Sanctum' Mysteries." *Publishers Weekly* 142, no. 1 (July 4, 1942): 30-31.

Radio Programming Profile. Washington, D.C.: BF Communications, 1967- (Quarterly).

Rhymer, Mary Francis, ed. *The Small House Halfway up in the Next Block.* New York: McGraw-Hill, 1972.

Rice, Craig. "What Is Wrong with Radio Drama?" *Radio Digest* 26-27 (May 1932): 30.

Riley, Donald W. "A History of American Radio Drama, 1914-1944." Ph.D. diss., Ohio State University, 1944.

Ringgold, Gene, and DeWitt Bodeen. *The Films of Cecil B. DeMille.* New York: Citadel Press, 1969.

Ross, Dale. "The 'Amos 'n' Andy' Radio Program, 1928-1937: It's History, Content, and Social Significance." Ph.D. diss., University of Iowa, 1974.

Rothel, David. *Who Was That Masked Man?* Cranbury, N.J.: A. S. Barnes, 1976.

Schroeder, Fred E. H. "Radio's Home Folks, Vic and Sade: A Study in Aural History." *Journal of Popular Culture* 12, no. 2 (Fall 1978): 253-56.

Seldes, Gilbert. "People and the Arts: The Production of 'Fall of the City.'" *Scribner's* 101 (June 1937): 61-62.

_____. *The Great Audience.* New York: Viking, 1951. Westport, Conn.: Greenwood Press, 1970.

_____. *The Public Arts.* New York: Simon and Schuster, 1956.

Segol, E. L. "No Need for Nostalgia in Kalamazoo." *Journal of Popular Culture* 12 (Fall 1978): 353-59.

Shankman, Arnold. "Black Pride and Protest: The Amos 'n' Andy Crusade." *Journal of Popular Culture* 12, no. 2 (Fall 1978): 236-52.

Shayon, Robert Lewis. "Along the Sustaining Culture Circuit." *Saturday Review of Literature* 34 (July 14, 1957): 34.

Shurick, E. P. J. *The First Quarter-Century of American Broadcasting.* Kansas City, Mo.: Midland Co., 1946.

Slate, Sam J., and Joe Cook. *It Sounds Impossible.* New York: Macmillan, 1963.

Stedman, Raymond William. *The Serials.* Norman: University of Oklahoma Press, 1972.

Stumpf, Charles. *Ma Perkins, Little Orphan Annie, and High-Ho Silver.* New York: Carlton Press, 1976.

Summers, Harrison B. *A Thirty-Year History of Programs Carried on National Radio Networks in the United States, 1926-1956.* Columbus, Ohio: Ohio State University Press, 1958. New York: Arno Press and the New York Times, 1971.

Terrace, Vincent. *Radio's Golden Years: The Encyclopedia of Radio Programs, 1930-1960.* La Jolla, Calif.: Barnes and Co., 1981.

"Theatre of the Air." *Radio Digest* 30-31 (January 1933): 46-47.

Thurber, James. *The Beast in Me and Other Animals.* New York: Harcourt, Brace, 1948.

Tyler, Poyntz, ed. *Television and Radio. The Reference Shelf,* vol. 36, no. 2. New York: Wilson, 1961.

Wertheim, Arthur Frank. "Relieving Social Tensions: Radio Comedy and the Great Depression." *Journal of Popular Culture* 10, no. 3 (Winter 1976): 501-19.

_____. *Radio Comedy.* New York: Oxford University Press, 1979.

Wolfe, G. Joseph. "'War of the Worlds' and the Editors." *Journalism Quarterly* 57 (Spring 1980): 39-44.

Wyatt, E. V. "Post-War Poets and the Theater: 'Fall of the City.'" *Catholic World* 145 (August 1937): 600.

Wylie, Max. "Amos 'n' Andy: A Loving Remembrance." *Television Quarterly* 2, no. 3 (Summer 1963): 17-24.

3   RADIO NEWS

The history of broadcast news is the story of a race between the broadcaster's imagination and the public's appetite for quick and dramatic information about major events. Although the beginning of this century saw the development of technology that would permit the broadcast of information from one location to another, it was a string of individual "big news stories" from 1920 to 1940 that created the public's insatiable appetite for up-to-the-minute news. The public's hunger for news sparked the ambition of the brightest people in the fields of technology and broadcast journalism, who sought better, faster, and flashier ways of bringing the big stories home. Their success further stimulated the public's desire for faster, more dramatic news, and so the cycle continues unabated today.

The fact that many major news stories such as conventions, elections, and political speeches are announced in advance gave the earliest experimenters with broadcast news both the laboratory subjects and the controlled environments they needed to produce newscasts that would beat the newspapers. There is some argument for crediting Lee De Forest with the first of the significant breakthrough newscasts with his 1916 broadcast of the presidential election results. However, most historians are more comfortable with 1920, coming down either on the side of Detroit's 8MK broadcast of the August Michigan primary results or KDKA's (Pittsburgh) broadcast of the November presidential election—a broadcast that has now passed into modern American folklore.

Since 1920 radio and broadcast news as we now know it has grown from three different sources. The first is the regularly scheduled newscast, which then, much as it does now, consisted of little more than a reading of headlines and leads of a few major stories—stories largely (and in the1920s exclusively) taken from newspapers or wire services. The newscast is still not a major component in the broadcast schedule of most radio stations. Most current radio newscasts take up no more than a few minutes per hour; radio newscasts in the 1920s took up no more than several minutes per day. Moreover, the charges of "rip and read" newscasting that still abound in the radio field indicate that to a large extent the straight radio newscast, even when it occurs in a major city, has not evolved considerably from its earliest forms. Compared to the growth of broadcast news in the other two areas, the straight newscast has all but remained stagnant for the past three generations.

The second source is the immediate broadcast of a major breaking story. Through the 1920s radio's increasing interest in developing ever-larger hookups for the broadcast of major stories played nicely into the hands of politicians who sought ever-larger audiences for their activities. In the 1920s and 1930s election returns, conventions, major speeches, and political advertising were used by broadcasters and politicians alike for the same, mutually self-serving purpose: to attract the largest possible audience to their event. Other events, such as the World Series and the Scopes trial, further encouraged the growth of network news. The rapid rise of these popular broadcasts and the corresponding expansion of their audiences grated on rival newspapers and wire services, who lost prestige and revenue during this period. Their feud with radio erupted in what has come to be known as the Press-Radio War of the 1930s. A discussion of that intriguing imbroglio appears later in this chapter.

The third source is the phenomenon of the news commentator, whose on-the-air persona became interwoven with the content of his commentaries. Broadcasters discovered early that a compelling (although not always learned and not always cordial) voice could attract listeners and advertisers to news on a regular basis. The history of the commentator is so important to the shaping of broadcast news (and, some have argued, to the shaping of American politics and policy) that a separate discussion of radio commentary is contained within this chapter.

Since radio news has been driven by the twin engines of charismatic radio commentators and compelling, instant coverage of breaking stories, it is not at all surprising that radio news (and possibly broadcast news) had its finest moments when the medium's most effective radio commentator covered the century's most important breaking story. A section on Edward R. Murrow's radio work—especially his work in Europe during World War II—follows the discussion of radio commentary.

GENERAL WORKS

The major sources on radio journalism include studies of broadcasting as well as studies of journalism. Erik Barnouw's three-volume *A History of Broadcasting in the United States* is the most important of these. The first volume, *A Tower in Babel,* is the most helpful in establishing the rise of radio news in the context of the history of broadcasting as a whole. Barnouw's volumes treat no subject in any depth, but in *A Tower in Babel* he stresses the impact of early newspaper ownership of radio stations on the development of broadcast news and sets forth the chronology of major news broadcasts and breakthroughs. For all his terseness, Barnouw effectively presents the importance of major broadcasts and the development of the public's desire for a national news—the kind of news that could only be handled by radio. *The Golden Web,* Barnouw's second volume covering 1933-1953, also provides the most solid general history of the medium during this period of time. Of particular use to scholars in radio journalism are his several discussions of Franklin Roosevelt's skill in using radio to his advantage and creating, it would seem for all time, the "media president." He also treats well the 1930s rivalry between NBC and CBS—particularly CBS's desire to use news as the means by which it would outperform its main competitor. The third volume, *The Image Empire,* covers the television age and thus does not provide a comparable amount of useful information in the area of radio news (or radio in general).

Gleason L. Archer's *A History of Radio to 1926*, the first major history of the medium, is particularly strong on the development of radio's use as a political tool but far less useful on the subject of the growth of news reporting within the broadcast industry. The book contains a superior discussion of Warren Harding's use (and success) with radio speeches. It is not unlike Barnouw's work in that it breaks its subject matter into many discrete subheadings, but Gleason's work reads much more slowly. Another early general history of radio that offers some valuable insights into the early news developments is E. P. J. Shurick's *The First Quarter-Century of American Broadcasting.* Shurick takes considerable pains to explain the advances in telephone wire hookups necessary for early presidential speeches. He also provides one of the earliest discussions of radio's role in local information and community action: law enforcement, flood emergencies, weather reports, farm reports, and so on.

Although it is not a comprehensive history of the medium or of radio news, Francis Chase, Jr.'s *Sound and Fury: An Informal History of Broadcasting* offers one of the earliest genuinely sophisticated analyses of the relationship between politics and radio. Chase's comparison of Hoover's and Roosevelt's radio styles is excellent. His discussion of the history of the program "Town Meeting of the Air" is a highly instructive case study of how radio in the 1930s was teaching itself and its audience new definitions of news and information broadcasting. Also included are well-researched sections on the Press-Radio War, Edward R. Murrow, and radio news' practice of raiding newspapers for its newscasters and reporters. Widely quoted in media and news studies, it is one of the best and most respected sources in the field.

Charles A. Siepmann's *Radio's Second Chance* is an excellent analysis of early radio news ventures. He is one of the few historians who incorporate fully into their general histories of radio news discussions of early censorship and freedom of speech cases. His is an economic and regulatory history of radio and radio news more than a programming history, and thus it complements nicely the other works cited.

Many books present original perspectives on the general history of radio news. Gilbert Seldes's *The Great Audience* offers an imaginative analysis of the formal evolution of the radio documentary; he pays particular attention to the role of playwright Norman Corwin in bringing a "poetic" quality to CBS's early documentary efforts. Mitchell V. Charnley's *News by Radio* contains a solid, compressed history of radio news. He is less taken than others with the role of Edward R. Murrow in advancing the quality of radio broadcasting during war; he assigns to Murrow no greater role or contribution than he does to any other major radio correspondent at the time. Charnley's book doubles as a textbook and contains chapters on how a radio newsroom operates and how a broadcast is formatted. Although dated (1948), much of this information (and Charnley's good sense) holds up well. Frank Luther Mott's *The News in America* is an imaginative and energetic (but not at all comprehensive) discussion of the state of news in America in the early 1960s. Of particular value is his chapter "WZZZ Airs the News," in which he takes us through the day of a fictitious city radio news operation. (The station is a composite of KGO in San Francisco and WHO in Des Moines.) Mott makes the telling point that small radio stations sometimes have larger commitments to airing and gathering news than do large ones—a key difference between radio news and television news, which are often lumped together in discussions of news after 1950. Paul F. Lazarsfeld's *Radio and the Printed Page: An Introduction to the Study of Radio and Its Role in the Communication of Ideas* contains two significant chapters on news. Concentrating his analysis on the radio audience, Lazarsfeld sees early radio news as the initial stimulant in the American consciousness for news beyond the local level. In addition, he provides some useful data on how the audience in the late 1930s perceived and used radio news. Harrison B. Summers's anthology *Radio Censorship* offers dozens of readings on radio censorship cases and law. The entire subject is critical to any discussion of radio news, although the readings in Summers's book cover news, entertainment, religion, and advertising.

Among the more recent histories of radio news, J. Fred MacDonald's "The Development of Broadcast Journalism," a chapter in his book *Don't Touch That Dial! Radio Programming in American Life, 1920-1960,* is excellent. Little new information is presented here (MacDonald is stronger in the area of entertainment programming), but the concise history of broadcasting presents efficiently (and in more readable fashion than do the more thorough but more encyclopedic Barnouw volumes) discussions on the rise of the commentator, radio censorship and World War II, the Press-Radio War, and postwar radio documentaries. He shortchanges Murrow somewhat—perhaps not wanting to add to the deluge—but otherwise provides a very good condensation of radio news' history. Peter Fornatale and Joshua E. Mills have an imaginative section

on radio news in their book *Radio in the Television Age.* The chapter, which is a
vigorous defense of radio news as the medium by which most people learn about
breaking stories (even in the television age), offers a cursory history of radio
news history highlights. In addition, Fornatale and Mills pay particular
attention to technological advances and their role in the growth of radio news in
the 1930s—a type of discussion usually associated with earlier sources on radio.
Steve Knoll's essay "Radio News—Promise and Performance" in Marvin
Barrett's anthology *The Politics of Broadcasting* makes the persuasive case that
the inflexibility of format radio in the 1970s and 1980s has stunted the growth of
radio news, implying that the flexible format of television programming has
given rise to growth and innovation in television news.

   Other studies that are less valuable but worth consulting as minor sources
include Judith C. Waller's *Radio: The Fifth Estate.* A standard summary history
of the medium, it is less thorough than most and is surprisingly stingy in its
information on news. Its one unique contribution is its discussion of the role of
women in braodcast news and its brief discussion of women's reactions to news
broadcasts. Scholars researching women and media studies will find it helpful.
Llewellyn White's *The American Radio: A Report on the Broadcasting Industry in
the United States from the Commission on the Freedom of the Press* contains, for
all the magnificence of its title, a good general history of radio, particularly on
the role of advertisers and advertising. This study can make the historical claim
of recommending in 1947 that radio not sell individual programs to individual
advertisers—thus ensuring that advertisers cannot gain control over news and
other programming. However, as a general source for radio history, it can be
used sparingly. Sammy R. Danna's "The Rise of Radio News" in Lawrence
Lichty and Malachi C. Topping's *American Broadcasting: A Source Book on the
History of Radio and Television* is a brief overview of radio news' early triumphs,
with particular emphasis between 1929 and 1933. Lloyd R. Morris's *Not So
Long Ago*, a self-confessed personal history of early twentieth-century America,
offers one-third of its considerable bulk to the rise of radio. Its freshness comes
from its personal tone rather than its new insights or information on radio or
radio news.

   Articles on radio news appear regularly in some of the standard academic
journals such as *Journal of Broadcasting* and *Journalism Quarterly.* David G.
Clark's "Radio in Presidential Campaigns: The Early Years (1924-1932),"
appearing in *Journal of Broadcasting* (Summer 1962), fleshes out nicely the
politicians' earliest ventures into political broadcasting, complete with
Democratic and Republican media advertising budgets for the early campaigns.
Michael Emery's "The Munich Crisis Broadcasts: Radio News Comes of Age"
in *Journalism Quarterly* (Autumn 1965) is valuable for the original insight that it
offers and its detailed account of what is generally agreed to be the greatest event
of radio news. Most often seen as Murrow's triumph for radio news, the Munich
crisis is viewed by Emery as radio news' triumph for itself. Radio news articles
in *Journal of Broadcasting* and *Journalism Quarterly* more frequently deal with

specific contemporary issues than they do with general history; examples are Howard H. Martin's "President Reagan's Return to Radio" in the winter 1984 issue of *Journalism Quarterly* or Theodore L. Glasser's "On Time-Compressed News" in the winter 1976 issue of the *Journal of Broadcasting*. But radio news-related articles appear in these journals with sufficient frequency to warrant regular checking of their indexes.

THE PRESS-RADIO WAR

One of the major stages in the evolution of broadcast journalism occurred in 1934 and 1935 when newspaper publishers, long both fascinated by and resentful of radio journalism, set about consciously to rid the airwaves of news-related broadcasts. In what was termed the Press-Radio War, newspapers vented so much hostility toward radio journalism that radio broadcasts became aware of how much potential they had as gatherers and disseminators of news. Paradoxically, by attempting to destroy radio journalism, the hostile newspapers advanced by decades radio's commitment to and capability for news broadcasting.

Years before the open conflict over radio's role in news broadcasting broke out between the press and radio, print journalists had expressed more than a few reservations about radio's ventures into political and information broadcasting. A 1922 article in *Wireless Age,* "What Newspaper Editors Say," published excerpts from newspaper editorials objecting vigorously to the considerable interest that politicians and radio broadcasters were beginning to show toward one another. In the *Milwaukee Journal* one could find:

When a candidate hires a hall, there's no law to make you go hear him. If a paper prints his speech, you can skip it and read something interesting in the next column. Usually you can dodge him on the street. But when he takes to the radio, he's got you. With the radio in the office, the club, the home, and the bathtub, on boats, trains, and automobiles, there's no escape from the spellbinder.

In an equally respectful editorial on the prospect of having congressional sessions broadcast over radio, the *Toledo News-Bee* argued:

One can let the *Congressional Record* lie in its wrapper. Or one can find out when something worthwhile has been said and read. . . . But in the place of the music, the lectures, market reports, weather reports and things of this sort, the congressional proceedings are as a whole not worth the time. Nobody but the man who is paid for it should have to stand the racket of Congress.

Even though in 1922 no stations had any newsgathering ambitions and few broadcast more than several minutes of news per day, this level of activity was sufficient to generate scorn among print journalists.

Scorn grew to fear and envy when broadcasters began reporting major stories with greater speed and impact than the newspapers or the wire services. Various scholars attribute to different individual stories the responsibility for enraging the print journalists and bringing them closer to a point of conflict with the broadcasters. Certainly the broadcast of election returns of every presidential election from 1920, major speeches by Presidents Hoover and Coolidge, the Scopes trial in 1925, and the Lindberg flight were among the major stories in the 1920s where the speed of radio provided unbeatable competition for the newspapers. Moreover, in the 1920s broadcasters were experimenting with chain and network hookups, thus giving their reporting expanded audiences. Newspapers, struggling with their local circulation figures, enjoyed no corresponding burst of energy or prestige during the same period. By the late 1920s the only thing preventing the newspapers from going for the throats of the radio broadcasters was that throughout the decade times had been good and there appeared to be enough advertising money available on the market to keep both newspapers and radio broadcasters well fed. Radio was costing print journalism some prestige and exclusivity in the reporting field, but there was not yet any widespread concern that radio was costing the papers a significant amount of revenue.

By the early stages of the depression that situation changed. War between the mediums broke out when financial rivalry merged with and ultimately overshadowed professional rivalry. In his article "The Origin of the Press-Radio Conflict," published in the June 1936 issue of *Journalism Quarterly,* Russell Hammargren sees 1928 as the year that the newspaper industry first began to perceive radio news (as well as radio advertising) as a major financial and professional threat. During the 1928 election, the Associated Press invested $250,000 to cover the election. As it had almost always done, AP turned over its information to the networks—a practice begun in the days when radio broadcast so little news that it was not even considered by the major papers and wire services to be a part of the journalism profession. However, by election night 1928 NBC and CBS were hooked up to some 120-plus stations between them and gleefully broadcast the fruits of AP's long hours and considerable expense. At last, the newspaper industry started to see radio news not as a frivolous plaything or a growing inconvenience, but as a genuine and life-threatening competitor.

Things might have come to a head even if there had been no depression, but the depression made confrontation inevitable. In the first several years of the depression the newspaper industry suffered significant advertising losses while the radio industry performed beautifully. Moreover, radio commentators (H. V. Kaltenborn, Floyd Gibbons, and others) were becoming very popular in the early thirties, and with them came the nearly earthshaking realization that radio news, at least in this format, could attract advertising revenue on its own.

In self-defense, newspapers began launching a few small, pathetic salvos. Resentful of the fact that listing radio schedules in the newspapers provided free advertising to radio sponsors, some papers refused to list radio programs whose titles included the name of the sponsor in their radio listings (thus "The Chase and Sanborn Hour" became "variety" or something similar) on the grounds that the papers would not give a free plug to advertisers who had abandoned them in hard times. Others refused to publish listings at all.

In 1933 the most serious battle line was drawn over the "ownership" of news. William Paley in *As It Happened: A Memoir* and T. R. Carskadon in his brilliant piece on the Press-Radio War for the *New Republic* (March 11, 1936) argue that what triggered the final escalation of hostilities was the radio coverage of the kidnapping of the Lindberg baby during the previous year—the biggest single news story in the then short history of radio news and arguably the biggest news story between the two world wars save only the stock market crash of 1929. CBS and NBC broadcast developments and updates around the clock for weeks. For scoops, immediacy, and impact, radio buried the newspapers. Live radio coverage of the Democratic convention in the summer of 1932 did nothing to soothe the badly frayed feelings of the newspapers.

Retaliation came swiftly. Under pressure from the newspapers, the wire services began cutting service to the radio stations, leaving the stations and the networks without their predominant (and in many cases their only) source of news. Left to their own devices, NBC and CBS quickly put together their own newsgathering operations, using stringers, contacts in major cities, foreign press, the telephone, and a great deal of imagination. In their highly readable and valuable accounts of putting together those early newsgathering operations, NBC's Abel Alan Schechter (*I Live On Air*) and CBS's Paul W. White (*News on the Air*) not only provided the best "in the trenches" histories of the radio journalists' plight during the Press-Radio War but revealed how many of broadcast news' standard practices grew out of the necessity of getting on the air without wire service bulletins (on-the-air interviews with highly placed government officials, eyewitness accounts of street events, the broadcast journalist's use of the telephone as his link to the outside world).

CBS's newsgathering operation, the Columbia News Service, was so successful that after only a few months it was keeping CBS fully competitive with the papers and the wire services. But NBC was not so successful, and the depression had finally taken a toll on radio. In December 1933 the wire services, the networks, and the American Newspaper Publishers Association sat down at the Biltmore Hotel in New York and hammered out the Biltmore Agreement—a short-lived exercise in uneven compromise that gave the networks access to preselected wire service news on the condition that broadcasters could air background news only (no spots), could broadcast only at times that would not allow radio news to "hit the streets" before the morning or evening papers, could not gather their own news, and could not have sponsors for news broadcasts.

As Keith P. Sanders notes in his *Journalism Quarterly* article (Autumn 1967) "The Collapse of the Press-Radio News Bureau" (the agency established to enforce the Biltmore Agreement), this attempt to control the growth of broadcast news was doomed to fail. The more than 60 percent of the radio stations that were not affiliated with the networks had no reason to honor it, the wire services themselves often made their news available to radio, and the networks began labelling their popular news commentary shows as "entertainment" and airing them at will. By 1936 radio news was accepted by everyone, including the newspapers, as an integral part of the business and profession of journalism.

No book-length discussions of the Press-Radio War have been published. None of the articles on the conflict is comprehensive, but en masse the body of literature fleshes out the details fully. Giraud Chester's "The Press-Radio War, 1933-1935" (*Public Opinion Quarterly*, Summer 1947) is more descriptive than analytical but discusses at some length the workings of the Press-Radio Bureau. "The Press-Radio War of the 1930's" (*Journal of Broadcasting,* Summer 1970) by George E. Lott, Jr., is the most recent of the scholarly treatments of the conflict and has the advantage of encompassing much of the previous literature. Lott traces the causes of the conflict, particularly the impact that the scope and variety of radio journalism experiments had upon a dumbfounded and later enraged newspaper establishment. Russell J. Hammargren's "The Origin of the Press-Radio Conflict" (*Journalism Quarterly,* June 1936), the first of the scholarly studies of the subject, is, for its brief three pages, shrewdly analytical; Hammargren makes an excellent connection between advertising rivalries and journalism rivalries as joint causes of the hostilities. Rudolph D. Michael's "History and Criticism of Press-Radio Relationships" in the September 1938 issue of *Journalism Quarterly* is particularly strong in documenting and analyzing the role of the wire services before and during the Press-Radio War. Keith P. Sanders' short article in the autumn 1967 issue of *Journalism Quarterly* ("The Collapse of the Press-Radio News Bureau") focuses exclusively on the bureau's doomed efforts to enforce the unenforceable. Sammy R. Danna's "The Press-Radio War" in Lichty and Topping's *American Broadcasting* gives an overview of the press-radio rivalry up to World War II, extending the generally accepted 1930-1935 dates for the conflict.

Various magazines reported on various aspects of the war. T. R. Carskadon's "The Press-Radio War" in the March 11, 1936, issue of *New Republic* is as insightful as it is wry. Most other popular periodical coverage would add little to what can be garnered from Carskadon and the other sources cited here.

Three first-person accounts of the warfare are worth noting. Paley devotes a full chapter to the conflict in *As It Happened: A Memoir,* portraying himself and his network as virtuous conquerors. In many respects his view is accurate, although there is evidence in other sources that Paley takes more personal credit for the triumph of the Columbia News Service than he may deserve. Schechter's *I Live on Air* and White's *News on the Air* both provide superior accounts of their respective roles in the conflict. Unfortunately, Schechter's is the more vivid and more detailed; it is Paul White's work with Columbia News Service that is truly history-making. Scholarship could use an extensive study of White's role here.

In addition to offering up the vicarious pleasures that all conflicts among industrial giants provide to those that study them, the Press-Radio War demonstrates that radio journalism and journalism as a whole came of age at about the same time. Carving out for themselves their individual areas of strength, radio (speed, impact, audience size) and newspapers (depth, breadth, and physical tangibility) produced from this conflict the occasionally uneasy but generally solid relationship between print and broadcast news that has characterized American journalism for the last fifty years. It is a marvelously revealing substudy in journalism history.

THE COMMENTATORS

By the 1950s television news had become so powerful that many discussions of radio news since that time have been subsumed under the category of broadcast news, with television news being the far greater of its two components. There is some justification for the orphaning of radio news during the television age. Television news brought to broadcasting all of the swiftness, immediacy, and dramatic impact that characterizes radio news. But it added pictures: first small fuzzy pictures, then large fuzzy pictures, then large clear pictures, then large color pictures, then giant pictures.

Even the newsgathering operations in radio and television differ more in degree than they do in kind. Radio news operations within the major networks and in large cities often share facilities and personnel with their co-owned television operations—with television broadcasting universally viewed as the more prestigious activity. The news philosophy, ethics, and practices are almost the same within the two media, as are the major stories and broadcast formats. While certainly the working procedures of the reporters, editors, and technicians in radio news must and do take into account the fact that their audience cannot see their stories, radio news and television news have developed along similar lines, with one notable exception: the radio news commentator.

The radio commentator—the well-spoken, well-known individual who interpreted the news and whose name became identified with those news stories he chose to elaborate upon—is central to the development of radio news. It is a phenomenon that knows no counterpart in television.

In his autobiography *Fifty Fabulous Years* H. V. Kaltenborn, a Harvard-educated editor for a Brooklyn newspaper, claims with some justification that he was the first radio commentator in 1923. Indeed, the controversies that Kaltenborn stirred up with sponsors, public officials, and the public at large over what would be considered today fairly mild fare speaks to the fact that in the 1920s people were not accustomed to hearing any news-related opinions on radio, even though they read such opinions daily in the newspapers. (Sometimes they read the exact same opinions; commentators such as Kaltenborn, Fulton Lewis, and Elmer Davis performed double duty as newspaper columnists and radio analysts.) Controversies notwithstanding, the good commentators were popular, and their numbers increased rapidly over the next decade. One source claims that by 1940 there were hundreds of them in America.

With their ever-increasing presence in radio came a concern over their influence and power, specifically a concern over the degree to which they could influence public opinion and public policy. The debate was never settled fully, even when the radio commentators' numbers and powers waned in the 1950s. The debate also helps to keep current scholarship active in the history of the commentator, for it is a central question in the development of broadcast journalism as a whole.

Two books form the center of the literature on the commentator. Irving Fang's *Those Radio Commentators* contains excellent, compressed biographies on Kaltenborn, Floyd Gibbons, Lowell Thomas, Father Coughlin, Boake Carter, Upton Close, Dorothy Thompson, Raymond Gram Swing, Elmer Davis, Fulton Lewis, Drew Pearson, Walter Winchell, and Hilmar Baukhage, as well as thumbnail sketches of regional and minor commentators. In the introduction of the book (charmingly entitled "The Excess Prophets") he surveys the history of the commentator—his rise to power, his flights with sponsors, the audience response, and the question of his influence.

The other book deals directly with the question of the commentators' influence as its central thesis. David H. Culbert's *News for Everyman: Radio and Foreign Affairs in Thirties America* argues that radio news, once having generated in the public an unprecedented interest in news in general and foreign affairs in particular, proceeded to shape public opinion and, in some cases, public policy through the persuasive, subjective analyses of its most influential commentators. Examining the careers of Carter, Kaltenborn, Swing, Davis, Lewis, and Murrow, he argues that each of these men altered American sentiment and that a few of them may have altered American policy in foreign affairs. In a thoroughly researched and energetically argued position, Culbert carefully tempers his assignations of responsibility, choosing wisely to show how commentators influenced the general climate of American thinking—a climate that may have allowed for a particular change in foreign policy. Culbert is quite careful not to attribute to any commentator the sole responsibility for any change in history; however, one gets a sense from the tone of the work that on occasion he would like to.

A very good companion study to Culbert's book is David Hosley's unpublished doctoral dissertation "The Men, the Instrument, and the Moment: The Development of Radio Foreign Correspondence in the United States through 1940" (Columbia University, 1982). Hosley's work is a social history of foreign correspondence tracing the transition from the network representative system (where news executives procured guest speakers to discuss foreign affairs on their programs) to the correspondent system (where reporters covered foreign affairs themselves). Hosley's narrative technique is reminiscent of popular novels and helps to capture the adventurousness of the men and their time. Moreover, his work nicely complements Culbert's in that Hosley successfully conveys the communal sense that the major correspondents developed about themselves and their mission, while Culbert concentrates on delineating individual styles and accomplishments.

Two other notable but less valuable treatments of the radio commentators include a discussion in Gilbert Seldes's *The Great Audience* that compactly details the rise of the commentator in the context of the rise of radio journalism in general. A rather curious treatment of radio announcers can be found throughout Ray Poindexter's *Golden Throats and Silver Tongues: The Radio Announcers*. Published by a tiny independent press, the book lacks editorial structuring. Announcers are announcers regardless of their quality or specialty, so one is likely to see discussions of Edward R. Murrow and H. V. Kaltenborn interspersed with biographies of Harry Von Zell and Art Linkletter. The lack of formal structuring and academic apparatus is unfortunate because the sheer volume of information on announcers and radio stations contained within this book is absolutely staggering.

Several articles on radio commentators document both the rise of the commentator and the character of the radio news commentators' heyday. Robert R. Smith's "The Origins of Radio Network News Commentary" (*Journal of Broadcasting*, Spring 1965) offers a wide range of explanations for the commentators' popularity in the 1930s, including the print journalist training of many of the leading commentators, the highly controversial New Deal legislation (which provided countless single issues and many major theoretical matters for debate), and the Press-Radio War, which led commentators to interpret newspaper stories out of fear of facing plagiarism charges from the papers if they read them straight. R. Franklin Smith's "The Nature and Development of Commentary" (*Journal of Broadcasting*, Winter 1961-1962 wrestles with some of the theoretical questions posed by the significance of commentary as part of radio news. Among his concerns are the definition of commentary and how it is distinguished from analysis. (Smith admits that this distinction has far more bearing on theoretical discussions of news than it does on practical situations.) On the issue of bias he observes that not only has CBS been the network most responsible for building up a stable of highly reputable news commentators, it has also been the network most responsible for the breaches of objectivity and most resistant to conservative commentators. Three articles that appeared in the 1940s define the parameters of the debate over how much influence commentators should have. Quincy Howe, in "Policing the Commentator: A News Analysis" (*Atlantic*, November 1943), fears the power of the sponsor far more than he fears the power of the commentator himself. Howe warns that the commentator's sponsor might cause news to be slanted according to the sponsor's whim. Giraud Chester, writing in *American Mercury* (September 1947), fears the ego of the commentator far more than he fears the sponsor. Documenting gross inaccuracies in sample copy presented by leading although unnamed commentators, he claims that the extraordinary adulation of the commentators by the public has swelled the commentator's head, making him eager to render judgments on subjects about which he has little knowledge. "Hearing Is Believing," Dixon Wecter's three-part article in *Atlantic Monthly* (June-August 1945) offers the stance of the patient who loves his doctor but hates the medical profession. Wecter, while praising lavishly the virtues of individual commentators, begins with the thesis that commentators have a tendency to "slant" the news and then argues that there are three culprits: the sponsor, the local station (although his reasoning here is murky), and the networks. His series recounts not only the major issues in the rise of the commentator (sponsors and legislation) but also some of the minor skirmishes, such as CBS news editor Paul White's ill-fated attempt in the early 1940s to rid CBS news of all commentaries. The third installment offers a fine profile of Fulton Lewis, Jr., and Upton Close as embodiments of the strengths and weaknesses of the commentator. Like the Chester and Howe pieces, Wecter's series is valuable as a primary source for journalism's fascination with the rapidly increasing power of the commentator in the 1930s and 1940s.

In addition to the resources on Edward R. Murrow, who will be discussed in a separate section, information on major commentators is in good supply. Owing to his preeminence in the early stages of radio and his own considerable paper trail, H. V. Kaltenborn has generated a sizable amount of useful information. Of his own works, the autobiography *Fifty Fabulous Years* is nearly as valuable as a history of radio commentary as it is as a history of the man himself. *I Broadcast the Crisis* is a self-edited collection of Kaltenborn's radio commentaries during September and October 1938, when CBS was deeply involved in covering the crisis in Europe. The collection is a marvelous resource and demonstrates that Kaltenborn is a good, although not infallible, predictor of events. *Kaltenborn Edits the News,* a collection of narrative world news updates written in 1937, is interesting only in what it reveals about Kaltenborn; it has little significance for the history of journalism or radio commentary. Biographical information on Kaltenborn is available in three doctoral dissertations: Giraud Chester, "The Radio Commentaries of H. V. Kaltenborn: A Case Study in Persuasion" (University of Wisconsin, 1947); David G. Clark's "The Dean of Commentators: A Biography of H. V. Kaltenborn" (University of Wisconsin, 1965); and Earl S. Grow's "A Dialogue on American International Involvement, 1939-1941: The Correspondence of H. V. Kaltenborn, His Sponsors, and His Public" (University of Wisconsin, 1964). Clark produced two very good articles for the *Journal of Broadcasting* from his dissertation: "H. V. Kaltenborn and His Sponsors: Controversial Broadcasting and the Sponsor's Role" (Fall 1962), a case study in sponsor-generated controversy; and "H. V. Kaltenborn's First Year on the Air," a very detailed narrative of the first year anyone ever spent as a full-fledged radio news commentator. Finally, Kaltenborn left a full set of papers to the State Historical Society of Wisconsin in Madison. The society has cooperated with several scholars who have sought to do research on early radio and on Kaltenborn in particular.

Memoirs and other information on major commentators are also available. Max Jordan, the head of NBC coverage of Europe during the war, documents his somewhat-forgotten adventures in his professional memoir *Beyond All Fronts.* Raymond Gram Swing's *Good Evening! A Professional Memoir* is often tedious in its detail but stands as the published statement of a major figure in radio commentary. William L. Shirer's *Berlin Diary: The Journal of a Foreign Correspondent, 1934-1941* is fascinating and valuable as a history of the war as well as a history of broadcasting. Many other commentators are the authors of autobiographies or subjects of biographical works, including Elmer Davis (*But We Were Born Free*), Galen Drake (*This Is Galen Drake*), and Walter Winchell (Bob Thomas's *Winchell*), among others. For a superior review of available literature on the major commentators, the reader is advised to consult the bibliographical information in Culbert's *News for Everyman: Radio and Foreign Affairs in Thirties America.*

In his article "The Rise and Fall of the Radio Commentator" (*Atlantic*, October 26, 1957), Quincy Howe argues that the combination of television and the absence of global warfare caused the radio commentator to decline in numbers and in influence. The fact that during the postwar era, radio and television stations began experimenting with station editorials (given by station management as the station's position and not by celebrity commentators) suggests that the broadcast journalism profession felt that it lost something vital when the radio commentator lost his prestige. While broadcast editorials survive (some delivered by such prestigious and well-known journalists as John Chancellor and Bill Moyers), they lack the power and the significance they once had. Whether a more sophisticated audience no longer feels the need for a personal interpreter or whether there is something indigenous to the commentator that makes his services more necessary in an ear-dominated news industry is not clear. What is clear is that the radio commentator gave to the character of broadcast news a permanent belief in the importance of subjective news analysis as well as a celebrity status to newspeople who can command the attention of the nation.

EDWARD R. MURROW

One generation after his death, the memory, achievements, and myth of Edward R. Murrow hold enormous influence over the way in which broadcast journalism sees itself and the world. If he was, as author David Halberstam has claimed, "as good as his legend," then he was very good indeed. Scholarship credits him with an enormous list of specific achievements in the area of broadcast journalism as well as a heroic stature that in the broadest possible way seems to bring credit and credibility to the work of all journalists everywhere. Future scholars may well take this generation of scholars and journalists to task for not casting the same jaundiced eye upon his record that they cast upon so many contemporary legends and heroes. But for now, the Murrow legacy is viewed as one of seminal, definitive, and even epochal achievement.

The definitive book on Murrow is A. M. Sperber's astonishing first book *Murrow: His Life and Times,* published in 1986. A twelve-year research project, *Murrow* captures the character of the man as effectively as it chronicles his career. Sperber's efforts are assisted greatly by information previously unavailable to other researchers, including the apparent full cooperation of Murrow's widow Janet. But Sperber's real triumph lies in the kinds of virtues that she admired in the work of Murrow: relentless pursuit of information, a keen ability to shape sensible character analysis from details, and remarkable skill in the telling of revealing anecodotes and stories. For example, Sperber writes of Murrow's religious upbringing. "The underside of that picture . . . was a sense of guilt, an awareness of sin, and the need for atonement, a dark view of the human condition. . . . Underlying formal piety, however, was the strong social conscience . . . the uncompromising sense of right and wrong; of the right to disagree." Owing to her self-confessed obsession with Murrow (as a college student Sperber saw Murrow's "See It Now" attack on Joseph McCarthy and was hooked), Sperber also picked up on salient details of Murrow's life and work that had been overlooked by earlier biographers. For example, Janet Murrow's failed attempt to orchestrate a reconciliation between the dying Murrow and his former friend and colleague William L. Shirer is both fascinating and moving. The primary source of the story is a Sperber interview with Shirer. The thirty-year-old story was always there for the telling, but no one before Sperber had succeeded in getting it out of Shirer. While Sperber's work may not quite render useless all other Murrow books and profile pieces, it is without question the place where a study of Murrow's life and career must begin.

Prior to the publication of the Sperber book, the most notable work on Murrow was Alexander Kendrick's biography, *Prime Time: The Life of Edward R. Murrow.* His is a less well researched but a somewhat more readable volume than Sperber's. Kendrick balances nicely the inevitable anecdotes with research that is solid but not exhaustive. The benefits of his collegial relationship with Murrow are apparent in his contrast between NBC's coverage of the Nazi rise to power in Germany (Kendrick appears to believe, as others have before him, that NBC's newspeople sought out Nazi friends and contacts in the hopes of getting the inside track on news stories) and Murrow's approach as head of the CBS team (he was mistrustful and critical of the Nazis from the outset and wanted absolutely no closeness with them—even if it cost CBS an occasional scoop). Kendrick further poses the theory that it was Murrow's coverage of D Day rather than the coverage of London, as is generally assumed, that established for CBS its "temperate yet crisp, dignified yet informed, understated . . . and always probing" style that marks its broadcast journalism to this day.

A highly original if limited book-length study of Murrow is R. Franklin Smith's *Edward R. Murrow: The War Years,* which is based largely upon the author's interviews with Murrow's friends and fellow journalists living or stationed in Europe during the war. While sporadically enlightening (one unimpressed social acquaintance sensed that Murrow hoped that the war would make him a star), the interviews are frequently cumbersome and ineffective. To Smith's credit, he details nicely Murrow's daredevil coverage of Hitler's takeover of Austria—the first on-the-scene coverage of a major crisis in history. In addition, the book is a marvelous, quasi-oral history of the nature and character of the BBC during Murrow's London years, 1937-1944.

In his two-part 1976 article in *Atlantic Monthly* entitled "CBS: The Power and the Profits" (which formed the basis for his CBS material in the best-selling book *The Powers That Be*), author and journalist David Halberstam offers a fresh perspective on Murrow's career. Although Halberstam is an unflinching admirer of Murrow, he notes pointedly that radio journalism was so new when Murrow rode herd over it that the networks had not yet built in the kinds of institutional checks and balances that would today prevent any journalist from dominating so completely the company's news policies and practices. Halberstam offers up a superior portrait of the Murrow/Fred Friendly relationship and credits Friendly's technical genius and fierce ambition with helping Murrow make what was for him a very difficult transition from radio to television. (Friendly touches on the awkwardness of that transition in the opening chapter of his 1967 best-seller *Due to Circumstances beyond our Control . . .* , a book that recounts in great detail the Murrow/Friendly relationship during the rise of CBS television news, but otherwise deals little with the subject of radio news.) Inasmuch as Halberstam's work is an institutional biography and Murrow is so often discussed as an individual who towered over his milieu—including his network—the Halberstam article casts the familiar stories of Murrow in the less familiar context of the growth of CBS. As a result, Halberstam's piece is of particular value to scholars interested in Murrow and radio news.

Another contextual analysis of Murrow's career is offered up by CBS's venerable owner and chief executive, William Paley, in his autobiography *As It Happened: A Memoir*. Since it is Paley's thesis that all of CBS's triumphs, including those in journalism, were triumphs for management in general and Paley in particular, Murrow's landmark achievements in his European broadcasts and later in his television broadcasts are described as team efforts on the part of directors, producers, reporters, and executives. Murrow, for whom Paley had enormous affection and admiration, is not given the "lone-star" status that his peers and other biographers so freely render unto him; there is an undertone in Paley's book that suggests that collective (and particularly executive) credit should be given where collective credit is due—and possibly where it is not.

The scholarship on Murrow is not at all limited to biography. Since he was broadcast journalism's olympian figure, his writings have been collected and analyzed closely. Two collections of Murrow's radio commentaries and broadcasts are significant. *This Is London,* a collection of many of the London-based reports prior to World War II, is notable both as a comprehensive anthology of Edward R. Murrow's historic broadcasts in 1939 and 1940 and as evidence of the early homage that the journalism field was paying to Murrow for that work. Published in 1941 and edited by Elmer Davis, it is an explicit tribute to Murrow's coverage, insight, and valor paid by a distinguished colleague. The second work is Edward Bliss, Jr.'s collection, *In Search of Light: The Broadcasts of Edward R. Murrow, 1938-1961.* Bliss's book is a generous selection of Murrow's radio and television reports. Bliss's brief essays introduce major broadcasts and trends, but he offers no genuine synthesis. His introductions are very good in spots, especially in the critical broadcasts of the bombing of London where Murrow made his mark on American broadcast journalism. Bliss's hope is that the essays reflect the style, philosophy, and compassion of Murrow; by and large he is correct. Many of Murrow's pre-1941 broadcasts are collected on tape at the University of Washington in the Milo Ryan Phonoarchives. A two-volume record-album series, "Edward R. Murrow, A Reporter Remembers," produced by Columbia, contains selections of broadcasts (volume 1 encompasses the war years, volume 2 the postwar years).

The most extensive study of Murrow's works is Thomas R. Woolley's widely quoted, unpublished doctoral dissertation "A Rhetorical Study: The Radio Speaking of Edward R. Murrow." This lengthy and at times labored examination of Murrow's work analyzes the rhetorical dimensions of Murrow's radio commentaries. Reminiscent of literary textual exegesis, the study yields some intriguing and valuable findings. Woolley breaks Murrow's radio career into two phases (Europe, 1938-1946, and America, 1947-1957) but finds no major differences in the rhetorical devices employed or the style that evolved in the two separate stages. Woolley notes that as influential and persuasive as he was, Murrow rarely used formal logic or deduction; he was persuaded by emotionalism and his own air of authority and integrity. Woolley also reminds us that while Murrow frequently preached the gospel of journalistic objectivity, he was often advocative in his reporting. (If nothing else, Murrow remains the hero for the current group of advocacy journalists in the broadcast media. In his 1988 book *Prime Times and Bad Times,* Ed Joyce, former president of CBS news, states that contemporary news broadcasters still invoke his name routinely.) Woolley's study also reveals just how independent Murrow was in his selection of material. Woolley observes that from 1947 to 1957 Murrow's interest in politics and foreign affairs and his relative disinterest in economics, culture, or disasters guided his content selection. Even when subjects that he did not find particularly interesting ended up as hard news in a given day or given week, Murrow was not prone to comment upon them.

As exhaustive as Woolley's study is, a few other scholars have explored the issue of Murrow as rhetorician and speaker. In his fascinating book *Documentary Expression and Thirties America,* William Stott discusses Murrow and the rise of radio in the 1930s as the "central medium" of reporting (pp. 75-91). David H. Culbert, in the Murrow chapter of *News for Everyman: Radio and Foreign Affairs in Thirties America* and in his article "This is London: Edward R. Murrow, Radio News, and American Aid to Britain" (*Journal of Popular Culture,* Summer 1976), offers two brief but formidable analyses of Murrow's speaking style. Given the limitations of written discussions on oral expression and oral style, Culbert argues effectively that Murrow's phrasing and pronunciation are vital to understanding the dramatic effect and persuasive force of his broadcasts. Lawrence Rudner's "Born to a New Craft: Edward R. Murrow, 1938-1940" (*Journal of Popular Culture,* Fall 1981) also analyzes Murrow's style as an outgrowth of his compassion for people and events but adds little to what is already known or thought about Murrow.

An extensive study of Murrow's specific contribution to radio journalism can be found in chapter 2 of Theodore John Bilsky's unpublished dissertation, "A Descriptive Study: Edward R. Murrow's Contributions to Electronic Journalism." Concentrating less on Murrow's vision and philosophy than he might have, Bilsky details specific, lasting achievements and advancements in radio journalism that Murrow developed either by himself or in conjunction with others. Bilsky numbers among these the first multipoint news broadcast (the now-familiar news roundup involving several reporters around the world, each pitching in before the broadcast returns to what we now call the anchorperson stationed in the newsroom headquarters), the hiring of broadcast journalists for their ability as journalists rather than their ability as speakers (although the careers of radio newspeople with less than spectacular voices—most notably Elmer Davis—suggest that this claim might be overstated), the development of on-the-spot newscasts, improvement or innovation in microphone techniques, and various technical advances, as well as breakthrough techniques and ideas for bringing realism to the broadcasting of unfolding events.

In the course of his life various popular magazines did profiles of Murrow. Among the more useful of these are Isabella Taves's "Edward R. Murrow" in the February and March 1954 issues of *McCall's,* and *Time's* cover story from September 30, 1957.

Not surprisingly, discussions about Murrow surface in books on other subjects. William L. Shirer's *Berlin Diary* has sporadic information about Shirer's dealings with Murrow when the author worked for Murrow during the war. Eric Sevareid's *Not So Wild a Dream* is cited often in Murrow bibliographies; for all its many virtues, it is not a significant sourcebook for Murrow research. Paul White's *News on the Air* also discusses Murrow now and again. Most of the useful material on Murrow in these books has been culled nicely in Bilsky's dissertation. Barbara Matusow's best-seller *The Evening Stars* contains a chapter on "The Murrow Legacy." While it pales in comparison to Halberstam's portrait of Murrow and his network, it offers a surprisingly sensitive account of Murrow's and CBS's transition from radio to television.

The primary collection of Murrow's papers is at the Edward R. Murrow Center of Public Diplomacy at Tufts University's Fletcher School (Medford, Massachusetts). CBS's library in New York has its own records of Murrow correspondence, memos, and press releases. Individual small collections of letters are scattered throughout the country.

Journalists and scholars may still be too close to the halcyon days of Murrow's radio reports to have gained sufficient perspective for a genuine and honest evaluation. But even now there is no doubting his influence and his boldness. Moreover, there is no arguing how profoundly he enhanced the impact and significance of radio news. For this reason, we can assume that future writers on the early days of journalism will always acknowledge his influence even if they choose not to propagate his myth.

MISCELLANEOUS SUBJECTS

The literature on radio news embraces many useful books and articles that do not fit comfortably into the broader categories already listed but do deserve mention. Walter Johnson's *The American President and the Art of Communication* as well as Glen Phillips's unpublished dissertation "The Use of Radio and Television by Presidents of the United States" (University of Michigan, 1968) flesh out in full detail the discussions of presidential politics and radio that are found in the general radio news histories discussed earlier in this chapter.

In the area of journalism ethics, most of the literature covers either journalism as a whole or broadcast media (with special emphasis on television). However, a few works have focused on the particulars of radio practice or radio technology. The best known of these is Ruth Brindze's 1937 muckraking *Not to Be Broadcast: The Truth about the Radio.* This alleged exposé constitutes a "sky-is-falling" condemnation of radio for allowing its journalists to be sponsored by big corporations, for permitting the influence of advertisers to shape the news, and for failing in the areas of accountability and record keeping. Too scathing to be taken too seriously, it is useful as an early venture into the dark jungle of journalism ethics. The Fairness Doctrine and its evolution through radio's network era is nicely handled in Gloria Swegman Brundage's article "Rationale for the Application of the Fairness Doctrine in Broadcast News" (*Journalism Quarterly,* Autumn 1972). This concise legislative history details the importance of the Radio Act of 1927 and the Communications Act of 1934 as well as other legislative landmarks in the Fairness Doctrine's somewhat tortured history. Lastly, an interesting Master's thesis by Robert William Mills, "Radio, TV, Film, and the Right of Privacy" (Indiana University, 1968), has an entire chapter surveying early radio journalism right-of-privacy cases. Of particular interest is a 1946 case against Drew Pearson in which the courts began to limit the privacy rights of public people—including noncelebrities who just happen to find themselves the subjects of news stories.

Two works on the general issue of oral delivery of radio news are worth noting, if only because "radio newsspeech" became a substudy in the research on Edward R. Murrow as analysts sought to account for his effectiveness. Clive J. Klinghorn's unpublished dissertation "A Study in the Use of Compressed Speech for Presentation of Radio News" (Oklahoma State University, 1979) shows the results of audience reaction to "compressed speech" (the conscious effort of broadcasters to utter more words than normal per minute while retaining natural pitch and articulation). Klinghorn comes to the rather unsurprising conclusion that while audiences have trouble maintaining comprehension and interest as speech rate is increased, they can be acclimated (up to a point) to more rapid than normal speech. In their survey of some of the more obscure literature on emphasis in delivery (as opposed to rapidity) and in their own study, Timothy P. Meyer and William C. Miller ("Emphasis and Non-Emphais in Radio Newscast Delivery," *Journalism Quarterly,* Spring 1970) suggest but do not firmly conclude that highly emphasized radio speech does not have a significant impact on listener comprehension of a newscast.

In what might be broadly classified as some behind-the-scenes glimpses of radio news, past and present, some worthwhile reading exists. David Brown and W. Richard Bruner's anthology *I Can Tell It Now* offers first-person recollections of journalism escapades that, for personal or national security reasons, had to be suppressed. Chapters by Kaltenborn and John Charles Daly are the only ones that deal with radio journalism per se. If anything, this 1964 volume serves as an unconscious documentation of how journalists once prided themselves (and now excoriate themselves) on their willingness to withhold information when larger considerations were at stake. James K. Buckalew's article "The Radio News Gatekeeper and His Sources" (*Journalism Quarterly,* Winter 1974) sought to determine the prevalence of the three basic editorial practices in programming radio news: "rip and read" (news off the wire services read as is), "re-write operations" (stories written in house from outside sources), and original news sources (news gathered and written in house). Buckalew uses his findings as evidence for dismissing industrywide charges of "rip and read" operations, claiming that radio stations are neither enamoured of nor repulsed by unretouched wire service stories. Bill Ohlemeier's short article "Editorial Practices of 107 Midwest Radio Stations" (*Journalism Quarterly,* Winter 1961) addresses the question of how, why, and under what circumstances radio stations draft editorials. The study is too old to be very useful now, but there seem to be no more recent published studies on precisely this subject. Someone needs to take Ohlemeier's work in the Midwest or elsewhere and do some updating. A similar area of study suffering a similar neglect in the last twenty years is the issue of public information programming on radio. Thomas H. Gubacs's "Public Issues Programs on Radio and Television, 1961" (*Journalism Quarterly,* Summer 1962) could well serve as a model for this kind of systematic publication.

In the area of new or original formats, one finds first the simultaneously prophetic and ironic article in *Radio Broadcast,* September 1925, James C. Young's "Is the Radio Newspaper Next?" Young details with great enthusiasm the likelihood that radio will serve as a full-blown adjunct to the newspaper before too long. Perhaps the omega study to Young's alpha is Stephen Price's unpublished dissertation "The Growth of All-News Radio: Participants' Perceptions of WCBS" (Columbia University, 1978). A detailed case study of WCBS as a model of other all-news stations and a competent discussion of the evolution of all-news radio in general, the dissertation is useful but often unconvincing in its claims that the all-news format (and its success in urban markets) reveals more than obvious information about the nature of American culture. A comparison work to Price's dissertation is the astonishing, esoteric "A Computer-based Analysis of All-News Radio Listening from a Structuralist Point of View," a doctoral dissertation by Michael Wool (Pennsylvania State University, 1984). It is too far out to be a news resource, but its use of all-news radio as text may be of fascination to hard-core researchers in communication theory.

The degree to which the radio talk show can be called a news vehicle is debatable, but it does provide—in a loosey-goosey manner—"information" broadcasting. For years, Larry King has been the most widely acclaimed call-in host—one of the few genuinely capable and comfortable with hard news issues. His autobiography, *Larry King,* tells more about himself and his brushes with the greats and near greats than it does about the medium of radio, but it is highly readable and even literate. Other available autobiographies in the same genre include Hilly Rose's *But, That's Not What I Called About*—a self-serving "my great life" book that does make a reasonably successful effort to document some of the impact that talk shows and call-in shows have had, particularly in the area of local news and local issues. Barry Gray's *My Night People* is a one-of-the-boys tale of the popular and occasionally controversial WMCA (New York) talk-show host of the 1960s and 1970s. Steve Post's *Playing in the FM Band* is the memoir of a hip talk-show disc jockey. A move to sexually frank call-in radio shows in the late 1970s and 1980s spawned cult heroes like Howard Stern and various sex therapists. The popular slick magazines, such as *Time* and *People,* gave these people generous coverage, and those articles are easily located through the *Readers' Guide to Periodical Literature.* The field of talk-show/call-in radio has produced some scholarly work. Eva M. Bronstein's doctoral dissertation, "Local Call-in Radio: A Study of the Search for Advice and Social Networks" (City University of New York, 1984), is a spirited defense of call-in programs and the much-maligned listeners who call these shows. Jane H. Bick's "The Development of Two-way Talk Radio in America" (University of Massachusetts, 1987) details the broadcast history of the increasingly popular and increasingly controversial format. Robert Avery et al.'s "Patterns of Communication on Talk Radio" (*Journal of Broadcasting,* Winter 1978) codifies host and listener exchanges ("generalizing," "description," "relationship clarification," and so on) and charts patterns. Buried within the tedious data one can find some genuinely creative and useful insights into how the seeming chaos of call-in radio talk actually has the makings of a sensible substructure.

The rise of television and television news has had the same devastating effect upon radio news literature as it has had on radio news budgets and visibility. Radio news is a study confined largely to the period between 1920 and 1950. Research in radio news inevitably becomes linked to the larger area of broadcast news, but researchers in radio must accept the fact that for now, and presumably forever, the agenda for that area will be set by the producers, reporters, editors, sources, and subjects of the television news industry.

BIBLIOGRAPHY FOR RADIO NEWS

Archer, Gleason L. *History of Radio to 1926.* 1938. Reprint. New York: Arno Press, 1971.

Avery, Robert K., Donald G. Ellis, and W. Glover. "Patterns of Communication on Talk Radio." *Journal of Broadcasting* 22 (Winter 1978): 5-17.

Barnouw, Erik. *A Tower in Babel: To 1933.* Vol. 1 of *A History of Broadcasting in the United States.* New York: Oxford University Press, 1966.

———. *The Golden Web: 1933 to 1953.* Vol. 2 of *A History of Broadcasting in the United States.* New York: Oxford University Press, 1968.

———. *The Image Empire: From 1953.* Vol. 3 of *A History of Broadcasting in the United States.* New York: Oxford University Press, 1970.

Bick, Jane H. "The Development of Two-Way Talk Radio in America." Ph.D. diss., University of Massachusetts, 1987.

Bilsky, Theodore John, Sr. "A Descriptive Study: Edward R. Murrow's Contributions to Electronic Journalism." Ph.D. diss., Case Western Reserve University, 1971.

Bliss, Edward, Jr., ed. *In Search of Light: The Broadcasts of Edward R. Murrow, 1938-1961.* New York: Knopf, 1967.

Brindze, Ruth. *Not to Be Broadcast: The Truth about the Radio.* 1937. Reprint. New York: Da Capo, 1974.

Bronstein, Eva M. "Local Call-in Radio: A Study of the Search for Advice and Social Networks." Ph.D. diss., City University of New York, 1984.

Brown, David, and W. Richard Bruner, eds. *I Can Tell It Now.* New York: Dutton, 1964.

Brundage, Gloria Swegman. "Rationale for the Application of the Fairness Doctrine in Broadcast News." *Journalism Quarterly* 49 (Autumn 1972): 531-37.

Buckalew, James K. "The Radio News Gatekeeper and His Sources." *Journalism Quarterly* 51 (Winter 1974): 602-6.

Carskadon, T. R. "The Press-Radio War." *New Republic* 86 (March 11, 1936): 132-35.

Charnley, Mitchell V. *News by Radio.* New York: Macmillan, 1948.

Chase, Francis, Jr. *Sound and Fury: An Informal History of Broadcasting.* New York: Harper and Bros., 1942.

Chester, Giraud. "Power of the Radio Commentator." *American Mercury* 65 (September 1947): 334-39.

———. "The Radio Commentary of H. V. Kaltenborn: A Case Study in Persuasion." Ph.D. diss., University of Wisconsin, 1947.

———. "The Press-Radio War, 1933-1935." *Public Opinion Quarterly* 13 (Summer 1949): 252-64.

Clark, David G. "Radio in Presidential Campaigns: The Early Years (1924-1932)" *Journal of Broadcasting* 6 (Summer 1962): 229-38.

———. "The Dean of Commentators: A Biography of H. V. Kaltenborn." Ph.D. diss., University of Wisconsin, 1965.

———. "H. V. Kaltenborn and His Sponsors: Controversial Broadcasting and the Sponsor's Role." *Journal of Broadcasting* 12 (Fall 1968): 309-23.

Culbert, David H. *News for Everyman: Radio and Foreign Affairs in Thirties America.* Westport, Conn.: Greenwood Press, 1976.

_____. "This Is London: Edward R. Murrow, Radio News, and American Aid to Britain." *Journal of Popular Culture* 10 (Summer 1976): 28-37.

Daly, John Charles. "A Death in the Family." In *I Can Tell It Now,* edited by David Brown and W. Richard Bruner, 95-99. New York: Dutton, 1964.

Danna, Sammy R. "The Press-Radio War." In *American Broadcasting: A Source Book on the History of Radio and Television,* edited by Lawrence W. Lichty and Malachi C. Topping. New York: Hastings House, 1976.

_____. "The Rise of Radio News." In *American Broadcasting: A Source Book on the History of Radio and Television,* edited by Lawrence W. Lichty and Malachi C. Topping, 338-343. New York: Hastings House, 1976.

Davis, Elmer H. *But We Were Born Free.* Indianapolis: Bobbs-Merrill, 1954.

Drake, Galen. *This Is Galen Drake.* Garden City, N.Y.: Doubleday, 1949.

Emery, Michael. "The Munich Crisis Broadcasts: Radio News Comes of Age." *Journalism Quarterly* 42 (Autumn 1965): 576-80.

Fang, Irving. *Those Radio Commentators.* Ames: Iowa State University Press, 1977.

Fornatale, Peter, and Joshua E. Mills. *Radio in the Television Age.* Woodstock, N.Y.: Overlook Press, 1980.

Friendly, Fred. *Due to Circumstances Beyond Our Control . . .* New York: Random House, 1966.

Glasser, Theodore L. "On Time-Compressed News." *Journal of Broadcasting* 20 (Winter 1976): 127-32.

Gray, Barry. *My Night People.* New York: Simon and Schuster, 1975.

Gross, Ben. *I Looked and I Listened.* New York: Random House, 1954.

Grow, Earl S. "A Dialogue on American International Involvement, 1939-1941: The Correspondence of H. V. Kaltenborn, His Sponsors, and His Public." Ph.D. diss. University of Wisconsin, 1964.

Gubacs, Thomas H. "Public Issues Programs on Radio and Television, 1961." *Journalism Quarterly* 39 (Summer 1962): 373-76.

Halberstam, David. "CBS: The Power and the Profits." *Atlantic Monthly* 237 (January 1976): 33-48.

Hammargren, Russell J. "The Origin of the Press-Radio Conflict." *Journalism Quarterly* 13 (June 1936): 91-93.

Hosley, David. "The Men, the Instrument and the Moment: The Development of Radio Foreign Correspondence in the United States through 1940." Ph.D. diss., Columbia University, 1982.

Howe, Quincy. "Policing the Commentator: A News Analysis." *Atlantic* 172 (November 1943): 72+.

_____. "The Rise and Fall of the Radio Commentator." *Atlantic* (October 26, 1957): 13-15+.

Johnson, Walter. *The American President and the Art of Communication.* Oxford: Clarendon Press, 1958.

Jordan, Max. *Beyond All Fronts.* Milwaukee: Bruce Publishing, 1944.

Joyce, Ed. *Prime Times and Bad Times.* New York: Doubleday, 1988.

Kaltenborn, H. V. *Kaltenborn Edits the News.* New York: Modern Age, 1937.

_____. *I Broadcast the Crisis.* New York: Random House, 1938.

_____. "The Broadcast That Almost Landed Me in Jail." In *I Can Tell It Now,* edited by David Brown and W. Richard Bruner, 93-94. New York: Dutton, 1964.

Kendrick, Alexander. *Prime Time: The Life of Edward R. Murrow.* Boston: Little, Brown, 1969.

King, Larry, and Emily Yoffe. *Larry King.* New York: Simon and Schuster, 1982.

Klinghorn, Clive J. "A Study in the Use of Compressed Speech for the Presentation of Radio News." Ph.D. diss., Oklahoma State University, 1979.

Knoll, Steve. "Radio News—Promise and Performance." In *The Politics of Broadcasting,* edited by Marvin Barrett. New York: Crowell, 1973.

Lazarsfeld, Paul F. *Radio and the Printed Page: An Introduction to the Study of Radio and Its Role in the Communication of Ideas.* New York: Duell, Sloan and Pearce, 1940.

Lott, George E., Jr. "The Press-Radio War of the 1930's." *Journal of Broadcasting* 14 (Summer 1970): 275-86.

MacDonald, J. Fred. "The Development of Broadcast Journalism." In *Don't Touch That Dial! Radio Programming in American Life, 1920-1960.* Chicago: Nelson-Hall, 1979

Martin, Howard H. "President Reagan's Return to Radio." *Journalism Quarterly* 61 (Winter 1984): 817-21.

Matusow, Barbara. *The Evening Stars.* New York: Ballantine Books, 1984.

Meyer, Timothy P., and William C. Miller. "Emphasis and Non-Emphasis in Radio Newscast Delivery." *Journalism Quarterly* 47 (Spring 1970): 144-47.

Michael, Rudolph D. "History and Criticism of Press-Radio Relationships." *Journalism Quarterly* 15 (September 1938): 176-84.

Mills, Robert William. "Radio, TV, Film, and the Right of Privacy." Master's thesis, Indiana University, 1968.

Morris, Lloyd R. *Not So Long Ago.* New York: Random House, 1949.

Mott, Frank Luther. *The News in America.* Cambridge, Mass.: Harvard University Press, 1962.

Murrow, Edward R. *This Is London.* New York: Simon and Schuster, 1941.

_____. "A Reporter Remembers." Sound Recording. New York: Columbia Records, 1969.

Ohlemeier, Bill. "Editorial Practices of 107 Midwest Radio Stations." *Journalism Quarterly* 43 (Winter 1961): 555.

Paley, William S. *As It Happened: A Memoir.* Garden City, N.Y.: Doubleday, 1979.

Phillips, Glen. "The Use of Radio and Television by Presidents of the United States." Ph.D. diss., University of Michigan, 1968.

Poindexter, Ray. *Golden Throats and Silver Tongues: The Radio Announcers.* Conway, Ark.: River Road Press, 1978.

Post, Steve. *Playing in the FM Band.* New York: Viking, 1974.

Price, Stephen S. "The Growth of All-News Radio: Participants' Perceptions of WCBS." Ph.D. diss., Columbia University, 1978.

Rose, Hilly. *But, That's Not What I Called About.* Chicago: Contemporary Books, 1978.

Rudner, Lawrence. "Born to a New Craft: Edward R. Murrow, 1938-1940." *Journal of Popular Culture* 15 (Fall 1981): 97-105.

Sanders, Keith P. "The Collapse of the Press-Radio News Bureau." *Journalism Quarterly* 44 (Autumn 1967): 549-52.

Schechter, Abel Alan. *I Live on Air.* New York: Stokes, 1941.

Seldes, Gilbert. *The Great Audience.* New York: Viking, 1951.

Sevareid, Eric. *Not So Wild a Dream.* New York: A. A. Knopf, 1946.

Shirer, William L. *Berlin Diary: The Journal of a Foreign Correspondent, 1934-1941.* New York: A. A. Knopf, 1941.

Shurick, E. P. J. *The First Quarter-Century of American Broadcasting.* Kansas City, Mo.: Midland Co., 1946.

Siepmann, Charles A. *Radio's Second Chance.* Boston: Little Brown, 1946.

Smith, R. Franklin. "The Nature and Development of Commentary." *Journal of Broadcasting* 6 (Winter 1961-1962): 11-22.

_____. "The Origins of Radio Network News Commentary." *Journal of Broadcasting* 9 *(Spring 1965):* 113-121.

_____. *Edward R. Murrow: The War Years.* Tallahassee, Fla.: New Issues Press, 1978.

Sperber, A. M. *Murrow: His Life and Times.* New York: Freundlich Books, 1986.

Stott, William. *Documentary Expression and Thirties America.* New York: Oxford University Press, 1973.

Summers, Harrison B., ed. *Radio Censorship.* New York: Wilson, 1939.

Swing, Raymond (Gram). *Good Evening! A Professional Memoir.* New York: Harcourt, Brace and World, 1964.

Taves, Isabella. "Edward R. Murrow." *McCall's* 81 (February and March 1954): 24-96, 53-105.

"This Is Murrow." *Time* 70 (September 30, 1957): 48-51.

Thomas, Bob. *Winchell.* Garden City, N.Y.: Doubleday, 1971.

Waller, Judith C. *Radio: The Fifth Estate.* Boston: Mifflin, 1946.

Wecter, Dixon. "Hearing Is Believing." Parts 1, 2, and, 3. *Atlantic Monthly* 175 (June 1945): 54-60; 176 (July and August 1945): 34-60, 58-63.

"What Newspaper Editors Say." 10 *Wireless Age* (July 1922): 46+.

White, Llewellyn. *The American Radio: A Report on the Broadcasting Industy in the United States from the Commission on the Freedom of the Press.* Chicago: University of Chicago Press, 1947.

White, Paul W. *News on the Air.* New York: Harcourt, 1947.

Wool, Michael. "A Computer-based Analysis of All-News Radio Listening from a Structuralist Point of View." Ph.D. diss., Pennsylvania State University, 1984.

Woolley, Thomas R. "A Rhetorical Study: The Radio Speaking of Edward R. Murrow." Ph.D. diss., Northwestern University, 1957.

Young, James C. "Is the Radio Newspaper Next?" *Radio Broadcast* 7 (September 1925): 28.

4   RADIO MUSIC

Whether radio music programming determines or is determined by American music preferences is a chicken-and-egg question. The development of radio music is so closely tied to the rise of popular, country, and classical music per se that the task of defining the literature on radio music as something distinguishable from the literature on modern American music is impossible. Put succinctly, the chicken is the egg.

Consequently, the material selected for discussion in this chapter includes not only works that deal primarily or exclusively with the subject of radio music (whose numbers are surprisingly small) but also works on music that incorporate radio into their discussions in a meaningful or significant fashion. It is in this latter group of works that some difficult judgment calls have been made since almost all works on contemporary music make some statement, at least implicitly, about the development of radio, even if the authors of these works are not always fully aware of that fact. Discussion of these works is limited to books and articles that yield substantial information about radio while making specific, direct reference to radio stations, programs, performers, audience taste, or legislation. Where exceptions appear in the discussion, they will be so noted. (For a full discussion of popular music, see Mark Booth's *Popular Music: A Reference Guide*.)

The categories of radio music to be discussed in this chapter are classical, country and western, jazz and pop, and rock. (Purists may object to having classical music introduced into a discussion that is oriented toward popular culture. However, the major rationale advanced for broadcasting classical music has been that networks, and occasionally sponsors, have tried to broaden the popular appeal of "serious" music. The financial return on such broadcasts has always been doubtful, although not always disappointing.)

GENERAL WORKS

Given that some two-thirds of all air time is devoted to music, it is astonishing that there have been only two major, full-length studies published on the broad subject of radio music as a whole. The more complete of these two fine works is Philip Eberly's *Music in the Air: America's Changing Tastes in Popular Music 1920-1980.* Eberly's book is an imaginative, intelligent exploration of American music tastes as a means of assessing popular tastes. He discusses most fully network broadcasting, FM radio, and Top 40. He provides as well an excellent discussion of black music and radio in the 1920s. The book also contains a superior discussion of the movement from live to "canned" music in the 1930s. There is an effective analysis of radio's role in the development of swing, showing the relationship of middle-class taste to the success of pop music. His discussion of classical music is also very good. Eberly's *Music in the Air* is simply the best book in the field.

Also quite good is Thomas DeLong's *The Mighty Music Box: The Golden Age of Musical Radio.* DeLong is stronger than Eberly in the area of classical music, devoting as he does a great deal of time to discussing early opera broadcasts in the context of record company efforts to keep singers off the air. (His chapter "Musical Thoroughbreds on the Air" is one of the few available discussions of the subject of broadcasting classical music.) Disappointing only in his less than thorough handling of jazz, DeLong provides a solid music-programming history of the major figures, decisions, promotions, and marketing efforts of radio music during the pre–rock and roll golden age.

Of limited value is Ernest La Prade's *Broadcasting Music,* which provides both a programmatic and technical history of broadcast music through the mid-1940s. La Prade provides more analysis of administrative structure than one might want from a discussion of such a programming-oriented subject as music, but given the paucity of information in the field, this book by NBC's director of music research in the 1940s is a good but not pivotal resource.

Substantial amounts of information on the general area of radio music are available in books on either radio as a whole or music as a whole. Some of the more significant of these include Erik Barnouw's three-volume *A History of Broadcasting in the United States,* although Barnouw is slightly stronger in the areas of news and variety than he is in the area of music. J. Fred MacDonald's discussion of the history of broadcasting in *Don't Touch That Dial! Radio Programming in American Life, 1920-1960* has some helpful information, but he, like Barnouw, is stronger and more thorough with the spoken word (radio news and radio drama) than he is with music. Francis Chase, Jr.'s *Sound and Fury: An Informal History of Broadcasting* contains a delightful history of bands in the 1920s and 1930s as well as an imaginative discussion of the role of the jukebox in the late 1930s as a phenomenon that came into being after the novelty of radio wore off. There is also a solid account of the American Society of Composers, Authors, and Publishers (ASCAP) radio war of 1941. Harrison B.

Summers's *A Thirty-Year History of Programs Carried on National Radio Networks in the United States, 1926-1956,* mentioned in the chapter on radio drama, is the standard publication of the network schedule for thirty years. Another valuable general study cited in the chapter on radio drama is John Dunning's *Tune In Yesterday: The Ultimate Encyclopedia of Old-Time Radio, 1925-1976,* which describes in short but exceptional essays the history of every regularly running radio show, including the music-oriented shows. Also of value is the chapter "Music out of Nowhere" in E. P. J. Shurick's well-respected book, *The First Quarter-Century of American Broadcasting.* Shurick provides a history of the first musical broadcast concerts (especially those conducted on KDKA), listing the music that was played and charting audience response. There is also a marvelously engaging discussion of how the earliest radio receivers responded best to high-pitched, sustained notes, thus leading the popularity of Hawaiian music and crooning. Although it contains less information on radio than one might expect, David Ewen's *History of Popular Music* provides a learned discussion of the legal disputes between recording companies and radio stations in the first twenty years of broadcasting. His chapter "Popular Music Becomes Big Business" reminds us that "Your Hit Parade" helped define the eventual role of radio in record and music promotion. Ewen also offers the inviting thesis that Muzak, started in 1931, helped saturate America with popular music and change its musical taste.

The single best source for radio music periodical literature is the *Music Index,* which has been accumulating annual periodical listings in music since 1949. Articles on various aspects of radio music appear under the headings "Radio Broadcasting," "Classical Music and Radio Broadcasting," "Country Music and Radio Broadcasting," "Popular Music and Radio Broadcasting," "Radio Orchestras," and "Radio Stations and Networks," among others. The radio music industry's key publications include *Billboard,* generally considered to be the bible of the music industry, as well as *Radio and Records* and the *Gavin Report.*

CLASSICAL MUSIC

During the 1920s, a decade that saw sales of millions of home radios, classical or serious music was perceived by many of its devotees as an art form for the educated elite—a stigma it still carries to a certain extent despite efforts on many fronts to broaden its appeal and alter its highbrow image. Although classical music was the first music that gained large-scale exposure on radio, most classical artists (until fairly recently) have attracted less press attention and even scholarly attention as broadcast personalities than have their counterparts in jazz, popular, country, and rock and roll. As a result, there is relatively little literature on classical music as radio programming, while there is an abundance of literature on classical music.

From the outset broadcasters saw the potential of spreading "good" music and elevating the taste of the American public. Charles Orchard, Jr.'s article "Is Radio Making America Musical?" which appeared in *Radio Broadcast Advertiser* in 1924, predicted that radio would elevate American taste to the level of that of Europe by filling the airwaves with symphony orchestra concerts, operas, and recitals. He also foresaw the educational value of such broadcasts. C. E. Massena's article "How Opera Is Broadcasted," appearing in *Radio Broadcast* in 1922, argues (probably correctly) that orchestras and artists are inspired by appearing on radio and thus perform better, adding to their popularity and ensuring their continued success. Other prophecies of how well radio could serve to spread good music appear sporadically in radio magazines throughout the twenties.

With the beginning of regular classical music broadcasts in 1926 came a selection of home study guides—musical appreciation courses built upon radio programming. Alice Keith's *Music for Radio* (1926), Hazel Gertrude Kinscella's *Music on the Air* (1934), Gilbert Chase's *Music in Radio Broadcasting* (1946), and Ben Jacobs's *Musica: The First Guide to Classical Music on American Radio Stations* (1976) are representative of the subindustry of "learn while you listen" publications that have followed classical music broadcasting throughout its history.

Of the few works that speak exclusively to radio and classical music as a whole, perhaps the most helpful is the most obscure. Robert Wilkins's "The Role of Serious Music in the Development of American Radio, 1920-1938" (Master's thesis, University of North Dakota, 1969) notes that the rise of radio music output is tied directly and predictably to the rise of networks. Wilkins states that before the network era radio music differed little from phonographs— short discrete selections or movements from larger works. But networks allowed broadcasting to graduate to full-length works. Early skepticism on the part of artists who feared that radio music would kill off their live careers evolved into a respect for the way the medium can enhance a career. Wilkins's dissertation is difficult to locate but worth the effort. In 1938 CBS published an in-house log entitled *Serious Music on the Columbia Broadcasting System: A Survey of Series, Soloists, and Special Performances.* This volume contains hard data: who performed, on what date, at what time, how many hours were devoted to serious music each year, how many programs, and so on. No interpretation is provided, but the data itself is comprehensive within its clearly stated parameters. Donald J. Bogue's frequently cited study *The Radio Audience for Classical Music: The Case of Station WEFM* is the best known of a small handful of individual station analyses that focus on some aspect of local classical music programs and audience response. Bogue takes as his mission to prove that there was in Chicago in the early 1970s enough evidence to argue against a proposed format change (away from classical) for WEFM. WEFM made the change anyway, but given Bogue's sense of urgency, his work reads more easily than do most audience survey studies.

Occasionally some historians of serious music give recognition to the role that radio has played in the development of their particular subject matter. Irving Sablosky's *American Music* does a very effective job of presenting radio's role in forming the transition between nineteenth-century and twentieth-century music. The discussion of radio is brief (confined largely to a chapter entitled "Bridge to the Present"), but it articulates clearly radio's role in the evolution of twentieth-century American taste in serious music. Christopher Pavlakis's *American Music Handbook, 1974* developed a wonderful idea. The book catalogs all the known stations and programs playing regularly scheduled classical music. This could have been a reliable research tool had the project been continued, but the idea was not pursued, and the dated information is not very useful except for those interested in information about 1974. Nicolas Slonimsky's *Music Since 1900* is a peculiar compendium and annotated diary of major events in the development of classical music. Many events relating to broadcast music are included but are neither presented with any organizing principle nor indexed in any manner that would make the information easily accessible or practical. Given the book's more than 1,500 pages, this is a sizable impediment to its usefulness.

Among the more helpful books focusing on narrower subject matter within the classical music field, John Briggs's *Requiem for a Yellow Brick Brewery: A History of the Metropolitan Opera* notes that the appearance of opera stars and concerts in the 1920s gave to radio programming an early respectability that it would not have received otherwise. In an entire chapter devoted to the Metropolitan Opera's broadcast history ("On the Air"), Briggs efficiently traces NBC's and CBS's early broadcast efforts with the company, including production and technical crises. This is a fine treatment of an often-overlooked dimension of classical music broadcasting. Howard Shanet's *Philharmonic: A History of New York's Orchestra* gives considerable attention to the foresight of Arthur Judson, the orchestra's chief administrator in the 1920s, who formed his own radio program corporation in anticipation of the orchestra's future in radio. (He later abandoned his corporation in order to tie himself to the fortunes of CBS and William Paley.) Judson developed "radio members," financial contributors to the orchestra recruited from the listening audience. Radio is not central to Shanet's book, but he does provide some useful information. Alan Levy's *The Bluebird of Happiness: The Memoirs of Jan Peerce* (which he coauthored with Peerce) offers a number of Peerce's recollections that are tied specifically to his work with "Radio City Music Hall on the Air" as well as Peerce's early, Jewish-oriented WVED program in New York. There are several career and personal anecdotes regarding Peerce's stint on "The A&P Gypsies" on NBC and "The Chevrolet Hour" on CBS. The information is good but not critical to the radio scholar.

Perhaps the place where classical music and radio broadcasting were most tightly linked was during the tumultuous years in which Arturo Toscanini led the NBC orchestra. This is a unique period in broadcast history because, rather than seeking to broadcast classical music that would have been performed live anyway, NBC chief David Sarnoff sought an impresario's hands-on role in the creation of a new musical force: an orchestra founded by the network specifically for broadcast purposes and led by the world's foremost conductor. Understandably, it is one of the most intriguing (and, thankfully, best-documented) episodes in the entire history of radio music.

In January 1937 Sarnoff sent Samuel Chotzinoff, a friend of Toscanini's and an employee of NBC, to Italy to entreat Toscanini, then in his seventies, to come out of retirement and lead the NBC orchestra—an orchestra created for him, composed of superior players from other orchestras. Sarnoff intended to make NBC and this orchestra the major force in elevating the musical taste of the American people by bringing to an American mass audience the work of that generation's—and arguably the century's—finest conductor. The relationship was a marvelous success, lasting as it did from 1937 to 1954, but not without difficulty every step of the way. That relationship and the difficulties it encountered make for some of the most intriguing reading in the entire field of radio music.

The best single piece of information on the birth and beginnings of this extraordinary experiment is a lengthy unattributed article in the January 1938 issue of *Fortune,* entitled simply "Toscanini on the Air." The article chronicles Sarnoff's early brainstorming sessions, the use of interloper Chotzinoff to sell the idea to Toscanini, the controversial raiding of other leading orchestras for top talent, and the technical preparations made by NBC to produce the weekly concerts. The article also contains a thumbnail history of the broadcasting of symphony concerts on the networks as well as some independently conducted audience research on the popularity of serious music broadcasts.

Later works fill out various aspects of the stormy but groundbreaking relationship between the almost laughably temperamental conductor and his very businesslike employers. Howard Taubman's *The Maestro: The Life of Arturo Toscanini* is the best-known biography of Toscanini that was written before the Maestro left NBC. Taubman devotes an entire chapter to the NBC years. Although Taubman is guilty of romanticizing his subject, he handles well the most complicated problem in that relationship—the reason why Toscanini left NBC and returned to Italy for the 1941-1942 season. (Speculations range from concern for the rise of fascism in his homeland to his fury at having to share his musicians with inferior guest conductors or his outrage at having to curtail the length of his rehearsals so that musicians in the NBC orchestra could meet other contractual commitments to the network. Apparently, the reason why the issue is so hard to sort out is that Toscanini exploded in anger on a regular basis and threatened to resign over one thing or another every year.) David Ewen's *The Story of Arturo Toscanini* contains an energetic retelling of the formation of the orchestra, but Ewen's compressed biography cannot compare with Taubman's full effort. Samuel Chotzinoff's often cloying and self-congratulatory *Toscanini: An Intimate Portrait* is still worthwhile since it is the first-person account of the man responsible for placing Sarnoff's dream into action. Much of the credit for the endurance of the seventeen-year relationship must go to Chotzinoff, who sees that it does. There are many anecdotes that fill in the details of the fiery artist's blood feuds with the broadcast bureaucrats, but the book disappoints in that for all the fly-on-the-wall recollections, it reveals precious little about the man himself. Chotzinoff's personal intrusions into his portrait of Toscanini infuriated B. H. Haggin, the "Music on the Radio" critic for the *Sunday Herald Tribune.* In his book *The Toscanini Musicians Knew,* which is primarily a collection of interviews with musicians who worked with Toscanini in the NBC orchestra and with the New York Philharmonic, Haggin denounces Chotzinoff's book as factually inaccurate (on some obscure and also some not-so-obscure points) and calls into question Chotzinoff's entire account of the NBC/Toscanini relationship. Of the two major recent biographies on Toscanini in English (we are leaving unexamined the generous amount of information available on Toscanini in Italian scholarship), George R. Marek's *Toscanini: A Biography* is far more thorough on the radio/broadcasting dimension of Toscanini's relationship with NBC than is Harvey Sachs's *Toscanini.* While Sachs views "the NBC" as just an orchestra that happened to be affiliated with a network, Marek provides some new details on the broadcast end of Toscanini's work, including letters between Sarnoff and Chotzinoff and publishing a copy of Toscanini's contract with NBC. The literature here reflects the grand success of broadcasting's most heroic and serious effort to fulfill the promise of its early prophets—to take classical music out of its drawing-room exclusivity and give it exposure to the entire nation. While the effort never did make of classical music a runaway best-selling product, it did make of Toscanini classical music's grandest radio star.

COUNTRY MUSIC

The chroniclers of the early history of country music have been very sensitive to the significant role that radio has played in the development of both the popularity and the content of country music. Running consistently throughout the major books on country and western, especially those dealing at least in part with the era before 1950, are discussions and acknowledgments of disc jockeys, stations, and programs that advanced the name and influence of key artists, records, or styles. Inasmuch as the country as a whole only "discovered" country music in a widely publicized "renaissance" of country music in the 1970s, major histories and studies of country music are likely to be produced in considerable numbers over the next few years. Among contemporary forms of radio music, country music has the best recent record for growth, change, and the discovery of new audiences.

The most satisfying history of country music, both for the student of radio music and the serious student of country music, is Nick Tosches's *Country: The Biggest Music in America.* Despite the lowbrow/high-hype title, this is a very serious study of country music, mercifully void of the sentimentality and uncritical cheerleading that marks so much current writing on country music. Tosches not only acknowledges the role of radio stations but shrewdly points out the influence of key disc jockeys at various stages of the discussion. The book is tough-minded (there is one chapter entitled "Cowboys and Niggers"), but it contains a collection of photographs strong enough to match the most commercially plotted, fan-oriented books. Bill C. Malone's *Country Music U.S.A.: A Fifty-Year History,* which is often heralded as the best of the recent studies in the country music field, is a solid comprehensive history of country music. Malone is careful to discuss the emergence of radio in the South (particularly as it served to combat the antirural bias in the music industry) as well as the history and influence of radio in the development of country and western music. Jack Hurst's *Nashville's Grand Ole Opry* is a coffee-table book that offers some very useful discussions of country music and radio, especially about the role that the "WSM Barndance" (the predecessor to the "Grand Ole Opry" radio show) and other small radio station barndances played in the development of the Opry. Although the book is about personalities rather than radio, it incorporates nicely the role of early southern radio exposure in the development of many stars' careers. Similarly, Irwin Stambler and Grelun Landon's *Golden Guitars: The Story of Country Music* interweaves radio exposure into the history of their subject matter. Since they devoted perhaps a disproportionate amount of their time and attention to radio station WSM in Nashville, the chapter on the "Grand Ole Opry" is more satisfying to the radio historian than are the other sections of the book. An especially strong book on the history of country music is Douglas B. Green's *Country Roots: The Origins of Country Music.* Incorporating key radio stations into every phase of the discussion (including small, obscure stations in addition to the landmark country music stations), Green clearly and thoroughly traces the contemporary styles of country music back through bluegrass, Cajun, gospel, and western swing. Most country music historians pay lip service to these roots, but few if any handle them as thoroughly as does Green. Green's is a vital although comparatively little known work. Other useful country and western histories include Colin Escott and Martin Hawkins' fascinating history of the most important record company in the development of both country music and white rock and roll, *Catalyst: The Sun Records Story.* Robert Shelton and Burt Goldblatt's *The Country Music Story,* Ken Griffis's *Hear My Song: The Story of the Celebrated Sons of the Pioneers,* Paul Hemphill's *The Nashville Sound,* and Charles Wolfe's *The Grand Ole Opry: The Early Years, 1925-35* are also very good histories of country music. A standard reference work in the field, Linnell Gentrey's *A History and Encyclopedia of Country, Western, and Gospel Music* pays close attention to radio's importance and influence throughout its text. In 1971 the Country Music Association began publishing *The Country Radio Station List,* which is an annual compilation of all-country or primarily country radio stations around the United States. Of course, celebrity biographies and autobiographies abound in the country music field just as they do in every other show business venue. For information on radio, few if any can match *Everybody's Grandpa—Fifty Years Behind the Mike* by Louis "Grandpa" Jones (with Charles Wolfe). Although nationally famous through his television work on "Hee Haw," the late comedian was a major country radio entertainer and "rube humorist" throughout the south in the 1940s and 1950s—well before the nation "discovered" country music and vaulted mainstays like Jones from novelty acts to major entertainer status. The book is generously illustrated with photographs from all phases of Jones' career.

In recent years journals and periodicals have begun to publish substantial offerings on the subject of country music and radio. Among the best of the easily accessible works is Richard P. Stockdell's "The Evolution of the Country Radio Format" (*Journal of Popular Culture,* Spring 1983). Stockdell's dense but brief history of country music's emergence on radio touches on virtually all of the landmark programs, defining four key stages: "The National Barndance," "The Grand Ole Opry," a growth phase (the 1930s and 1940s), and the all-country radio station. Although no part of the history is discussed in depth, Stockdell's interviews with key country radio people make the article quite valuable. Less personal in its approach is George O. Carney's comprehensive piece "Country Music and the Radio: An Historical Geographic Assessment" in the *Rocky Mountain Social Science Journal* (April 1974). Carney traces the radio broadcasting history and migratory patterns of country music styles (bluegrass, west coast sound, honky-tonk, and Texas swing) through the chronology of broadcast programming. Maps of the broadcast patterns discussed in the text are very useful: this is a skillful handling of a tricky body of information. A lovely piece on the early "WLS Barndance" is George Biggar's "The WLS National Barn Dance Story: The Early Years" in *John Edwards Memorial Foundation Quarterly* (1971). Also useful is D. K. Wilgus's "Current Hillbilly Recording: A Review Article" in the *Journal of American Folklore* (1957). Perhaps the best of the academic journals for country radio music is *Journal of Country Music,* which regularly publishes articles on country radio history, such as Timothy A. Patterson's "Hillbilly Music among the Flatlanders: Early Midwestern Radio Barndances" (Spring 1975), as well as excellent biographies of country musicians that incorporate radio fully into their texts, such as Bob Pinson's "Bob Wills and His Texas Playboys on Radio" (Winter 1974). Commercial periodical information on country music and country music radio can be found in *Music City News* and *Spotlight on Country.*

JAZZ AND POPULAR MUSIC

In contrast to the histories of country music, the histories of jazz music are surprisingly lacking in full, solid discussions of the role of radio broadcasting. Enormously sensitive to the role of records, jazz historians have all but ignored the role of radio in the major jazz histories. Astonishingly, there seems to be no full-length published study on jazz music and radio broadcasting in America. Jack Wheaton's unpublished dissertation, "The Technological and Sociological Influences on Jazz as an Art Form in America" (University of Northern Colorado, 1976), includes radio in its discussion of how jazz grew through the growth of technology in all phases of the music industry. Wheaton's discussion of how radio disseminated black music during the Swing Era is particularly good.

Among the general jazz histories that incorporate at least some discussion of radio into the history of jazz, Neil Leonard's *Jazz and the White Americans: The Acceptance of a New Art Form* is the best of a bad lot. His chapter on "The Impact of Mechanization" pays homage to the radio boom in the early twenties and notes in passing an impact on jazz, but his information is limited to the number of radios sold and hours programmed. There is no analysis to speak of. Barry Ulanov's *A History of Jazz in America* offers some sporadic integration of radio's role in jazz development, as does Frank Tirro's *Jazz: A History.* Brian Rust's *The Dance Bands* is filled with radio historical information in its compressed but solid survey of dance bands, but most of this information is directed at British radio since jazz music in Britain is Rust's focus here. Billy Taylor's imaginative *Jazz Piano: History and Development,* a history of piano styles, gives some notice of radio's contribution to their development. However, none of these books is nearly as thorough or effective as Eberly's *Music in the Air: America's Changing Tastes in Popular Music, 1920-1980* or DeLong's *The Mighty Music Box: The Golden Age of Musical Radio,* both discussed earlier in this chapter under "General Works."

Other books on jazz that contain valuable information for the radio music enthusiast include Sheldon Harris' *Blues Who's Who: A Biographical Dictionary of Blues Singers,* a tour de force with encyclopedic biographical entries of over 600 blues artists. A radio index cross-lists all performers with their known radio appearances. (Similar indexes appear for film, television, and records.) Gary Giddins, the erudite jazz critic for the *Village Voice,* writes perceptively and sensitively on Bing Crosby's radio work in "Bing for the Millions," a column anthologized in his book *Riding on a Blue Note: Jazz and American Pop.* Joel Vance's biography of Fats Waller, *Fats Waller, His Life and Times,* contains a marvelous discussion of Waller's radio career—a career that serves as a parable for the survival of radio in the 1930s at the expense of the recording industry and live big-band performances. Walter C. Allen's *Hendersonia: The Music of Fletcher Henderson and His Musicians,* apart from being an astounding compendium of the day-to-day events of Hendersons' career, contains within its massive contents the details of Hendersons' radio performances—times, stations, programs, and so on. Rudy Vallee's *Let the Chips Fall* is in many ways a typical (and thus regrettable) celebrity autobiography, but the chapter on his radio career ("Radio's Child") is highly anecdotal and amusing. It tells much about Vallee and radio but relatively little about radio itself. Thomas DeLong's *Pops: Paul Whiteman, King of Jazz* takes some pains to discuss Whiteman's radio career. Anita O'Day's autobiography *High Times, Hard Times* and Helen Foster's autobiography *I Had the Strangest Dream* both include, along with discographies, a log of live radio appearances. Jessica Dragonette's *Faith Is a Song: The Odyssey of an American Artist* is an occasionally mawkish but generally informative autobiography from the woman who was arguably NBC's first major musical star. Kate Smith's *Living in a Great Big Way* devotes no fewer than three chapters to radio, including one surprisingly good chapter on how a musical radio show is put together and some of the hazards and adjustments a stage singer must take into account when moving into the radio medium. Carroll Carroll's reminiscences, appearing under the almost funny title *None of Your Business; or, My Life with J. Walter Thompson (Confessions of a Renegade Radio Writer)* is a general radio memoir, but inasmuch as Carroll was pivotal in bringing "Kraft Music Hall" into being, his discussions of that program and his tenure with it are very useful to radio music enthusiasts.

Periodical writing on jazz and radio broadcasting is confined almost exclusively to short-term news and feature profiles on such subjects as stations, format changes, disc jockeys, and special broadcasts (for example, "Voice of America"'s overseas jazz broadcasts, which attracted much press attention in the 1950s). In the last thirty years this beat has been covered regularly by *Downbeat, Billboard, Billboard Music Week,* and even *Variety* on occasion. In the last ten to fifteen years these staples have been joined by some less well known publications, including *Radio Free Jazz, Jazz Echo,* the U.S.-based *Jazz Magazine* (there is a European-based magazine by the same title), and *Jazz Times.* Jazz and radio broadcasting stories are published less regularly in *Jazz Journal, Jazz and Pop,* and *Second Line.* Among the foreign jazz journals, *Melody Maker* (England) and *Coda* (Canada) include regular reporting on jazz radio. There are a few exceptional periodical articles that cover a broader scope of radio jazz. Frank Kahn's "Jazz Radio: Milestones and Millstones" in *Jazz and Pop* (August 1967) is a very good compressed history of jazz on radio, rivaling any other single source of information on the subject. Willis Conover's "Jazz in the Media: A Personal View" in *Jazzforschung—Jazz Research* (1980) is a rambling, minimally informative overview of jazz's uneasy relationship with mass media (radio, television, and film), but Conover deserves credit for trying, if with only partial success, to give his article some breadth.

ROCK AND ROLL

The one area in which radio music literature can be accused of reaching overkill and uncontrollable repetition is in the area of rock music and radio. The reasons for this abundance are varied, but probably the most important is the inescapable fact that radio has a relationship with rock music that is in its nature and scope unlike that which radio has ever had with any other form of music—or, for that matter, any other form of programming. Unlike classical, jazz, or country music, rock and roll had no clearly established audience before it became a radio staple. Although it has clear roots in black rhythm and blues and various country music styles—both of which had ethnic and regional audiences that knew the music outside of radio—rock and roll was born, nurtured, and discovered on the radio. Rock music also has a unique place in the advertising history of radio because it gave radio sponsors their first understanding of the emergence of postwar American teenagers as major consumers. Because rock and roll music was defining itself while it was a mainstay of radio programming, the rock and roll disc jockey took on an enormous amount of power and celebrity. That power and celebrity led to rock and roll's central place in the radio payola scandals in the late 1950s—a series of convulsive events from which neither the record business nor the radio business has fully recovered. Although at times it has appeared that radio and rock music have been bent on destroying one another, the fact is that each owes the other the lion's share of gratitude for its prosperity since World War II. This astonishing bond between radio and one dimension of its programming has not gone unnoticed by the chroniclers of popular music or the history of radio.

There are dozens of histories of rock and roll, and several of them include important historical information on both the music and its relationship to radio. One of the most highly regarded is Carl Belz's *The Story of Rock*. Belz observes astutely the central role of early radio in the success of rock singers who could not perform well live. Inevitably, all rock/radio histories cover the disc jockeys, and Belz's discussion of the disc jockey as folk artist constitutes an original and insightful handling of a well-worn topic. Equally learned and important is Charlie Gillett's *The Sound of the City: The Rise of Rock and Roll,* a sociocultural discussion that recounts deftly pioneer disc jockey Alan Freed's calculated attempt to bring black rhythm and blues into the white lower middle-class consciousness and marketplace. Gillett also handles nicely the historical wars between ASCAP (the song writers' performance rights protection organization) and rock radio stations. R. Serge Denisoff's sprawling *Solid Gold: The Popular Record Industry* depends heavily on up-to-the-minute anecdotes and often seems more dated than the earlier Gillett and Belz books. But Denisoff knows his stuff, and his chapter on disc jockeys ("The Gatekeepers of Radio") provides an excellent historical bridge between the emergence of the powerful rock disc jockey and his predecessors such as big-band jockeys and the omnipotent Arthur Godfrey. Much of this chapter is based on material that Denisoff researched in preparation for "The Evolution of Pop Music Broadcasting, 1920-1970" in *Popular Music and Society* (Spring 1973), an efficient historical compression of the disc jockey and the rise of the pop music program. Very impressive as well is Steve Chapple and Reebee Garofalo's *Rock 'n' Roll Is Here to Pay: The History and Politics of the Music Industry,* which not only discusses early rock and roll radio in some detail but also handles well rock radio's AM/FM schizophrenia. Clive Davis's best-seller *Clive: Inside the Record Business* devotes a great deal of time to the relationship between record companies (where Davis served considerable time as producer and executive) and rock radio stations.

Other worthwhile but not necessarily critical histories of rock music include Roger Karshner's *The Music Machine,* an energetic exploration of the music business that is less detailed but more easily skimmed than are the histories previously mentioned. C. A. Schicke's *Revolution in Sound: A Biography of the Recording Industry* is a stripped-down, lean but good analysis of the recording industry without any attempts to glamourize it. Radio is generally well integrated into the discussion. Ian Whitcomb's uneven but engaging *After the Ball: Pop Music from Rag to Rock* suffers under the weight of "new journalism" excess that was popular in the early 1970s, but there are some gems in it, including a terrific discussion of the development of the microphone and its influence on song style as well as a shrewd discussion of Rudy Vallee as the prototypical radio music personality. Tony Russell's *Blacks, Whites, and Blues* is a jewel of a book that traces the blues through folk, country, and other popular music idioms and sheds much light on radio's role in the development of blues music. Arnold Shaw's *The World of Soul: Black America's Contribution to the Pop Music Scene* has less information on radio than one would hope for, although discussions of Della Reese's unwillingness to "kiss up" to white disc jockeys (and the consequent impact upon her career) and the story of Motown's efforts to crack the WABC (New York) playlist before it had the Supremes offer unique and important insights into race and the radio business. (Some additional material on race and rock radio will be discussed later.)

A handful of book-length publications focus almost exclusively on the disc jockeys and program directors (the so-called gatekeepers to air access). Without question the best of these is Arnold Passman's *The Deejays,* a meticulous discussion of the job and men (mostly) who hold it. An allusion to the Greek hero Perseus as the first deejay belies Passman's merciful lack of hype. More importantly, he takes his time with the early subject matter: the early ASCAP/radio wars and pre-rock and roll disc jockeying. The fact that Passman is in no hurry to get to the more widely known rock and roll music makes this book invaluable. There is much information in this book that is not readily available elsewhere. By contrast, Larry Lujack's narcissistic *Superjock,* a scatological, off-the-cuff autobiography, often appears on music bibliographies even though it has no informational value to speak of.

Program direction and the decision-making process of playlisting have been the subject of two doctoral dissertations. Joseph Johnson's "Radio Music—The Gatekeepers" (Michigan State University, 1970) compares the program directors of music stations to news editors. He interviews several program directors and finds predictable results: they are guided by personal taste, record sales, and intuition about audience preferences. Similar conclusions are reached by David Bob Kelliher's "The Decision-Making Process of the Radio Music Gatekeeper: A Path Analytical Approach" (University of Oregon, 1981), which seeks to quantify factors in determining playlists drawn up by a number of program directors in three western states.

Owing to the importance of music formats in rock and contemporary music, a sub-bibliography on format-related literature has begun to spring up in the last several years. The most important work in this area is Edd Routt, James McGrath, and Fredric Weiss's *The Radio Format Conundrum.* The authors not only provide a solid, in-depth discussion of the history of format radio but also demonstrate brilliantly how the formatting issue is integrated into every phase of radio broadcasting: advertising, promotion, economics, technology, the writing of disc jockey copy, and so on. The book comes very close to making other materials on the subject obsolete. The most comprehensive study on the all-pervasive Top 40 format is David MacFarland's *The Development of the Top 40 Radio Format,* a dissertation published in the Arno Press series of communications dissertations. MacFarland's book is a massive narrative and compendium of the development of Todd Storz's concept and the complete history of the stations and broadcast groups that picked it up, complete with how each one introduced and marketed the format. Another book on radio formats with an emphasis on rock and roll music is Peter Fornatale and Joshua E. Mills's *Radio in the Television Age,* which offers a helpful primer on the range of music formats in contemporary radio. Several journal articles relating to formats and format changes are available. Bruce M. Owen's "Regulating Diversity: The Case of Radio Formats" in the *Journal of Broadcasting* (Spring 1977) is an economist's analysis of legal intervention into the issue of formats. Taking the courts to task for rulings that hold format diversity in a listening area to be in the public interest, Owen argues vigorously that there exists no relationship between format diversity and "consumer well-being."

Since rock radio has lived and died on record popularity charts, the basic charts have become fundamental resources in rock radio literature. The most important of these are the *Billboard* ratings that Joel Whitburn has been collecting for the last several years. His most recent edition is *The Billboard Book of Top 40 Hits, 1955 to Present.* This compilation and other similar Whitburn publications are authorized and published by *Billboard,* whose listings are now, as they have been for over thirty years, the definitive ratings listings for radio. Nevertheless, others have gotten into the act. Frank Hoffman collects *Cash Box Magazine's* listings in *The Cash Box Singles Charts, 1950-1981* and *The Cash Box Album Charts, 1975-1985* with George Albert. Charles Miron's *Rock Gold: All the Hit Charts from 1955-1976* aspires to a comprehensiveness that the others do not have, and Elston Brooks's *I've Heard Those Songs Before: The Weekly Top Ten Tunes for the Past Fifty Years* offers the earliest published listings that we know about. An eye-opening companion resource to the various listings is Peter Hesbacher's article "Sound Exposure in Radio: The Misleading Nature of the Station Playlist" in *Popular Music and Society* (1974). Hesbacher attacks the playlist formula as being subjective and self-fulfilling. He calls for a more objective way of gathering a playlist together. Another helpful companion to the playlists is Hesbacher, Robert Downing, and David Berger's two-part article "Sound Recording Popularity Charts, Parts I and II" in *Popular Music and Society* (1975) which discusses very clinically just how charts are put together.

It is impossible to chronicle the magazine articles that are written about rock and roll radio. Station news, programming trends, disc jockey professional activities, and promotional matters are all covered regularly by *Variety, Billboard, Cash Box,* and *Broadcasting,* to name the major vehicles. *Rolling Stone* frequently reports radio-related news and will, on occasion, assign its energetic and talented feature writers a long story on some aspect of rock radio, such as Ben Fong-Torres's "Radio: Ups, Downs in the FM Ozone" (July 6, 1972). *Rolling Stone* has some relatively insignificant competition in the form of "serious" rock magazines, but none has *Rolling Stone's* longevity or credibility.

PAYOLA

The payola scandal of the late 1950s is so central to the history of rock radio and the history of radio broadcasting as a whole that a separate treatment of payola literature is warranted. The radio industry is still not quite certain what to make of the payola scandals. Contemporary assessments treat the scandals as everything from a thorough and much-needed cleansing of a fraud-ridden industry to a circus of finger pointing and blame placing or an outrageously unfair regulation of the kind of normal lobbying and promotion practices that occur in most large businesses. With public attention turned to the broadcast medium through a famous television quiz show scandal (in which selected, telegenic contestants—including the son of an internationally known humanities scholar—won hundreds of thousands of dollars on shows where they had been given answers and questions in advance), Congress took up an investigation of various suspect radio practices. These investigations focused primarily but not exclusively on the issues of how radio station managers and disc jockeys decide which of the overabundance of records released each week will receive precious airplay. In 1959 Congressman Orrin Harris headed a committee that interrogated disc jockeys, radio executives, music publishers, and others on the two central issues of payola: pay for play (direct payment for airing a record and consultantship) and compensation to a disc jockey or radio station employee to take time to listen to a particular record. Often forgotten is that the Harris Committee, which was overwhelmed by the amount of work it had bitten off, also delved into other issues such as ASCAP and Broadcast Music Incorporated (BMI) control over broadcast music, copying of playlists between stations, the degree of public service that surrounded station public service activities, and forged playlists distributed by promotion people. The impact of the hearings has yet to be fully measured or comprehended.

All of the major rock and roll radio histories mentioned earlier contain sections on payola, but perhaps the best single discussion on the broad issue is Russell Sanjek's *From Print to Plastic: Publishing and Promoting America's Popular Music (1900-1980),* a two-part discussion that places the payola scandals in the context of the history of the ASCAP/BMI wars and the earliest conflicts between radio and the creators of live music and sheet music. Along the way, Sanjek notes historical parallels between music and book publishing, the roots of "pay for play" in vaudeville, and the rise of the music industry's formal hit-making machinery. Dick Clark's autobiography *Rock, Roll, and Remember* is significant because it contains Clark's public defense of his own behavior. Clark, who owned considerable interests in companies that published or produced the music he aired on his trend-setting television show "American Bandstand," was a central witness in the congressional hearings. Although he was not charged criminally, his career in the 1950s has become something of a case study of conflicting interests within the music business. The official record of the hearings of the congressional subcommittee is documented in *Responsibilities of Broadcasting Licensees and Station Personnel*, a two-part collection of testimony of the committee's witnesses. A committee staff report, *Song Plugging and the Airwaves: A Functional Outline of the Popular Music Business*, serves as a primer for the organization of both the music industry and the congressional investigation. The investigations were front-page news in and out of the broadcasting business and were covered in great detail throughout 1959 by *Variety, Billboard, Broadcasting,* and major periodicals such as the *New York Times, Look, Life, Time,* and others.

MISCELLANEOUS SUBJECTS

Some other useful sources in the area of radio music include Algin Braddy King's doctoral dissertation "The Marketing of Phonograph Records in the United States: An Industry Study" (Ohio State University, 1966), which looks at the relationship between radio and record companies from an economic point of view (rather than that of show business or popular culture) in the postpayola era. Another useful business-oriented publication is Peter Hesbacher, Robert Rosenow, Bruce Anderson, and David Berger's "Radio Programming: Relating Ratings to Revenues in Major Market" in *Popular Music and Society* (1975), which examines closely the relationship of ratings to station income in Philadelphia's radio stations. Two works that provide useful information on copyright matters are Sidney Shemel and M. William Krasilovsky's *This Business of Music*, a contemporary textbook on payola, copyright, legal issues, and other basic information for the musician, and Laurence Simpson's "The Copyright Situation As Affecting Radio Broadcasting," a brief, accessible updating of early copyright law through the 1920s that appeared in the *New York University Law Quarterly Review* in 1931. Simpson's article is valuable for its interpretation of the 1909 copyright law that gave broadcasting companies permission to play records through 1930.

In the last ten years research on ethnic programming, especially black radio stations (whether black owned or black oriented), has begun to gather and analyze specific information on an issue that has been at the center of rock radio from its inception—the interrelationship between black music, white music, black audiences, and white audiences. Among the more substantial studies in this area are Theodore Grame's book *Ethnic Broadcasting in the United States,* a comprehensive analysis of primarily regional as well as ethnic trends in radio and television broadcasting. Stuart Surlin's "Black-Oriented Radio Programming to a Perceived Audience" in *Journal of Broadcasting* (1982) examines the sometimes-imprecise practice of defining the tastes of black audiences. In his doctoral dissertation "A Comparative Analysis of the Programming Practices of Black-Owned, Black-Oriented Radio Stations and White-Owned, Black-Oriented Radio Stations" (University of Wisconsin, 1982), James Phillip Jeter discusses the differences that arise between white and black station owners when both try to program for black audiences. Norman Spaulding's dissertation "The History of Black Oriented Radio in Chicago, 1929-1963" (University of Illinois, 1981) is more than a local study, for Spaulding poses the thesis that black-oriented radio programming was the first black mass communications medium to transcend the boundaries of illiteracy and class within the black community and thus served as a unifying element in that community. Graham Vulliamy's "The White R&B Audience and The Music Industry 1952-1956," in *Popular Music and Society* (1975) offers a solid discussion of race attitudes in pop music, as does the profoundly unscholarly, occasionally pornographic *The Life and Times of Little Richard* by Charles White. White makes generous use of explicit interviews with the musically and sexually adventurous "Little Richard" Penniman, thus making this an oral biography in more ways than one.

Although the amount of literature available on radio music is plentiful, some areas require further study. The literature on radio music does not adequately recognize the role that all facets of radio—technological developments, programming history, advertising conflicts, audience response—play in the continuing development of musical taste. Certainly there are exceptions, such as the well-documented payola scandals and the evolution of contemporary radio formats. But such questions as the popularization of classical music, the spread of country music into urban markets, the tension between disco music and "straight rock" in the 1970s, and the rise of "funk" music in reaction to Motown's efforts to sell black acts to middle-class white audiences all lack comprehensive analyses from the perspective of radio broadcasting history.

BIBLIOGRAPHY FOR RADIO MUSIC

Allen, Walter C. *Hendersonia: The Music of Fletcher Henderson and His Musicians.* Jazz Monograph Series. Highland Park, N.J.: Walter C. Allen, 1973.

Attwood, W. "Age of Payola." *Look* (March 29, 1960): 34-36ff.

Barnouw, Erik. *The Golden Web: 1933 to 1953.* Vol. 2 of *A History of Broadcasting in the United States.* New York: Oxford University Press, 1968.

_____. *The Image Empire: From 1953.* Vol. 3 of *A History of Broadcasting in the United States.* New York: Oxford University Press, 1970.

Belz, Carl. *The Story of Rock.* New York: Oxford University Press, 1969.

Biggar, George. "The WLS National Barn Dance Story: The Early Years." *John Edwards Memorial Foundation Quarterly* (1971): 105-12.

Bogue, Donald J. *The Radio Audience for Classical Music: The Case of Station WEFM.* Chicago: Community and Family Study Center of the University of Chicago, 1973.

Booth, Mark W. *American Popular Music: A Reference Guide.* Westport, Conn.: Greenwood Press, 1983.

Briggs, John. *Requiem for a Yellow Brick Brewery: A History of the Metropolitan Opera.* Boston: Little, Brown, 1969.

Brooks, Elston. *I've Heard Those Songs Before: The Weekly Top Ten Tunes for the Past Fifty Years.* New York: Morrow, 1978.

Carney, George O. "Country Music and the Radio: A Historical Geographic Assessment." *Rocky Mountain Social Science Journal* 2, no. 2 (April 1974): 19-32.

Carroll, Carroll. *None of Your Business; or, My Life with J. Walter Thompson (Confessions of a Renegade Radio Writer).* New York: Cowles, 1970.

Chapple, Steve, and Reebee Garofalo. *Rock 'n' Roll is Here to Pay: The History and Politics of the Music Industry.* Chicago: Nelson-Hall, 1977.

Chase, Francis, Jr. *Sound and Fury: An Informal History of Broadcasting.* New York: Harper and Bros., 1942.

Chase, Gilbert. *Music in Radio Broadcasting.* New York: McGraw-Hill, 1946.

Chotzinoff, Samuel. *Toscanini: An Intimate Portrait.* New York: Knopf, 1956.

Clark, Dick. *Rock, Roll, and Remember.* New York: Crowell, 1976.

Conover, Willis. "Jazz in the Media: A Personal View." *Jazzforschung—Jazz Research* 12 (1980): 35-40.

The Country Music Association Radio Station Survey. Nashville: Country Music Association, annual publication.

Davis, Clive. *Clive: Inside the Record Business.* New York: Morrow, 1975.

DeLong, Thomas. *The Mighty Music Box: The Golden Age of Musical Radio.* Los Angeles: Amber Crest Books, 1980.

_____. *Pops: Paul Whiteman, King of Jazz.* Piscataway, N.J.: New Century Publishers, 1983.

Denisoff, R. Serge. "The Evolution of Pop Music Broadcasting 1920-1970." *Popular Music and Society* 2, no. 3 (Spring 1973): 202-26.

_____. *Solid Gold: The Popular Record Industry.* New Brunswick, N.J.: Transaction Books, 1975.

Dragonette, Jessica. *Faith Is a Song: The Odyssey of an American Artist.* New York: McKay, 1951.

Dunning, John. *Tune In Yesterday: The Ultimate Encyclopedia of Old-Time Radio, 1925-1976.* Englewood Cliffs, N.J.: Prentice-Hall, 1976.

Eberly, Philip. *Music in the Air: America's Changing Tastes in Popular Music, 1920-1980.* New York: Hastings, 1982.

Escott, Colin, and Martin Hawkins. *Catalyst: The Sun Records Story.* London: Aquarius, 1975.

Ewen, David. *The Story of Arturo Toscanini.* New York: Holt, 1951.

_____. *History of Popular Music.* New York: Barnes and Noble, 1961.

Fong-Torres, Ben. "Radio: Ups and Downs in the F. M. Ozone." *Rolling Stone* (July 6, 1972): 22+.

Fornatale, Peter, and Joshua E. Mills. *Radio in the Television Age.* Woodstock, N.Y.: Overlook Press, 1980.

Foster, Helen. *I Had the Strangest Dream.* New York: Coward, McCann, and Geohagen, 1981.

Gentry, Linnell, ed. *A History and Encyclopedia of Country, Western, and Gospel Music.* 2nd ed. Nashville: McQuiddy Press, 1969.

Giddins, Gary. *Riding on a Blue Note: Jazz and American Pop.* New York: Oxford University Press, 1981.

Gillett, Charlie. *The Sound of the City: The Rise of Rock and Roll.* New York: Outerbridge and Dienstfrey, 1970.

"Gimme, Gimme, Gimme on the Old Payola." *Life* 47 (November 23, 1959): 45-48.

Grame, Theodore. *Ethnic Broadcasting in the United States.* Washington, D.C.: American Folklife Center, Library of Congress, 1980.

Green, Douglas B. *Country Roots: The Origins of Country Music.* New York: Hawthorn, 1976.

Griffis, Ken. *Hear My Song: The Story of the Celebrated Sons of the Pioneers.* Los Angeles: John Edwards Memorial Foundation, 1974.

Haggin, B. H. *The Toscanini Musicians Knew.* New York: Horizon, 1967.

Harris, Sheldon. *Blues Who's Who: A Biographical Dictionary of Blues Singers.* New Rochelle, N.Y.: Arlington House, 1979.

Hemphill, Paul. *The Nashville Sound.* New York: Simon and Schuster, 1970.

Hesbacher, Peter. "Sound Exposure in Radio: The Misleading Nature of the Station Playlist." *Popular Music and Society* 3, no. 3 (1974): 189-202.

Hesbacher, Peter, Robert Downing, and David Berger. "Sound Recording Popularity Charts." Parts 1 and 2. *Popular Music and Society* 4, no. 1 (1975): 3-18; 4, no. 2 (1975): 86-99.

Hesbacher, Peter, Robert Rosenow, Bruce Anderson, and David Berger. "Radio Programming: Relating Ratings to Revenues in a Major Market." *Popular Music and Society* 4 (1975): 208-24.

Hoffman, Frank. *The Cash Box Singles Charts, 1950-1981.* Metuchen, N.J.: Scarecrow Press, 1983.

Hoffman, Frank, and George Albert. *The Cash Box Album Charts, 1975-1985.* Metuchen, N.J.: Scarecrow Press, 1987.

Hurst, Jack. *Nashville's Grand Ole Opry.* New York: H. N. Abrams, 1975.

Jacobs, Ben. *Musica: The First Guide to Classical Music on American Radio Stations.* Edison, N.J.: Musica Publishing Co., 1976.

Jeter, James Phillip. "A Comparative Analysis of the Programming Practices of Black-Owned Black-Oriented Radio Stations and White-Owned Black-Oriented Radio Stations." Ph.D. diss., University of Wisconsin, 1982.

Johnson, Joseph. "Radio Music—The Gatekeepers." Ph.D. diss., Michigan State University, 1970.

Jones, Louis. "Grandpa" with Charles Wolfe. *Everybody's Grandpa—Fifty Years behind the Mike.* Knoxville: University of Tennessee Press, 1984.

Kahn, Frank. "Jazz Radio: Milestones and Millstones." *Jazz and Pop* 6 (August 1967): 12-16.

Karshner, Roger. *The Music Machine.* Los Angeles: Nash Publishing, 1971.

Keith, Alice. *Music for Radio.* Boston: Brichard, 1926.

Kelliher, David Bob. "The Decision-Making Process of the Radio Music Gatekeeper: A Path Analytical Approach." Ph.D. diss., University of Oregon, 1981.

King, Algin Braddy. "The Marketing of Phonograph Records in the United States: An Industry Study." Ph.D. diss., Ohio State University School of Business, 1966.

Kinscella, Hazel Gertrude. *Music on the Air*. New York: Viking, 1934.

La Prade, Ernest. *Broadcasting Music*. New York: Rinehart, 1947.

Leonard, Neil. *Jazz and the White Americans: The Acceptance of a New Art Form*. 1962. Reprint. Chicago: University of Chicago Press, 1988.

Levy, Alan, and Jan Peerce. *The Bluebird of Happiness: The Memoirs of Jan Peerce*. New York: Harper and Row, 1976.

Lujack, Larry. *Superjock*. Chicago: Henry Regnery, 1975.

MacDonald, J. Fred. *Don't Touch That Dial! Radio Programming in American Life, 1920-1960*. Chicago: Nelson Hall, 1979.

MacFarland, David. *The Development of the Top 40 Radio Format*. New York: Arno Press, 1979.

Malone, Bill C. *Country Music U.S.A.: A Fifty-Year History*. Austin: University of Texas Press, 1968.

Marek, George R. *Toscanini: A Biography*. London: Vision, 1976.

Massena, C. E. "How Opera Is Broadcasted." *Radio Broadcast* (August 1922): 285-93. Abridgement reprinted in *American Broadcasting: A Source Book on the History of Radio and Television*, edited by Lawrence W. Lichty and Malachi C. Topping. New York: Hastings House, 1976.

Miron, Charles. *Rock Gold: All the Hit Charts from 1955 to 1976*. New York: Drake, 1977.

The Music Index. Detroit, Mich.: Information Coordinators, 1949-.

O'Day, Anita. *High Times, Hard Times*. New York: Putnam, 1981.

Orchard, Charles, Jr. "Is Radio Making America Musical?" *Radio Broadcast Advertiser* 5, no. 6 (October 1924): 454-55.

Owen, Bruce M. "Regulating Diversity: The Case of Radio Formats." *Journal of Broadcasting* 21 (Summer 1977): 305-19.

Passman, Arnold. *The Deejays*. New York: Macmillan, 1971.

Patterson, Timothy A. "Hillbilly Music among the Flatlanders: Early Midwestern Radio Barndances." *Journal of Country Music* 6, no. 1 (Spring 1975): 12-18.

Pavlakis, Christopher. *The American Music Handbook, 1974*. New York: Free Press, 1974.

Pinson, Bob. "Bob Wills and His Texas Playboys on Radio." *Journal of Country Music* 5, no. 5 (Winter 1974): 134-93.

Routt, Edd, James McGrath, and Fredric Weiss. *The Radio Format Conundrum*. New York: Hastings House, 1978.

Russell, Tony. *Blacks, Whites, and Blues*. New York: Stein and Day, 1970.

Rust, Brian. *The Dance Bands*. London: Ian Allen, 1972.

Sablosky, Irving. *American Music*. Chicago: University of Chicago Press, 1969.

Sachs, Harvey. *Toscanini*. London: Weidenfeld and Nicolson, 1978.

Sanjek, Russell. *From Print to Plastic: Publishing and Promoting America's Popular Music (1900-1980)*. Brooklyn, N.Y.: Institute for Studies in American Music, 1983.

Schicke, C. A. *Revolution in Sound: A Biography of the Recording Industry*. Boston: Little, Brown, 1974.

Serious Music on the Columbia Broadcasting System: A Survey of Series, Soloists, and Special Performances, 1927-1938. New York: CBS, 1938.

Shanet, Howard. *Philharmonic: A History of New York's Orchestra.* Garden City, N.Y.: Doubleday, 1975.

Shaw, Arnold. *The World of Soul: Black America's Contribution to the Pop Music Scene.* New York: Cowles, 1970.

Shelton, Robert, and Burt Goldblatt. *The Country Music Story.* Indianapolis: Bobbs-Merrill, 1966.

Shemel, Sidney, and M. William Krasilovsky. *This Business of Music.* 4th ed. New York: Billboard Publications, 1979.

Shurick, E. P. J. *The First Quarter-Century of American Broadcasting.* Kansas City, Mo: Midland Publishing Co., 1946.

Simpson, Laurence. "The Copyright Situation As Affecting Radio Broadcasting." *New York University Law Quarterly Review* 9, no. 2 (December 1931): 181-97.

Slonimsky, Nicolas. *Music since 1900.* 4th ed. New York: Scribners, 1971.

Smith, Kate. *Living in a Great Big Way.* New York: Blue Ribbon Books, 1938.

Spaulding, Norman. "The History of Black Oriented Radio in Chicago, 1929-1963." Ph.D. diss., University of Illinois, 1981.

Stambler, Irwin, and Grelun Landon. *Golden Guitars: The Story of Country Music.* New York: St. Martin's, 1972.

Stockdell, Richard P. "The Evolution of the Country Radio Format." *Journal of Popular Culture* 16, no. 4 (Spring 1983): 144-51.

Summers, Harrison B. *A Thirty-Year History of Programs Carried on National Radio Networks in the United States, 1926-1956.* 1958. Reprint. New York: Arno Press, 1971.

Surlin, Stuart. "Black-Oriented Radio: Programming to a Perceived Audience." *Journal of Broadcasting* 16 (Summer 1972):289-98.

Taubman, Howard. *The Maestro: The Life of Arturo Toscanini.* New York: Simon and Schuster, 1951.

Taylor, Billy. *Jazz Piano: History and Development.* Dubuque, Iowa: Wm. C. Brown, 1982.

Tirro, Frank. *Jazz: A History.* New York: Norton, 1977.

"Toscanini on the Air." *Fortune* 17 (January 1938): 62-66ff.

Tosches, Nick. *Country: The Biggest Music in America,* Briarcliff Manor, N.Y.: Stein and Day, 1977.

Ulanov, Barry. *A History of Jazz in America.* New York: Viking, 1952.

U.S. Congress, House Committee on Interstate and Foreign Commerce. *Responsibilities of Broadcast Licensees and Station Personnel.* 2 vols. Washington, D.C.: Government Printing Office, 1960.

_____. *Song Plugging and the Airwaves; A Functional Outline of the Popular Music Business.* Washington, D.C.: Government Printing Office, 1960.

Vallee, Rudy. *Let the Chips Fall.* Harrisburg, Pa.: Stackpole Books, 1975.

Vance, Joel. *Fats Waller, His Life and Times.* Berkeley, Calif.: Berkeley Publishing Company, 1979.

Vulliamy, Graham. "The White R&B Audience and the Music Industry, 1952-1956." *Popular Music and Society* 4, no. 3 (1975): 70-85.

Wheaton, Jack. "The Technological and Sociological Influences on Jazz as an Art Form in America.'' Ph.D. diss., University of Northern Colorado, 1976.

Whitburn, Joel. *The Billboard Book of Top 40 Hits, 1955 to Present.* New York: Billboard Publications, 1983.

Whitcomb, Ian. *After the Ball: Pop Music from Rag to Rock.* New York: Simon and Schuster, 1972.

White, Charles. *The Life and Times of Little Richard.* New York: Harmony Books, 1984.

Wilgus, D. K. ''Current Hillbilly Recording: A Review Article.'' *Journal of American Folklore* 78 (1965): 267-286.

Wilkins, Robert. ''The Role of Serious Music in the Development of American Radio, 1920-1938.'' Master's thesis, University of North Dakota, 1969.

Wolfe, Charles. *The Grand Ole Opry: The Early Years, 1925-35.* London: Old Time Music, 1975.

5   RADIO COMEDY AND VARIETY

More than any other form of programming, it was the comedy/variety show that created radio stars: celebrities whose fame and influence sprang directly from the medium. In contrast to soap operas, news, mysteries, and even scripted comedies (such as "The Rise of the Goldbergs" and "Amos 'n' Andy"), whose popularity among audiences relied at least as much on format or specific content as on star appeal, the variety show rose or fell with the fortunes of the star whose name often formed the title of the program. Thus in reputation and in character Fred Allen, Jack Benny, Groucho Marx, Henry Morgan, Bob Hope, and others became inseparable from their radio shows and their radio show personas.

Not surprisingly, then, the bibliographical material on the comedy/variety show is housed principally in autobiographies, biographies, and magazine profiles. Recognizing clearly that the variety show was a showcase for a personality, the chroniclers of this form of programming carved away at all manner of biography, short and long; fan magazines, commercial publications, and scholarly works; profiles of stars and profiles of obscure part players. Perhaps more than any other form of programming, the radio variety show (and most certainly the written record of the radio variety show) is the sum of its various personality parts.

Nonetheless, some important general works are worth noting. Erik Barnouw's first two volumes of *A History of Broadcasting in the United States* (*A Tower in Babel* and *The Golden Web*), which covers the comings and goings of major radio personalities at networks as part of its overall history, are very helpful for keeping chronologies in order and keeping the growth of variety programming in perspective with key elements in the rise of radio. Gilbert Seldes's *The Great Audience*, a standard theoretical work in popular culture, also incorporates some discussion of entertainment personalities in a broad context.

There are three major reference works with important material on variety radio programming. John Dunning's *Tune In Yesterday: The Ultimate Encyclopedia of Old-Time Radio, 1925-1976* offers a one-page outline of every program during the golden age with details of cast and opening and closing dates; each entry contains an anecdotal and/or critical history. Harrison B. Summers's *A Thirty-Year History of Programs Carried on National Radio Networks in the United States, 1926-1956* lists the major network schedules for those years and is indispensable to any study of variety programming. Frank Buxton and Bill Owen's *The Big Broadcast, 1920-1950* is more valuable for its stature than its wealth of information, but with its generous photography and informal sketches of major golden age programming, it is an irrepressible if not indispensable resource for variety program information.

There are two major and several minor book-length studies that address the broad subject of comedy and/or variety programming. Arthur Frank Wertheim's *Radio Comedy* is the best single volume on the subject. Wertheim makes no distinction between scripted comedy and stand-up comedy. There is a superior chapter on early "song and patter" shows, which served as precursors to the variety show format. A moving chapter on Ed Wynn as the focal point of the natural transition from vaudeville to radio and a superb discussion on Jack Benny's humor as a guide to the maturation of radio humor beyond vaudeville are among the more deft features of this excellent volume. Although some of Wertheim's classifications are strained ("The Zanies," "The Scatterbrains"), the discussion is comprehensive, well written, and extremely insightful.

Jim Harmon's *The Great Radio Comedians* is a distant second behind Wertheim's book. Harmon shows the scholar's ability to dig but discards the historian's pose because it spoils the fun (and, one suspects, because he is both unfamiliar and uncomfortable with scholarly methodology). Specifically, the fault here is that no sources are cited, and one is forced to take his word for everything. There is a weak attempt to identify a type of comedy style that is indigenous to radio and to which Stan Freberg, Bob Newhart, and Bill Cosby are the modern heirs. The point is probably valid, but no solid case is made. The chapter on Bob Hope is too casual. Harmon delivers a lovely section on the largely ignored subject of W. C. Fields's radio career and a strong chapter on ethnic groups. There are so few book-length studies in the field that any such study is important, and thus Harmon's book is a fundamental if flawed resource.

There are several other general works, both books and magazine articles, that provide background to the more specific biographies. The best of these is Steve Allen's *The Funny Men,* which begins with two intriguing essays on the transition from radio comedy to television comedy. Allen discusses with considerable authority the reluctance of many of the most successful radio comedians to make the jump to television. He also points out that in the late 1940s, at the birth of the television age, radio comedy was losing its punch and popularity. As a result, both the performers and the networks were inhibited by the prospect of bringing established radio comedians to the new medium of television. Instead, the first comedy slots on television went to unknowns and far less popular comedians (Sid Caesar, Dave Garroway, Robert Q. Lewis, Sam Levenson, and Wally Cox). Allen's individual profiles of the major radio comics are interesting but are of relatively little value as broadcasting history. A notable exception is his discussion of Fred Allen's failure to make the transition to television while others—Jack Benny, George Burns and Gracie Allen, Groucho Marx—fared very well. Steve Allen's frankness reveals as much about Fred Allen as it does about the revolutionary success-oriented star-making process in early variety television programming.

Also very helpful is Jack Gaver and Dave Stanley's *There's Laughter in the Air! Radio's Top Comedians and Their Best Shows,* arguably the first book ever published on the subject. Written in 1945, it has a fine introduction, which gives a compressed history of radio comedy up to that time. The authors assert that (Billy) Jones and (Ernie) Hare are the first successful radio comedy team, playing out of WEAF (New York). (It has been observed elsewhere in this reference book that claims for firsts in early radio are as frequent as they are unreliable. However, such claims do serve the purpose of providing a format, if not an excuse, for putting little-known early pioneers in radio history before the public.) The remainder of the book contains brief chapters on various comedy stars, which provide alternately useful and worthless information (the Edgar Bergen chapter delves into Charlie McCarthy's fictitious "will" and thus is guilty of advancing Bergen's performance rather than discussing it). Perhaps the strongest dimension of the profiles, which include Fred Allen, Ed Wynn, Bob Hope, and Jack Benny, is that Gaver and Stanley make a creditable attempt to contrast the styles of the various comics, and as a result, the sample scripts from each comic's programs make very good reading.

Some general background works that cover areas related to variety and comedy in radio include several books on vaudeville. The best of these is Douglas Gilbert's *American Vaudeville: Its Life and Times,* which is a well-established work in the field of American theater history. By tracing vaudeville comedy acts and formats, Gilbert brings a sound historical context to the emergence of radio comic formats. Three chapters are particularly informative: "Great Comics of the 1900's," which features profiles on Ed Wynn and Fred Allen, among others; "The Comic Character Artists: Tramp, Blackface, Negro, and Jew," which shows the roots of some staple radio comedy and dramatic characters; and "The Single, Two, and Four Acts," which discusses comedy routine formats, many of which became staples of radio. Also very important is John E. DiMeglio's article "Radio's Debt to Vaudeville" in the fall 1978 issue of *Journal of Popular Culture.* DiMeglio offers a historical overview of career paths of vaudevillians who crossed over from vaudeville to radio. He makes very good use of fan-magazine material (especially *Radio Guide*) to show how these entertainers had come to be recognized as radio rather than vaudeville personalities by the early 1930s. Although he denies that vaudeville was essential to the rise of radio comedy, he concedes that it was a strong influence.

He enlists Eddie Cantor's autobiography in his defense of letting studio audiences into comedy/variety shows—a major contribution to radio from the vaudevillians, who grew up on live stages and who associated comedy performances with live audiences. In sum, DiMeglio delineates the legacy vaudeville left to live radio: a wealth of stage-trained comedic talent.

Also helpful, but decidedly less valuable than the works just cited, is Abel Green and Joe Laurie, Jr.'s *Show Biz: from Vaude to Video,* a pastiche of alternately intriguing and boring show-business history. Treading the line between abject trivia and rare information, the book's radio section tells us, among other things, that the first technical enhancement of dance steps occurred when a WOR (New York) sound effects man put marble slabs under the feet of in-studio dancers. More significantly, we learn that in the 1930s radio amateur nights with cash prizes broke out all at once throughout the country, a result of low production costs and talent scarcity. This phenomenon seems to have whetted the American audience's appetite for that particular genre of broadcast entertainment, which is still a staple of television ("Star Search," "You Can Be A Star," and so on). Also helpful in documenting the rise of radio talent from the ranks of vaudevillian performers is Bill Smith's *The Vaudevillians.* The most scholarly book-length treatment of vaudeville is Albert F. McLean's *American Vaudeville as Ritual,* which is more valuable as theater history than as background to variety programming in radio.

A few other general materials in the area of radio comedy and variety programming are worthy of mention but are not indispensable. Two books by Larry Wilde, *The Great Comedians Talk about Comedy* and *How the Great Comedy Writers Create Laughter,* include interviews with major figures, including Ed Wynn, Jack Benny, and George Burns. The books attempt to serve the same function as Steve Allen's *The Funny Men*, but Wilde does not have Allen's knowledge of the field or sensitivity to the complexity of the comics he analyzes.

Although significant general and background sources are usually confined to books or book-length materials, an exception can be made for Jack Gould's wonderful *New York Times Magazine* article "How Comic is Radio Comedy?" (November 21, 1948). Gould, the radio and television editor of the *Times*, cites format changes in some of the leading radio comedy programs of the late 1940s as a sign that the technical and artistic difficulties inherent in performing radio comedy eventually forced the most talented and successful radio comics to realize how difficult it is for them to combat staleness in their own programs. Gould analyzes the theoretical problems inherent in radio comedy and thus offers something very closely akin to a theoretical background for programming changes.

Comedy and variety programs in the network era and the golden age (the 1920s through the 1950s) were very much the way their most sentimental and nostalgic fans remember them—the projection of the stage personalities of a handful of star entertainers, some of whom were possessed of extraordinary gifts. Their influence upon our national consciousness and the nature and content of our television and stage entertainment is unmistakable. Moreover, as the first of the great media stars, they (and the fan magazines that deified them) can be said to have contributed almost as much to the current interest in celebrities as did the much-vaunted studio systems in Hollywood. Thus the substantial bibliographical history of comedy and variety programming can be said to be the sum of its parts. Information is most readily available about the most popular and thus the most influential of the stars. Prominent among these are Jack Benny, Fred Allen (whose enigmatic appeal to historicans and biographers is probably greater than that of Jack Benny, although Benny was a far more powerful star), Bob Hope, and George Burns and Gracie Allen, among others.

A caveat on the biographical and profile material on these stars is worth offering. Scholars desiring to separate fan material or promotional puff pieces from hard historical biographical scholarship are going to be disappointed. Although the language and sophistication differ between fan profiles and serious histories, the fact of the matter is that virtually all of these stars were revered by their serious biographers. Moreover, if there are skeletons in the closets of the likes of George Burns or Jack Benny, they have attracted neither the interest nor the scrutiny of those who have chronicled their careers for the sake of history. Whether these people were in a medium whose informality neutralized the impact of their private lives upon their audience or whether their lives were relatively free of the celebrity excesses to which show business history seems otherwise addicted is not clear. But the information that comprises the biographical literature, whether found in best-selling biographies or in check-out-counter tabloids, is almost ceaselessly admiring.

By and large the amount of copy generated about radio stars did not equal the amount of copy generated about movie stars (even when the former ventured successfully into television), but if any radio personality came close to achieving "Hollywood" copy, it was Jack Benny. He was a fan-magazine favorite in the radio era when his was the most highly rated of the comedy variety shows. His astonishing financial success and the loyalty of his cast and crew brought extra attention (virtually all of it laudatory in the extreme) from the serious news reporters as well as the fan-magazine writers. His enormous success in television started the cycle all over again (although the aging Benny was not a big television fanzine item, generating as he did relatively little of the indispensable sex appeal that sold these publications). Finally, upon his retirement the authors found him—and he found himself among them.

There is indeed excess in the annals of Benny literature, but not too much of it is wretched. Benny had enough going for him as a talent, a businessman, a husband, and a human being to generate some worthwhile copy. For information on his radio career, the best book is Milt Josefsberg's *The Jack Benny Show*. This loving and clearly subjective remembrance by one of Benny's writers is priceless because it concentrates on everything about Benny—from his work to his personal life—from the perspective of the weekly show. The recollections of

Benny's generous behavior to his staff (in marked contrast to many other radio personalities) is rendered here less to puff the late comedian's legend than to indicate how Benny used his considerable humility and interpersonal skills to keep his staff happy and stable in the often-unhappy and unstable world of radio comedy. Josefsberg writes convincingly of the influence that Benny's behind-the-scenes kindness had on the success of the program. The backstage insights regarding how comedy bits and sketches were worked out, tested, and evaluated reveal an enormous amount about the nature of radio comedy and bring out effectively the paradoxical process of thinking out humor to be delivered in Benny's offhanded manner. Many examples of individual bits are discussed: how they were worked and reworked and, eventually, how they succeeded or failed. Benny's legendary imbalance of gifts (he was alleged to be a poor writer and ad-libber but a great editor and deliverer) are fleshed out convincingly here, removing from Benny the idiot savant image that sometimes attends even the praise of his admirers. Most importantly, the relatively little time devoted to Benny's personal life is refreshing. Two other books are worthwhile, although not quite as good as Josefsberg's work as far as radio history is concerned: Irving Fein's *Jack Benny: An Intimate Biography* and, of course, Mary Livingstone Benny's (Mrs. Jack Benny) memoir *Jack Benny*. Both are valuable and document more information about Benny than one can ever possibly remember.

Outside of these books, some of the more intriguing information on Benny can be found in magazine profiles. Admittedly, most of the profiles on Benny are forgettable "back stage with the big star" pieces. But more than a few magazine writers were able to find some strong angles, especially where Benny's groundbreaking business sense and success were concerned. The first serious piece on Benny as businessman and power broker was in Hubbell Robinson and Ted Patrick's "Jack Benny" profile in the March 1938 issue of *Scribner's Magazine*. Their thesis, that Benny's mere popularity is insufficient to explain his financial success and power, proceeds to make of Benny a shrewd financial mastermind behind the facade of affability. His uniqueness among vaudevillians (ear gags rather than eye gags) is seen as a distinguishing virtue. His on-stage persona becomes for Robinson and Patrick a self-creation designed to "widen the lead" between himself and rival performers. Benny is portrayed as an innovator of situational comedy while rivals languish in question-answer routines and other tired formats. By the end of the piece Benny is both the Picasso and the D. H. Lawrence of his field—the consummate master. What Robinson and Hubbell offer is a bit much in the way of veneration, but they show the earliest recognition of Benny as a preeminent force on some very serious levels: finances, creativity, and performance.

Perhaps the most historically solid of the magazine pieces (in terms of broadcast history) is James Rorty's "Storm Warnings on the Air Waves" in the December 17, 1948, issue of *Commonweal*. Rorty examines Benny's industry-shaking move to CBS after spending the bulk of his career with NBC. As background, the article goes into considerable detail about the generally unrecognized fact that this move to CBS, which primed the pump for other network switches by major stars, was a contest for Benny's considerable corporate control and holdings of his related enterprises and not simply a bidding war for his talent. Rorty's profile reveals Benny as an astonishingly shrewd and powerful businessman—one of the first media entertainers to hold considerable control over his own projects and thus to gain commensurate negotiating leverage with the networks.

A somewhat more facile look at Benny's financial life on the radio can be found in Cleveland Amory's highly clever piece "Jack Benny's $400 Yaks" in the *Saturday Evening Post* of November 6, 1948. Here Amory provides a dollar-by-dollar breakdown of Jack Benny's "joke factory" (the show and its economics) in what amounts to an extremely informative analysis of how a star-centered program is financed. Amory begins with how Benny spent his still-impressive $27,000 weekly salary, the gross figure from which he paid his team of actors and writers. Dividing Benny's net income by the number of minutes he was on the air and the number of jokes or "laugh lines" Benny was likely to produce, Amory comes to the facile conclusion that Benny was paid $400 per laugh. Although Amory appears to be appalled or in awe, he delivers a fairly comprehensive look at the week-by-week finances of the medium's most successful variety show.

It was inevitable that *Life* would do one of its profile pieces on Jack Benny. Anyone familiar with *Life*'s typical work on its celebrities would be tempted to dismiss the Benny piece without reading it, because certainly a distressingly large number of *Life*'s entertainment profiles over the years were nothing more than slick fan-magazine puff pieces. But the piece they did on Benny in the issue of February 3, 1947, was a rare exception. First of all, it rendered an honest evaluation of the program that was, although generally laudatory, not entirely uncritical. Second, it did what *Life* traditionally did best; it presented an excellent photo display of the program in process and in progress. (Perhaps the hidden benefit of this article is that it demonstrates how clearly the relatively underappreciated medium of still photography can help illuminate the history of America's great aural medium.) Profiles on the writers and the cast, albeit brief, help flesh out a vivid portrait of comedy/variety's flagship program. Other profile material abounds, especially in *Radio Guide* and other fan magazines, but much of this material is predictable and repetitive. Benny's popularity created a wealth of information about his work and his legend. The abundance of material is both exhausting and exhaustive.

The biographical interest in Jack Benny is rivalled only by that in one other radio comedy performer, Fred Allen, the host of the very popular "Town Hall Tonight" (later "Allen's Alley"). Allen, although not nearly as successful as Benny during the 1930s and 1940s, has held an enigmatic fascination for radio buffs and historians. There are several reasons for this. Probably the most important is that Allen was the one major radio comedian possessed of a contemporary sensibility who did not attain success on television. (By contrast,

Eddie Cantor, a very popular radio star, really did not have a comedy style that could have sustained the demands of a television audience.) Thus, unlike Benny, Burns and Allen, Milton Berle, Bob Hope, and even lesser lights such as Henry Morgan, Allen is a part of "ancient" broadcasting history. The impulse to honor him as a forefather is seen not only in the plethora of written information about him but in the frequency with which major television personalities, such as Johnny Carson, Steve Allen, and Dick Cavett, invoke his name in olympian terms.

Allen is also enigmatic because of the uniqueness of his work. Unlike virtually all of the other comedians, who had a staff of writers, Allen did all of his own writing. This heroic feat clearly has put his peers in awe of him. It is also this feat that is alleged to have killed him prematurely. Finally, Allen's contentiousness (comparable only to radio bad boy Henry Morgan's cynicism) made him attractive to intellectuals, who adored his sophisticated ribbing of the middle-brow establishment.

Allen's literary legacy includes two autobiographies, *Treadmill to Oblivion* (1954) and *Much Ado about Me* (1956), of which *Treadmill* is more important from the standpoint of radio history. The book is simply the history of Allen's radio career. Starting from his own assessment of how he (along with many other Broadway comics) decided to make the crossover from Broadway to radio ("it's dough—let's go"), Allen analyzes carefully the distinctions between stage humor and radio humor (and in the process comes down quite hard on Eddie Cantor and others for failing to make that distinction). The book begins with his venture into radio shows for Linit and Sal Hepatica and proceeds eventually to his two major programs "Town Hall Tonight" and "Allen's Alley." Along the way he offers a jaundiced but enormously incisive history of radio comedy. In addition to chronicling the crossover phenomenon of Broadway comics to radio comics, Allen produces a generous amount of information on the role of sponsors and advertisers (with whom his hate-hate relationship is legendary), the work, style, and craft (or lack thereof) of other radio comedians, the importance of fan mail to network and advertiser support of radio programs (which was why Allen introduced into his programs several letter-inducing "bits" such as the Etiquette Department and the Question Box), the endless task of writing, and the rise of his one immortal radio persona, Senator Claghorn. The book is a jewel, indispensable not only as a text on Allen but as a text on radio comedy.

Much Ado about Me is properly titled, and although it is comprehensive as an autobiography, the book is guilty of the sort of wretched excesses and self-indulgences that Allen so loathed in others. His family history and early career in vaudeville are all there. The book is important for scholars interested in Allen himself, but it is not a significant contribution to radio history. Of considerably greater importance than *Much Ado about Me* is Joe McCarthy's edition of *Fred Allen's Letters,* which is a marvelous companion volume to *Treadmill to Oblivion.* This widely acclaimed volume of personal correspondence contains an engaging section on radio, "The Radio Treadmill." Herein are exchanges with cowriters Bob Welch and Harry Turgend as well as friend Don Quinn (the creator of "Fibber McGee and Molly"). In his letters Allen often lets down his studied cynical view of life and reveals some genuine frustration. The pace of his work load, the object of his mocking derision in *Treadmill to Oblivion,* genuinely gets to him. On the other hand, Allen favored his correspondents with the same cleverness with which he delighted his radio audiences, and thus the letters are immensely pleasurable. Moreover, they offer a clear sense of the chaotic energy that informed Allen's own radio broadcasting career.

In addition to his own considerable output of autobiographical material, Allen inspired many very good magazine articles. Among the serious think pieces on Allen is Alan R. Havig's "Critic from Within: Fred Allen Views Radio" in the fall 1978 issue of *Journal of Popular Culture.* Havig seeks to articulate and analyze formally Allen's much-vaunted role as radio critic. It is Havig's view that "radio needed thoughtful criticism," a hard thesis to dispute, but the suggestion implies that there was a shortage. (Not so; virtually every major big-city newspaper had radio and television criticism during the 1940s and 1950s. Havig could have made a better case for a shortage of criticism within the industry.) However, Havig does offer the insight that Allen was one of several people who came to radio when both he and the industry were under serious financial pressures, a combination that does little to ease the relationship between any artist and any entertainment medium. Havig's article is more ambitious than are other academic treatments of Allen in that he makes a creditable effort to present Allen in the context of theories of popular culture. Luther F. Sies's "Tally-Ho, Mr. Allen," published in the same issue of *Journal of Popular Culture,* is a solid, compressed biography of Allen and his career. Sies makes good use not only of previously published materials but also of program scripts and a 1956 NBC radio biography of Allen, "Fred Allen—A Biography in Sound." Sies ties Allen to the humor traditions of Ambrose Bierce and William Cowper Brann in addition to the humor of Mark Twain and Will Rogers.

John K. Hutchens's "Fred Allen: Comedian's Comedian" in the May 1942 issue of *Theatre Arts Monthly* is noteworthy as a solemn piece on Allen in that it enumerates the reasons for Allen's mythical status among his peers and fans. Hutchens points out that Allen writes the bulk of his own material, whereas Cantor, Hope, and others rely far more heavily on a staff of writers. Allen's delivery is relatively free of show-biz polish and panache, and thus he can sustain a full hour of entertainment more readily than can his peers (a highly debatable assertion). Hutchens cites as well the learned level of Allen's banter (current events, Swinburne, and Shakespeare as well as normal run-of-the-mill radio talk). Allen's relatively low listener ratings are viewed by Hutchens as a tribute to Allen's ability to rise above mediocrity. The value of Hutchens's article lies in the generally sensible foundation that it lays for the mythic dimensions of Fred Allen's reputation, both during his career and most certainly afterward.

Of the various popular profiles on Allen, two possess some lasting value. Joseph Bryan III's "Eighty Hours for a Laugh" in the October, 4, 1941, issue of *Saturday Evening Post* captures Allen's genuine discomfort with radio almost as effectively as do Allen's own letters. Bryan offers a clearheaded discussion of just how much of Allen's highly popular commentary on the medium of the radio reflected his own disposition. Although it is a point made often, the Bryan article reveals perhaps better than any other biographical piece Allen's shyness, his disdain for the business that nurtured him, his quirkiness, and, as is suggested elsewhere, his early death on account of that genuine torment. Pale by comparison but not without its virtues is George Sessions Perry's "Backstage at Allen's Alley" in the January 4, 1947, issue of *Saturday Evening Post.* Written in the sixteenth year of Allen's success on the air, the article, while adding little to what is available in other sources, does make the intriguing observation that Allen's most famous character, Senator Claghorn, is never on the air for more than seventy seconds per one hour. Unfortunately, Perry does not pursue that marvelous insight to discuss its implications for the power of well-drawn characters to exist through radio with a life of their own. Except for the discovery of that gold mine (lamentably left unearthed), the article is a predictable *Saturday Evening Post* behind-the-scenes piece: relentlessly if cheerfully descriptive and avoiding analysis like the plague.

Several other major radio personalities were the subjects of autobiographies, biographies, and profiles whose value as radio history ranges from priceless to useless. Among the most helpful (and most enjoyable) of this collection is George Burns's *I Love Her, That's Why.* Although the book emphasizes Burns and Allen's vaudeville and stage careers, the three chapters covering their radio careers are both fun and informative. Burns reveals that the duo was not even invited as guest stars on other people's radio programs until they had been completely successful as stage comedians. Moreover, it was Gracie who broke them into radio when she was given a guest appearance on Eddie Cantor's "Chase and Sanborn Hour." Soon afterwards they became regulars on "The Guy Lombardo Show" and took over the program when Lombardo left CBS. The famous "long lost brother" bit, in which Gracie sustained a running gag for months of searching for her lost brother, was so powerful that she used it not only as leverage to obtain guest appearances on other CBS programs (where she would enter in search of her long-lost brother, a continuation of the plot of her own show) but also once on a rival NBC program. Burns claims that the "long-lost brother" routine was the first crossover of fictional plots from one show to another. (The crossover is now part of the television "spin-off" phenomenon, where programs such as "Rhoda," "Maude," and "The Jeffersons" inherited characters and story lines borrowed from parent programs.) An equally arresting revelation is Burns's account of the evolution of their domestic comedy out of their "Boy and Girl" routines from vaudeville and early radio—a function of their advancing ages and their inability to appear on stage as doting sweethearts when the public already knew that they were married and raising children.

Biographical material on Bob Hope is readily available, although not plentiful as far as his radio career is concerned. For scholarship in popular culture, his career has inspired a doctoral dissertation, William Robert Faith's "Bob Hope and the Popular Oracle Tradition in American Humor." Although Faith's emphasis is not on radio in particular, he does incorporate all of Hope's comedic work into his critical framework. Hope himself has written several autobiographies; *Have Tux, Will Travel: Bob Hope's Own Story* has the most information on his radio career. For biographies, *The Amazing Careers of Bob Hope: From Gags to Riches* by Joe Morella, Edward Z. Epstein, and Eleanor Clark covers his radio career but does not provide the kind of thorough treatment of the industry that Josefsberg's book on Jack Benny does.

Eddie Cantor has produced two autobiographies, the completely forgettable *My Life Is in Your Hands* ("as told to David Freedman"), and the somewhat more helpful *Take My Life* (with Jane Kenser Ardmore, 1957). The latter book offers a good section on radio audiences, but the thrust of the book suggests that Cantor was far more fond of his theater career than his radio career. Other biographies and autobiographies on radio stars that seem to provide surprisingly little information on their radio careers include Mae West's *Goodness Had Nothing to Do with It* and Milton Berle's *Milton Berle*. Although not a radio comedy star in the conventional sense, Will Rogers did have an impact on radio comedy, a fact that is disappointingly underplayed in his own autobiography *(The Autobiography of Will Rogers)* and his major biographies and critical studies, including Paul Alworth's *Will Rogers*. However, Rogers himself published a collection of his radio talks *(Twelve Radio Talks Delivered by Will Rogers during the Spring of 1930 through the Courtesy of E. R. Squibb and Sons)*, and various tapes and recordings of his radio appearances are available. (The chief source for these is the Will Rogers Memorial Commission, Claremore, Oklahoma.)

Although he was not a star of the magnitude of Burns, Hope, or Benny, Henry Morgan was enough of an iconoclast (his particular claim to fame was the bald-faced insulting of his own sponsors) to attract more than his share of attention from writers and scholars. Three of these are worth noting. Arthur Wertheim's "The Bad Boy of Radio: Henry Morgan and the Censors" in the fall 1978 issue of *Journal of Popular Culture* traces Morgan's bouts with his sponsors. Wertheim stretches the term censorship by implying that a sponsor's decision to withdraw sponsorship from a program because the program fails to promote a product in a favorable light is a form of censorship. The article may merit some attention because of Wertheim's prominent position as a scholar in the radio field, but it does not edify or clarify the tricky issue of censorship. This piece could have been far more important than it is. Two magazine pieces written in 1947 during the height of Morgan's radio career are Murray Schuhmach's "Triple-Threat Morgan" in the *New York Times Magazine* (September 14) and Robert Lewis Taylor's "Henry Morgan: Radio's Freshest Wit Makes a Business of Kidding His Sponsors" in the April 14 issue of *Life*. Schuhmach goes overboard in his comparison of Morgan to the great American humorists in history, but the article reveals, if somewhat unintentionally, why Morgan, along with Fred Allen, was something of a darling among the intelligentsia. Taylor's piece is surprising for *Life* in that it is a genuine article and not a sneak peek behind the glamorous life of a celebrity. Forsaking photography for text, *Life* and Taylor pay an ironic tribute to the rebellious, intellectual, but ultimately harmless spearer of sponsors and one of the first "hip" personalities who jabbed the medium as part of his form of entertainment. Taylor's perspective, without the benefit of hindsight or distance, provides a more realistic view of Morgan's place in the scheme of things than does Wertheim's. Morgan was simply cutting the edge for irreverent comedy; he is neither a martyr to the first amendment nor a victim of real censorship.

Other helpful biographical profiles on variety and comedy personalities include two solid *New Yorker* pieces on well-known radio comics and a 1943 *American Magazine* profile on a radio character actor. Whitney Balliett's "Their Own Gravity" in the September 24, 1973, issue of the *New Yorker* is a superb, erudite portrait of Bob and Ray. Although inspired by their 1970s Broadway show, *The Two and Only,* the article faithfully recounts their early radio beginnings in the 1940s on WHDH (Boston), their many short-lived engagements with most of the major New York radio stations and networks (NBC, ABC, Mutual, and WOR) and their triumphant return to radio in the 1960s after achieving success in television in the 1950s. On April 4, 1977, the *New Yorker* published Mark Singer's "Profiles—Goody," a retrospective on comedy writer and actor Goodman Ace. "What's His Name?," an article by Jerome Beatty in the July 1943 issue of *American Magazine,* is on its surface a routine profile of a radio character actor. But the article offers confirmation of the thesis that vocal familiarity in radio worked as much as facial familiarity works in television and movies, and that a radio performer with a distinctive voice (but no name recognition) could be as familiar as those dozens of screen actors whose faces are familiar but whose names are virtually unknown to the public.

Although the bulk of the bibliographical information on comedy and variety programming is housed in general texts and biographies of the performers, there is a modest supply of useful works on miscellaneous concerns. The staggering number of gags and jokes that came over the radio each week produced an interest in the art, craft, and business of radio comedy writing. Jerome Beatty's "From Gags to Riches" in the March 1936 *American Magazine* is a surprisingly useful article on the background of comedy writing in radio. Tracing the first radio jokes to witless song cues ("I have a friend who should take the advice of this next singer and 'Drink to Me Only with Thine Eyes'"), the article focuses on the development of radio joke production. Brief profiles are presented of successful writers (including Hal Horne, the most successful free-lance radio joke writer of the late 1930s, and David Freeman, Eddie Cantor's chief writer and the owner of a 50,000-entry joke file) as well as some observations on the pressures of producing the extraordinary amount of material necessary to fill the demand. Milton MacKaye's "The Whiskers on the Wisecracks" in the August

17, 1935, issue of the *Saturday Evening Post* is a satiric but substantial discussion of the industry of gag and comedy writers. In addition to discussing the financial rewards for success in the field (Harry Cohn, Jack Benny's head writer, is the highest-paid one-show writer at $1,750 per week), MacKaye is very good on the subjects of American humor (for example, how its tendency toward timeliness burdens most jokes with a short half-life) and the gagman's debt to vaudeville, jokebooks, and college humor magazines. An unattributed article, "Pun and Punch," appeared in the March 27, 1937, issue of *Literary Digest,* offering the underdeveloped but intriguing thesis that radio comedy influenced common speech in America and turned America into "what Europe thinks it is—a nation of wisecrackers." The article is chiefly a discussion of how radio humorists' one-line tags and sayings work their way into common conversation (a phenomenon familiar to contemporary television audiences, who adopted Don Adams's "Would you believe," Steve Martin's "Excuuuuuse me," and John Belushi's "But nooooo" in much the same manner). Goodman Ace's half-serious "The Old Badger Game" in the *Saturday Review of Literature* (February 3, 1951) provides a spirited and deliberately overwrought defense of comedy writers who are occasionally berated collectively on the air by comics when jokes do not go over. Ace seeks either credit for writers for gags that work or a moratorium on comedians' criticism. Edwin O'Connor's "No Laughing Matter" in the September 1946 *Atlantic Monthly* is an offhanded but useful discussion of the structure of radio comedy shows. O'Connor not only asserts that the format of comedy and variety radio shows is remarkably similar from show to show but also suggests that the format is more important than the quality of the content for determining the success of the program. Although offered as a satiric piece, the article is a competent if compressed analysis of the radio comedy and variety format. Robert Yoder's "Don't Shoot Father. Save Him For Laughs" in *Saturday Evening Post* (August 14, 1948) proves to be an oddly prophetic if lighthearted analysis of sex roles in radio comedy, particularly with regard to the father as a fool or buffoon. Citing " Ozzie and Harriet," "The Life of Riley," and "The Great Gildersleeve," Yoder concludes that fathers may well be the schlemiels that radio portrays them to be but winces while winking about the fact that their foibles are cannon fodder for radio comics. While not a compelling piece by any means, the article is a harbinger of future serious-minded content analyses of sexual stereotyping and role modeling in the media.

Perhaps it is because comedy and variety programs succeeded on the basis of intangibles such as personality, charisma, chemistry, and timing more than tangible factors such as scripts, songs, or even good jokes that the bibliographical material available is somewhat thin. Nevertheless, these programs are probably the most enduring aspect of the nation's collective memory of radio. Certainly television borrowed heavily in the 1950s and 1960s from the radio variety show of the 1930s and 1940s, transplanting the format, many of the stars, and many of the writers into the new medium. Moreover, the comedy/variety stars themselves are remembered for their presence, whereas other radio immortals (Murrow, Welles, and so on) are often remembered for particular moments. The radio comedy and variety program, then, may have made its largest contribution to American popular culture by giving a home entertainment medium a means of generating entertainment, celebrity, and fame on a par with that created by movie theaters. Benny, Burns and Allen, Allen, Cantor, Wynn, and others seem to have served the same function for radio that Gable, Monroe, and Grant served for the movies—they were the industry's chief entree into the consciousness of the American public.

BIBLIOGRAPHY FOR RADIO COMEDY AND VARIETY

Ace, Goodman. "The Old Badger Game." *Saturday Review of Literature* 34 (February 3, 1951): 26.

Allen, Fred. *Treadmill to Oblivion*. Boston: Little, Brown, 1954.

_____. *Much Ado about Me*. Boston: Little, Brown, 1956.

Allen, Steve. *The Funny Men*. New York: Simon and Schuster, 1956.

Alworth, Paul. *Will Rogers*. New York: Twayne, 1974.

Amory, Cleveland. "Jack Benny's $400 Yaks." *Saturday Evening Post* 221 (November 6, 1948): 24-25.

Balliett, Whitney. "Their Own Gravity." *New Yorker* 49 (September 24, 1973): 42-50.

Barnouw, Erik. *A Tower In Babel: To 1933*. Vol. 1 of *A History of Broadcasting in the United States*. New York: Oxford University Press, 1966.

_____. *The Golden Web: 1933 to 1953*. Vol. 2 of *A History of Broadcasting in the United States*. New York: Oxford University Press, 1968.

Beatty, Jerome. "From Gags to Riches." *American Magazine* 123, no. 3 (March 1936): 14-15+.

_____. "What's His Name?" *American Magazine* 136, no. 1 (July 1943): 36-37ff.

Benny, Mary Livingstone, and Hilliard Marks. *Jack Benny*. Garden City, N.Y.: Doubleday, 1978.

Berle, Milton. *Milton Berle*. New York: Dell, 1975.

Bryan, Joseph, 3rd. "Eighty Hours for a Laugh." *Saturday Evening Post* 214 (October 4, 1941): 22-23ff.

Burns, George, with Cynthia Hobart Lindsay. *I Love Her, That's Why!* New York: Simon and Schuster, 1958.

Buxton, Frank, and Bill Owen. *The Big Broadcast, 1920-1950*. New York: Avon, 1973.

Cantor, Eddie, as told to David Freedman. *My Life Is in Your Hands*. New York: Blue Ribbon, 1932.

Cantor, Eddie, with Jane Kesner Ardmore. *Take My Life*. Garden City, N.Y.: Doubleday, 1957.

DiMeglio, John E. "Radio's Debt to Vaudeville." *Journal of Popular Culture* 12, no. 2 (Fall 1978): 228-35.

Dunning, John. *Tune In Yesterday: The Ultimate Encyclopedia of Old-Time Radio, 1925-1976*. Englewood Cliffs, N.J.: Prentice-Hall, 1976.

Faith, William Robert. "Bob Hope and the Popular Oracle Tradition in American Humor." Ph.D. diss., University of Southern California, 1976.

Fein, Irving. *Jack Benny: An Intimate Biography*. New York: Putnam, 1976.

_____. *Fred Allen's Letters,* edited by Joe McCarthy. Boston: Little, Brown, 1956.

Gaver, Jack, and Dave Stanley. *There's Laughter in the Air! Radio's Top Comedians and Their Best Shows.* New York: Greenberg Press, 1945.

Gilbert, Douglas. *American Vaudeville: Its Life and Times.* New York: Dover, 1968.

Gould, Jack. "How Comic Is Radio Comedy?" *New York Times Magazine,* November 21, 1948, 22-23ff.

Green, Abel, and Joe Laurie, Jr. *Show Biz: From Vaude to Video.* New York: Henry Holt and Co., 1951.

Harmon, Jim. *The Great Radio Comedians.* Garden City, N.Y.: Doubleday, 1970.

Havrig, Alan R. "Critic from Within: Fred Allen Views Radio." *Journal of Popular Culture* 12, no. 2 (Fall 1978): 328-39.

Hope, Bob. *Have Tux, Will Travel: Bob Hope's Own Story.* New York: Simon and Schuster, 1954.

Hutchens, John K. "Serious Business This Radio Humor." *New York Times,* March 15, 1942, 16-17.

_____. "Fred Allen: Comedian's Comedian." *Theatre Arts Monthly* 25, no. 5 (May 1942): 307-13.

"Jack Benny, Inc." *Life* 42 (February 3, 1947): 85-86+.

Josefsberg, Milt. *The Jack Benny Show.* New Rochelle, N.Y.: Arlington House, 1977.

MacKaye, Milton. "The Whiskers on the Wisecracks." *Saturday Evening Post* 208 (August 17, 1935): 12-13.

McLean, Albert F. *American Vaudeville as Ritual.* Lexington: University of Kentucky Press, 1965.

Morella, Joe, Edward Z. Epstein, and Eleanor Clark. *The Amazing Careers of Bob Hope: From Gags to Riches.* New Rochelle, N.Y.: Arlington House, 1973.

O'Connor, Edwin. "No Laughing Matter." *Atlantic Monthly* 128, no. 3 (March 1938): 11-15ff.

Perry, George Sessions. "Backstage at Allen's Alley." *Saturday Evening Post* 219 (January 4, 1947): 14-15.

"Pun and Punch." *Literary Digest* 123, no. 13 (March 27, 1937): 20.

Robinson, Hubbell, and Ted Patrick. "Jack Benny." *Scribner's Magazine* 103, no. 3 (March 1938) 11-15.

Rogers, Will. *Twelve Radio Talks Delivered by Will Rogers during the Spring of 1930 through the Courtesy of E. R. Squibb and Sons.* New York: Squibb and Sons, 1930.

_____. *The Autobiography of Will Rogers.* Boston: Houghton Mifflin, 1949.

Rorty, James. "Storm Warnings on the Air Waves." *Commonweal* 49, no. 10 (December 17, 1948): 11-15.

Schuhmach, Murray. "Triple-Threat Morgan." *New York Times Magazine,* September 14, 1947, 20ff.

Seldes, Gilbert. "Sixty-Percent Entertainment." *Saturday Review* 39 (March 24, 1956): 32.

_____. *The Great Audience.* New York: Viking, 1956. Westport, Conn.: Greenwood Press, 1970.

Sies, Luther F. "Tally-Ho, Mr. Allen." *Journal of Popular Culture* 12 (Fall 1978): 164-89.

Singer, Mark. "Profiles—Goody." *New Yorker* 4 (April 4, 1977): 41-46+.

Smith, Bill. *The Vaudevillians.* New York: Macmillian, 1976.

Summers, Harrison B. *A Thirty-Year History of Programs Carried on National Radio*

Networks, 1926-1956. Columbus: Ohio State University Press, 1958. Reprint. New York: Arno Press and the New York times, 1971.

Taylor, Robert Lewis. "Henry Morgan: Radio's Freshest Wit Makes a Business of Kidding His Sponsors." *Life* 22 (April 14, 1947): 59-64.

Wertheim, Arthur Frank. "The Bad Boy of Radio: Henry Morgan and the Censors." *Journal of Popular Culture* 12, no. 2 (Fall 1978): 347-52.

_____. *Radio Comedy.* New York: Oxford University Press, 1979.

West, Mae. *Goodness Had Nothing to Do with It.* New York: Putnam, 1970.

Wilde, Larry. *The Great Comedians Talk about Comedy.* New York: Citadel, 1968.

_____. *How the Great Comedy Writers Create Laughter.* Chicago: Nelson-Hall, 1976.

Yoder, Robert. "Don't Shoot Father. Save Him For Laughs" *Saturday Evening Post* 211 (August 14, 1948): 28+.

6   RADIO SPORTS

The area of radio sports broadcasting may be the one aspect of radio history where the amount of available literature is most out of proportion to the degree of audience interest. By all accounts the interest in sports broadcasting has shown steady audience growth since its beginnings in the early 1920s. Nevertheless, it is a subject to which both sports historians and radio historians devote surprisingly little attention—perhaps because each believes that the subject is the principal domain of the other.

The material that is available can be broken down into two major categories: material on historical events in sports (usually associated with a particular sport or a single competition within a particular sport) and material on or by individual sports announcers. It is this second category that has for the last sixty years yeilded by far the largest amount of published information on sports broadcasting. Before proceeding to examine the information, we should note that despite the fact that the term ''sports'' seems to be all-encompassing, for practical purposes the term must be limited to the sports that form the nucleus of radio sports broadcasting, especially from 1920 to 1959: baseball, boxing, and football.

HISTORICAL INFORMATION

It is safe to conclude that the early history of radio sports broadcasting is the history of baseball broadcasting. Although boxing and then football proved to be programming staples as well, it was baseball that taught the radio stations, both major and minor, how to broadcast sports, how to cultivate sports broadcasters, how to compete with the newspaper sports pages, and how to turn sports broadcasting into a lucrative part of station programming.

In 1987 Curtis Smith filled a longstanding void in sports broadcasting history with the publication of his book *Voices of The Game: The First Full-Scale Overview of Baseball Broadcasting, 1921 to the Present.* The book's subtitle, for all its immodesty, is quite accurate. There is nothing else in the otherwise sparsely populated literature of sports broadcasting that approaches its breadth and depth. Although Smith's approach is narrative, his writing occasionally seems encylopedic; the dual burden of setting down the vital information while still spinning a genuinely intriguing tale sometimes gets the better of him. But overall the book is quite readable. To his considerable credit, Smith remembers that the early days of baseball on the radio did not begin and end with New York and east coast-based broadcasts. Pioneering baseball broadcasting in Chicago, Cincinnati, and Kansas City are all given their due. Moreover, unlike many historians who cover "broadcasting" by skimming quickly over radio to get to the more fertile fields of television, Smith devotes a hefty portion of his nearly 600-page text to radio. At the back of the book is a helpful bibliography (although it is more sports-oriented than broadcast-oriented) and a mind-boggling annotated chronology of over sixty events in baseball broadcasting history. Thus far, Smith's book is the only full-length, genuinely indispensable source for baseball's radio history and, indeed, for all sports on radio.

Of the available shorter material, Wayne Towers's monograph *World Series Coverage in New York City in the 1920s,* published in the University of Kentucky Journalism Monographs series, is far and away the best. Towers observes shrewdly how the dominance of New York teams in the 1920s (including three "Battle of Broadway" World Series between the Giants and the Yankees) stimulated both the New York newspapers and the New York radio stations to increase their coverage. The coincidence of the World Series enthusiasm emanating from the center of radio experimentation stimulated radio's interest in baseball broadcasting. He also observes how baseball's own efforts in the 1910s to make the game more offense oriented (elimination of the spitball, changing the interior and exterior of the ball to make it livelier) simultaneously made it more adaptable to radio broadcasting.

In terms of general mention of early baseball coverage, the next best sources are the biographical and autobiographical materials on various sports announcers. Erik Barnouw's *A Tower In Babel* (volume 1 of his three-volume history of American broadcasting) mentions only briefly the pioneering efforts of KDKA (Pittsburgh), WJZ (Newark), and WEAF (New York) in sports broadcasting. While most baseball histories scarcely mention radio's role at all, there is some nominal material in David Quentin Voigt's *American Baseball,* volume 2, and in J. Roy Stockton's chapter "Baseball" in Alison Danzig and Peter Brandwein's anthology *Sports Golden Age: A Close-Up of the Fabulous Twenties.* However, none of this material compares with the depth and intelligence of Smith's book or Towers's monograph.

The periodical literature from 1920 to 1950 would on occasion pick up on general issues related to the broadcasting of baseball. The most valuable of these is Francis Wallace's long piece in *Collier's* in 1951, "Are the Major Leagues Strangling Baseball?" The article reviews thoroughly and intelligently the imbroglio that followed a 1950 Department of Justice ruling that individual baseball clubs in major and minor leagues had complete territorial rights to broadcast coverage within a fifty-mile radius of their local franchises. Although the legislation has changed dramatically since then, Wallace provides a clear blueprint for the difficult and complicated economic balance of fan attendance, general revenues, and radio broadcasting. Smaller articles appear in the standard news magazines, and occasionally even in *Business Week* or *Nation's Business* when baseball strikes occur, but they do not offer the kind of depth that the Wallace article provides.

Another major magazine piece on the history of baseball broadcasts over radio defies classification but is probably the best writing ever done on sports broadcasting by anyone. Willie Morris's childhood memoirs of listening to the Dodgers on radio while he was growing up in Mississippi is a first-rate literary biography. "Memoirs of a Short-Wave Prophet," which appeared in the *New Yorker,* details the young Morris's experiments with his father's shortwave radio. Morris discovered that through shortwave he could pick up a baseball broadcast four innings ahead of the standard delayed broadcast, which was recounted "live" from his local station. Morris would use this information to bedevil friends who were stunned at the youngster's ability to "predict" not only the final score but what players would do in the last half of the game.

Even more so than with baseball, the broadcast history of boxing is fragmented. Barnouw makes mention of the broadcast of the Dempsey/ Carpentier championship, but the only thorough account of that first historic broadcast is J. Andrew "Major" White's first-person account in *Reader's Digest* (December 1955). Hyperbolically entitled "The First Big Radio Broadcast," the article details how White, the former editor of *Wireless Age,* was invited by David Sarnoff to broadcast the fight. The fight ended up doing more for White than for boxing, since he soon went with Sarnoff as a full-time sports announcer and is now considered to be one of the genuine pioneers in the field. A substantial and very useful *Literary Digest* article in 1935 ("World at Ringside by Proxy," unattributed) detailed the first international broadcast of a boxing match (Joe Lewis versus Max Baer). The article provides a considerable amount of information on how the arrangements were made to give radio accounts to Japanese wire services.

Only two periodical articles are even worthy of mention in the early broadcast history of radio football: "Does Radio Cut the Football Gate?," an unattributed article in *Literary Digest* (July 16, 1932) discussing the trauma of college athletic officials over the impact on attendance of the new practice of broadcasting football games, and "Regulation or Strangulation," an unattributed article in *Collier's* (November 17, 1951) detailing the Department of Justice's fight against the National Football League's efforts to restrict coverage of its games.

PERSONALITIES

For better or for worse, the best source material for information on radio sports is found in the biographies, autobiographies, and profile pieces on individual sports announcers, who developed their own celebrity status when executives like Sarnoff and Paley discovered that audience reaction and response to sports broadcasting was tied to the appeal of the sports reporter. It is generally agreed that J. Andrew "Major" White, the aforementioned broadcaster of the first boxing match ever broadcast, was the first radio personality whose celebrity was identified exclusively with sports broadcasting. It is also generally agreed that Graham McNamee of WEAF in New York was both the father of the now unshakable fast-talk, fast-paced entertainment style of sportscasting and the first sportscaster to attain major celebrity status.

McNamee is one of only a handful of radio broadcasters about whom there exists even a measurable amount of useful printed material. The largest body of work concerns (Walter L.) Red Barber, the venerable Dodgers and later Yankees broadcaster. Ted Husing is also the subject of a few pieces, and Lindsey Nelson, the New York broadcaster most closely associated with the Mets, is the author of two lengthy commercial autobiographies. Biographical material is omitted on one Ronald Reagan, former sports reporter for WHO in Des Moines, Iowa, and former play-by-play man for the Chicago Cubs, who eventually found employment in other fields. The two books by, and much of the information about, the indefatigable Howard Cosell offer very little in the way of insight into radio. Although he has had his own radio program for years, Cosell's impact clearly has been through television.

Red Barber's book *The Broadcasters* is an excellent source on radio sportscasters. It is an informative if occasionally cloying memoir. It has several useful short sketches of major sports radio figures, including an uncharitable picture of CBS legend Ted Husing and a salute to McNamee, who received 50,000 pieces of fan mail the day after the first World Series game ever broadcast. Barber knows his business and was a practicing print journalist throughout most of his career. One result of his professionalism is a splendid discussion about how competition among the networks inflated beyond proportion the importance of college bowl games as CBS and NBC found themselves in a prestige war to see who could gobble up the rights to the best games. A promising chapter on the relationship between sponsors and sports broadcasting turns into straight description. (Barber, writing in 1970, gives the impression here that he is loath to offend the people with whom he was working at the time.) That flaw aside, *The Broadcasters* is a well-written, important book. In 1962 Barber also wrote a serious, two-part piece on interviewing technique for the *Saturday Review,* the second of which spelled out specific differences between radio and television techniques ("TV and Radio Aren't the Same").

There are several magazine profiles on Barber, probably because of his enormous popularity and because the print press recognized him as a colleague in a way that they did not recognize other sportscasters. Among the best of these profiles is Richard G. Hubler's "The Barber of Brooklyn" in the March 21, 1942, edition of the *Saturday Evening Post,* which was written when Barber was "the verce" of the Brooklyn Dodgers. It is hard to know if Hubler is engaging in the mythmaking that has been the unyielding benchmark of *Saturday Evening Post* interviews, but backing himself up with facts, he argues that Barber was responsible not only for enormous increases in attendance at Ebbetts Field but also, through the popularity of his broadcasts, for creating the cultural affection for the Dodgers that was to become both national and international in scope. Quentin Reynolds, another powerful New York print journalist in the 1940s and 1950s, lionized Barber in his 1954 *Reader's Digest* profile, "The Two Lives of Red Barber." Writing during the year that Barber left the Dodgers (after fifteen years) to come to the Yankees, Reynolds fondly but perceptively analyzes Barber's appeal and style. He also notes that Barber's Yankee contract allowed him to broadcast only at home so that he could give time to his other career as an Episcopal lay reader. The reverence with which the broadcasting field looks upon him and the uniqueness of his style and delivery are deftly summed up in William Taafe's "Back in the Catbird Seat" (*Sports Illustrated,* July 23, 1984). Reporting on Barber's weekly radio appearances on National Public Radio, Taafe gives a most laudatory account of Barber's legacy to the sport. Barber's obituary is likely to offend by comparison.

Less well known than Barber, but arguably far more influential, was Graham McNamee, the first major sportscaster star, although he did report news and other events as well. McNamee's autobiography, *You're on The Air,* coauthored with Robert Gordon Anderson in 1926, is in and of itself a recognition of the early power and celebrity of the successful sportscaster. Although there is a condescending air in McNamee's writing ("I know you are sitting in little farm houses or in city apartments with your headphones over your ears") and enough self-congratulation to become occasionally annoying, the book provides some very helpful insights into early radio history. For one thing, the book can stand as a commendable station history of WEAF, since McNamee was with that station almost from its beginning and stayed with it throughout his career. McNamee also analyzes the source of his sports style, which he said he fashioned after the earliest boxing broadcasts; the fast action of a punch-by-punch boxing match provided a pace and rhythm that McNamee adopted for himself and that the profession later took on as its own. Finally, McNamee reveals some solid broadcasting savvy when he discusses the nuances of broadcasting football games as opposed to baseball games. His analysis of how he must make use of outpost reporters throughout the stadium to send back reports on the same play from different angles foreshadows the coming of high-tech, multicamera football coverage. In addition, McNamee boasts of his innovation of interviewing fighters in their training camps days before a broadcast fight. McNamee would take notes and then, before the fight and between rounds, would disseminate portions of the interviews. This is precisely the way that ABC Television, the leading broadcaster of boxing matches, combines interviews and the fights. McNamee, although pleased with the technique, could have had no idea how influential it would be. Two years after his book was published, McNamee wrote a lengthy piece for *American Magazine* entitled "My Adventures in Broadcasting Sporting Events." It is a highly anecdotal piece that reveals something of McNamee's devil-may-care persona and, by virtue of publishing fan letters (some negative, some positive), offers some early but inconclusive evidence of the development of the fan's relationship to the sportscaster. Biographical information on McNamee is not easy to come by, and his *New York Times* obituary (T. R. Kennedy, Jr.'s "A Voice to Remember," May 10, 1942) is as good as anything available.

Of the major pioneer sportscasters, Ted Husing is the one to whom history appears to have been least generous. Evidence suggests that this may have much more to do with Husing's personality than with the fickleness of history. Husing's autobiography, entitled improbably *My Eyes are in My Heart,* is filled with so much name-dropping and horn-blowing that it blurs Husing's genuine contributions to the history of sportscasting. Claiming, among other things, the invention of on-the-spot news coverage by virtue of his having taken a microphone to a nearby fire, he asserts that his ability to cover news was CBS' "biggest break." He speaks frequently of Paley's admiration for him, although Paley, in his autobiography *As It Happened,* said that Husing was so bad as an office manager that he had to ship Husing to Chicago, where his sportscasting career began in earnest. The central thesis of Husing's book, confirmed nowhere else in radio literature, is that he single-handedly brought CBS to the forefront of sports broadcasting. One useful profile on Husing is Julian Bach's "Hold 'Em Husing" in the November 16, 1937, *Literary Digest.* Bach follows Husing as he prepares to broadcast a college football game. Like the chapter on the same subject in McNamee's *You're on the Air,* written eleven years earlier, the article gives a reasonably good description of the technology and techniques of the art of football broadcasting in the late 1930s.

Lindsey Nelson, an agreeable and competent but by no means pivotal broadcaster, becomes important to the radio bibliographer simply because he took the trouble to write two genuinely informative books, *Backstage at the Mets* in 1966, a press-box denizen's view of the Mets' first four dismal seasons, and *Hello Everybody, I'm Lindsey Nelson* (1985), a detailed autobiography that devotes several chapters to Nelson's early days in radio. The latter book, which is far more useful to the radio historian than the former, is refreshing in that Nelson, who is duly modest about his own role in broadcast history, writes as a skilled observer relatively free of self-serving agendas. His observations on how one breaks into radio and on life among the vagabond broadcasters of the 1940s make this one of the more useful memoirs on radio broadcasting as a whole and certainly on sports broadcasting.

More significant than Nelson, but less helpful as a broadcast historian, Mel Allen, "The Voice of the Yankees," has been the subject of several profile pieces. Among the best of these Huston Horn's "Baseball's Babbling Brook" in the July 9, 1962, *Sports Illustrated.*

Inasmuch as radio sportscasters have been bona fide celebrities in their own right since the 1920s, many lesser lights have been the subjects of various personality profiles, interviews, and feature articles over the last sixty years. These articles have appeared in an astonishing range of magazines: *Ms.*, *American Magazine, Saturday Evening Post,* the *New Yorker, New York, Sports Illustrated, Time, Newsweek,* and so on. Although many are superficial, there are a few of sufficient length and substance that they deserve mention. If only because Peter Martin's celebrity profiles in the old *Saturday Evening Post* are historical benchmarks in feature reporting, his 1946 piece on Philadelphia announcer Byrum Saam, himself a "discovery" of Ted Husing, is worth consulting. The article does make the surprising statement that despite conventional wisdom and literature to the contrary, broadcasting a baseball game over radio is more difficult than broadcasting a football game. Frank X. Tolbert's 1951 *Saturday Evening Post* profile of Dizzy Dean ("Dizzy Dean—He's Not So Dumb!") reveals relatively little about sports broadcasting itself but is a rare look at the broadcast career of the language-chopping former pitching great who announced his departure from radio (to television) by saying, "I'm through talkin' about things people ain't seein'." Frederic A. Birmingham's long article "Voice of the '500': Sid Collins" (*Saturday Evening Post,* Summer 1972) is a welcome departure from the dominant celebrity of baseball, football, and, to a lesser extent, basketball announcers.

Since the early 1970s the best source of magazine profiles on radio sportscasters has been *Sports Illustrated,* whose occasional column, "TV and Radio," sometimes offers hard-nosed news articles on radio personalities from various parts of the country, thus providing radio sportscasters not based in New York with the only national print exposure they are likely to receive anywhere. Among the individuals who have been profiled in the "TV and Radio" column since the early 1970s are Pete Franklin (sportstalk host and insult doyen previously on Cleveland's WWWE, now handling evening drive-time on New York's WFAN), Cawood Ledford (University of Kentucky play-by-play man who in the early 1980s became nationally known through his broadcast of NCAA Division I basketball games), Bob Uecker (the former baseball player and Milwaukee Brewers play-by-play radio and television announcer who eventually found fortune and fame as a mainstay of the Miller Lite Beer repertory company), Joe Nuxhall (former baseball pitcher who converted to Cincinnati Reds broadcaster), and Jaime Jarrin ("la Voz de los Dodgers" on KTNQ, the Los Angeles Spanish-speaking station). In 1984 the column also featured a unique article on the Syracuse University FM radio station, which has an extraordinary record of producing professional radio sportscasters ("The Voices from Syracuse" by William Taafe).

In the last thirteen years *Sports Illustrated* has also produced two long features (the only ones of their kind in major, readily accessible national publications) on radio personalities. "See No Evil, Hear No Evil . . . Ha!" which appeared in September 1972, made a legend of WBZ's (Boston) *Sports Huddle,* an irreverent, even caustic radio call-in show that, along with Howard Cosell's broadcasts, encouraged the American sports fan to reject his or her traditional posture of hero worship for uncompromising social criticism and truculent consumerism. The piece, by Herman Weiskopf, is a superb case study on the immense power of a local media celebrity within his or her own community. In 1984 Bruce Newman's article "From High above the Western Sideline" sought to portray Chick Hearn, the voice of the Los Angeles Lakers, in a highly favorable light but managed to show how a successful egotistic media celebrity can exert power over the sports he covers—even to the point of affecting the outcome of a game.

SATIRICAL PIECES

Perhaps nothing confirmed the rise and power of the radio sportscasters as much as the spate of satirical pieces on them that appeared in various magazines in the 1920s and 1930s. There is a certain sameness to them all, and so mere listing of those that appeared in national magazines should suffice: John Tunis's "Sports and the Radio," *Outlook and Independent,* October 16, 1929; "Left Wing" 's "Public Enemy No. 64B: The Football Broadcaster," *Nation,* October 9, 1935; Paul Perella's "Sports Broadcast," *Atlantic,* October 1945; Arthur J. Harris, Jr.'s "The Baseball Experts," *Atlantic Monthly,* July 1954; and Ralph Schoenstein's "Talk Me out of the Ball Game, *Saturday Review,* April 11, 1964.

Radio sportscasting is a field in which all the right articles but not many of the right books are available. The personality profiles abound, the memoirs are there, and the five or six major breakthrough events have been duly recorded. But aside from Smith's powerful *Voice of the Game* the kind of searching analysis of the entire field is still largely undone. Even the pivotal works in radio programming history, such as those of Barnouw or MacDonald, leave sports broadcasting all but untouched. Until such works appear, a substantial portion of radio history will continue to be undiscovered and largely unknown.

BIBLIOGRAPHY FOR RADIO SPORTS

Bach, Julian. "Hold 'Em Husing." *Literary Digest* 124, no. 16 (November 6, 1937): 22-23.
Barnouw, Erik. *A Tower in Babel.* Vol. 1 of *A History of Broadcasting in the United States.* New York: Oxford University Press, 1966.
Barber, Red. "TV and Radio Aren't the Same." *Saturday Review* 45 (March 10, 1962): 50-52.
———. *The Broadcasters.* New York: Dial, 1970.
Birmingham, Frederic A. "Voice of the '500': Sid Collins." *Saturday Evening Post* 244 (Summer 1972): 60-61ff.

"Does Radio Cut the Football Gate?" *Literary Digest* 114 (July 16, 1932): 32-33.

Fimrite, Ron. "La Voz de Los Dodgers." *Sports Illustrated* 54, no. 25 (June 15, 1981): 62.

Harris, Arthur J., Jr. "The Baseball Experts." *Atlantic Monthly* 194, no. 1 (July 1954): 87-88.

Horn, Huston. "Baseball's Babbling Brook." *Sports Illustrated* 17, no. 2 (July 9, 1962): 54-63.

Hubler, Richard G. "The Barber of Brooklyn." *Saturday Evening Post* 214 (March 21, 1942): 34ff.

Husing, Ted. *My Eyes Are in My Heart.* New York: Bernard Geis, 1959.

Kennedy, T. R. "A Voice to Remember." *New York Times,* May 10, 1943, 43.

Left Wing. "Public Enemy No. 64B: The Football Broadcaster." *Nation* 141, no. 3666 (October 9, 1935): 405-6.

Lublin, Joanne. "Mary Shane: Baseball's New Motor Mouth." *Ms.* 6, no. 4 (October 1977): 94-95.

MacDonald, J. Fred. *Don't Touch That Dial! Radio Programming in American Life, 1920-1960.* Chicago: Nelson-Hall, 1979.

McNamee, Graham. "My Adventures in Broadcasting Sporting Events." *American Magazine* 106 (July 1928): 46-47ff.

McNamee, Graham, with Robert Gordon Anderson. *You're on the Air.* New York: Harper and Brothers, 1926.

Martin, Peter. "He Talks a Wonderful Touchdown." *Saturday Evening Post* 219 (October 12, 1946): 94-95.

Morris, Willie. "Memoirs of a Short-Wave Prophet." *New Yorker* 39 (November 1963): 117-32.

Nelson, Lindsey. *Backstage at the Mets.* New York: Viking, 1966.

_____. *Hello Everybody, I'm Lindsey Nelson.* New York: William Morrow, 1985.

Newman, Bruce. "From High above the Western Sideline." *Sports Illustrated* 60, no. 15 (April 9, 1984): 80-90.

Paley, William S. *As It Happened: A Memoir.* Garden City, N.Y.: Doubleday, 1979.

Perella, Paul. "Sports Broadcast." *Atlantic* 176, no. 4 (October 1945): 122-23.

Phillips, H. I. "Hold 'Em Mike." *Saturday Evening Post* 209 (October 1, 1936): 25-26.

Reed, William F. "The Wildcats Come In Loud and Clear." *Sports Illustrated* 52, no. 7 (February 18, 1980): 46.

"Regulation or Strangulation." *Collier's* 128 (November 17, 1951): 86-87.

Reynolds, Quentin. "The Two Lives of Red Barber." *Reader's Digest* 65 (August 1954): 102-6.

"Rookie of the Year." *New York* vol. 18, no. 31 (August 12, 1985): 22.

Schoenstein, Ralph. "Talk Me out of the Ball Game." *Saturday Review* 47 (April 11, 1964): 82-83.

Smith, Curtis. *Voices of The Game: The First Full-Scale Overview of Baseball Broadcasting, 1921 to the Present.* South Bend, Ind.: Diamond Communications, Inc., 1987.

Star, Jack. "Bob Elson, Voice of the White Sox." *Look* 26, no. 10 (May 8, 1962): 64a-64c.

Stockton, J. Roy. "Baseball." In *Sport's Golden Age: A Close-up of the Fabulous Twenties,* edited by Allison Danzig and Peter Brandwein. New York: Harper and Brothers, 1948.

Taafe, William. "The Mouth That Always Roars." *Sports Illustrated* 57, no. 22 (November 22, 1982): 68.

_____. "The Voices from Syracuse." *Sports Illustrated* 60, no. 11 (March 12, 1984): 65.

_____. "Back in the Catbird Seat." *Sports Illustrated* 61, no. 5 (July 23, 1984): 52.

_____. "Baseball's Lovable Shnook." *Sports Illustrated* 61, no. 11 (September 3, 1984): 48.

Tolbert, Frank X. "Dizzy Dean—He's Not So Dumb!" *Saturday Evening Post* 224 (July 14, 1951): 25+.

Towers, Wayne. *World Series Coverage in New York City in the 1920s.* Journalism Monographs, no. 73. Lexington, Ky.: Association for Education in Journalism, 1981.

Voigt, David Quentin. *American Baseball.* Vol. 2. Norman: University of Oklahoma Press, 1970.

Wallace, Francis. "Are the Major Leagues Strangling Baseball?" *Collier's* 127 (March 10, 1951): 18-21ff.

Weiskopf, Herman. "See No Evil, Hear No Evil . . . Ha!" *Sports Illustrated* 37, no. 10 (September 4, 1972): 26-32.

White, J. Andrew. "The First Big Radio Broadcast." *Reader's Digest* 67 (December 1955): 881-85.

"World at Ringside by Proxy." *Literary Digest* 120 (September 28, 1935): 25-26.

7 SHORT WAVES: MISCELLANEOUS SUBJECTS

WOMEN IN RADIO

As is the case in other areas of the literature on broadcasting, much of the work on women in broadcasting emphasizes television broadcasting at the expense of discussion and information on women in radio. Fortunately, there are some exceptions.

No book-length study of the role of women in radio has yet been written. The book most closely associated with the early achievements of women in radio is Judith Cary Waller's *Radio: The Fifth Estate,* published in 1946. This book is important not only because it is a full-length treatment of early radio broadcasting by one of the most important women in broadcasting history but also because it contains a substantial section on women in radio and radio journalism. Several good journal articles and sections of books are available. Among the best historical pieces is Catharine Heinz's "Women Radio Pioneers" in the *Journal of Popular Culture* (Fall 1978), which offers a series of brief, informative anecdotal profiles on Judith Waller, Dorothy Gordon (a singer and later producer and musical director of such programs as CBS's "American School of the Air" and "Children's Corner"), and Edythe J. Meserand (newswoman and journeyman production and promotion executive for WEAF, NBC, and WOR in New York). The brevity of the article belies both its value and the author's considerable legwork in digging up dozens of local clippings and obscure interviews with these legendary women. In another Heinz article, "The Voice of Authority; or, Hurrah for Christine Craft," written for *Feedback*'s special spring 1984 issue on women in broadcasting, the author uses the famous case of a female television anchor allegedly fired for her lack of attractiveness to viewers as a launching point for a history of newswomen in television and radio. One of the more valuable early histories can be found in "The Women's Role in Broadcasting" chapter in E. P. J. Shurick's *The First Quarter-Century of American Broadcasting,* which discusses both early pioneering efforts (particularly those of Waller and Kate Smith) and early programming for women.

The biographies and autobiographies of such major radio personalities as Kate Smith, Jessica Dragonette, and Gertrude Berg provide an enormous amount of information on key women in radio. These works are discussed in the radio music (Smith and Dragonette) and radio drama (Berg) chapters of this volume. A short biographical piece worth noting is Pat Mawer's "Ruth Crane: Early Days in Broadcasting," a chapter in Maurine Beasley and Sheila Silver's anthology *Women in Media: A Documentary Sourcebook.* Mawer's article profiles the career as writer and on-the-air personality of Crane, who worked with WJR (Detroit) and WMAL (Washington, D.C.).

A wonderful article that seeks to assess the general state of women and radio in more recent times (women-oriented programming, radio ownership by women, international efforts to make radio responsive to the feminist movement, and so on) is Anne Karpf's "Women and Radio" in the British journal *Women's Studies International Quarterly* (1980). A fairly recent survey on the issue of women station owners was published by John D. Abel in the spring 1984 issue of *Feedback,* in which information gathered from an FCC Ownership Report was published to show that women are indeed participating in ownership (whether through outright ownership or stockholdings). However, the study would have been far more informative if comparisons with previous years and projections for the future had been included. As women on-the-air personalities increase in number, personality profiles of women radio performers, especially disc jockeys, have begun appearing with increasing frequency in local newspapers and popular magazines.

The field of radio has many areas that cry out for additional research and resource material. Arguably the first among these is the subject of women in radio, which could use much additional work in both scholarly and popular forums.

RADIO ADVERTISING

The act of placing radio advertising into a discrete section is self-defeating because radio advertising is a part of virtually all aspects of radio history, including technology, corporate history, and programming. This truism is reflected in the bibliographical history of the medium. Among the best available sources on radio advertising are works ostensibly on some other aspect of radio or on radio in general. Erik Barnouw's *A History of Broadcasting in the United States,* Eugene Lyons's *David Sarnoff,* Gleason Archer's *History of Radio to 1926,* William Peck Banning's *Commercial Broadcasting Pioneer: The WEAF*

Experiment, 1922-1926, Jim Harmon's *The Great Radio Heroes,* and Fred Allen's *Treadmill to Oblivion* are all cases in point.

Nonetheless, there are several important sources that focus on advertising and sponsorship in radio as their main thrust and, predictably, often yield valuable information on other aspects of radio history. The more comprehensive studies tend to deal with the pretelevision years. The most important book on advertising in the pioneer and network eras is Orrin E. Dunlap, Jr.'s *Radio Advertising,* which was published in 1931. In nearly 400 pages it covers almost every aspect of radio advertising, including economic issues, legal issues, audience research, and comparisons with advertising in print media. Dunlap is the logical starting place for research into radio advertising before the television era. Gleason L. Archer's *Big Business and Radio* treats the rise of radio as a struggle of corporate giants (AT&T, RCA, and others). However, readers should be aware of Archer's friendship with David Sarnoff, who turned over his records to Archer, presumably with the expectation that treatment in this volume would be favorable. (It was.) A wonderful companion to Archer's book is Susan Renee Smulyan's dissertation " 'And Now a Word from Our Sponsors . . .': Commercialization of Broadcast Radio, 1920-1934.'' Smulyan traces the toe-by-toe process by which radio waded into the anguish of deciding to sell airtime to sponsors and walks deftly through the early investment calls, appeals for goodwill donations, proposals for government sponsorship of radio, and so on. The particular value in her work lies in the fact that her narrative has the effect of slowing down time as it persuades us that what is often seen as a hastily arranged shotgun marriage between radio stations and time-buying advertisers was really the end result of much careful planning, trial and error, and a cautious measuring out of options for financing radio. A particularly nice feature of the dissertation is the chapter on sources, which provides a very helpful guide to relevant sources and collections.

An untraditional but arresting source for information on radio advertising is Fred Wakeman's 1946 novel *The Hucksters,* a tale set in the corrupt amoral world of the radio adman. Its success and its impact upon the radio industry at the time are the subjects of an excellent article by Alan Havig: "Frederick Wakeman's *The Hucksters* and the Post-War Debate over Commercial Radio" in *Journal of Broadcasting* (Spring 1984). As Havig reminds us, Wakeman's advocacy for the removal of sponsor control of radio programming, launched from the forum of a popular novel and, in 1947, a popular film, generated intense debate and criticism within the industry. Havig dutifully stops far short of giving Wakeman credit for the eventual reduction of the role of the sponsor in radio programming (many had argued for that position long before Wakeman's novel appeared), but he reasonably credits the novel with enhancing the interest in and the intensity of the discussion.

Other more traditional sources include Elizabeth Heighton and Don Cunningham's *Advertising in the Broadcast Media.* A college text, the book contains a solid chapter on radio advertising through 1946 (as well as a second chapter on advertising in the television age). Erik Barnouw's *The Sponsor,* principally a book on television advertising, offers a superior, scholarly chapter ("Rise") on the evolution of radio advertising. His copious notes on this subject would provide any graduate student with a guidepost to master's or doctoral work in the field of radio advertising. Tony Schwartz's *The Responsive Chord,* an analysis based on communications theory of how broadcast advertising persuades, is both intriguing and persuasive. Schwartz, whose debt to Marshall McLuhan is properly acknowledged, offers the theory that radio listeners "bathe" and "sit in" the sound of radio; they do not merely hear it. Thus, according to Schwartz, the radio listener responds to recall stimuli rather than "name recognition." Schwartz argues that this insight escapes many ineffective radio advertising copywriters and producers. Although Schwartz is theoretical in his approach, he keeps the communications research esoterica to a minimum and renders his highly original and provocative judgments completely accessible to scholars in nontheoretical fields and to lay readers.

Two "adman" biographies are very valuable. Carroll Carroll's widely known *None of Your Business; or, My Life with J. Walter Thompson (Confessions of a Renegade Radio Writer)* reads with all the romping speed of a show-business biography (which in some measure it is) while providing firsthand glimpses into life in one of the major agencies servicing radio during its golden era. Somewhat less important is James Rorty's *Our Masters Voice,* published in 1934. Rorty's book offers both a comprehensive overview of the advertising industry in the 1930s and a brief but surprisingly thorough chapter on radio advertising. His style shifts awkwardly from informality to textbook number crunching, but his ability to synthesize law, censorship, technology, and the idiosyncracies of the early advertising business into a single cogent essay is admirable.

There are some specialized publications on radio advertising that can be helpful to the seeker of hard-line statistical information on the subject. James Duncan, Jr.'s annual *American Radio* and *Duncan's Radio Market Guide* are standard trade sources that analyze stations by the size of their markets and other related data. Hugh Malcolm Belville, Jr.'s *Audience Ratings: Radio, Television, and Cable* devotes two early chapters to radio in which he offers a competent, compressed history and analysis of the standard ratings services (including the early Hooper and Nielsen ratings), explaining the growth of their role and influence over radio advertising and commercialization. The unattributed *Public Sentiment toward Wartime Advertising,* a 1943 study published by the Association of National Advertisers, is the end result of an extensive public opinion survey on how the public felt about the efforts of companies and corporations to help "win the war" through various broadcasting and advertising initiatives. The effort may be more fascinating than the analysis since the methodology for data collection and review cannot be determined clearly from the publication. (Incidentally, the public in general responded favorably to these various initiatives on the part of the companies.)

Various trade and commercial journals, both current and out of print, have focused upon radio advertising. Among the key early publications are *Radio Broadcast* (1920-1930) and *Broadcast Advertising* (1929-1932), which detailed almost every aspect of radio development in the 1920s but concentrated very heavily on sponsorship and ownership matters. *Advertising Age* charted a similar course in the 1930s and 1940s. *Sponsor* (1946-1968) covered radio advertising issues in more recent times.

RELIGIOUS RADIO BROADCASTING

A series of scandals in the late 1980s involving the moral and fiscal responsibility of television ministers and the entry of a television evangelist as a serious and effective candidate into the 1988 Republican presidential race will doubtless stimulate additional scholarship throughout the 1990s in the here-tofore generally small subfield of religious radio broadcasting in America. Although never fully ignored in radio histories and scholarship, it tends to be viewed as an area that has had very little influence in defining either the cultural or the sociological impact of the medium in this country. From the perspective of the student of popular culture, there is some truth in that assertion; the character of American radio would have changed little if religious broadcasting had never aired on it. (The same cannot be said for music, drama, comedy, news and information, or even sports.)

By contrast, in the area of international radio broadcasting there is extensive literature on religious broadcasting in other countries—especially in the third world. Like the missionary educators before them, religious radio broadcasters are often the first to bring both their message and their medium into third world regions. But back home, religious radio is a relatively small if fascinating area.

Of the research literature available, the most common, the most fascinating, and the most useful works tend to be those with biographical information on the charismatic and controversial radio preachers, the predecessors and colleagues of the now-infamous television evangelists. Not surprisingly, a review of some of the literature available on these men teaches us much about their more famous television counterparts, who are very much at the center of contemporary popular culture interests. One sees in the studies of these forefathers the egotism and power that is part of the image and reality of the television minister.

Carl McIntire, a highly contentious, ultraconservative preacher from New Jersey, has been the subject of two doctoral dissertations: one covering his early career (Robert Joseph Mulholland's "Carl McIntire: The Early Radio Years [1932 to 1955]") and one emphasizing his more well known period in the 1960s, when his weekly "Twentieth Century Reformation Hour" fed off the political abundance provided by the cold war, the civil rights movement, and the social agendas of liberals (William Howe Cianci's "Carl McIntire: A Study of His Philosophy and Use of the Mass Media"). Both dissertations are well executed.

They are less insightful than they claim to be when they assess the relationship of McIntire's theology to the medium (the attraction of a charismatic evangelical to a mass medium is almost painfully obvious), but their research (especially Mulholland's) yields some fascinating behind-the-scenes squabbles with CBS, the National Association of Broadcasters, and the Federal Communications Commission. The history of these confrontations, which show McIntire as frequently victorious and never really vanquished, reveal the remarkable degree of power that a single local minister with an adoring radical following can bring to bear on the giants of the broadcast industry.

Charley Orbinson's article "Fighting Bob Schuler: Early Radio Crusader" in *Journal of Broadcasting* (Fall 1977) takes the unusual approach of defending a historically vilified moral radio crusader. Orbinson takes the position that Schuler, whose uncompromising editorials against Los Angeles officials in the 1920s eventually cost him his station, was in fact a victim of the bureaucracy and not a monger of dissent and character assassination. He claims that the 1930 case brought against Schuler by the Federal Radio Commission for intemperate remarks was a landmark case in radio regulation because it allowed the federal regulatory agencies to consider past programming as part of a decision for license renewal. Orbinson challenges persuasively the validity of the FRC ruling that removed Schuler's license. (Usually, historians recounting the warfare between the regulating bodies and the radio ministers try to remain neutral on the issue of license battles, if indeed they can conceal their glee at the setbacks for the ministers—a point Orbinson notes particularly in Schuler's case.) Laments Orbinson, "It is unfortunate that Schuler [occupies] a place of disdain in broadcast history."

Father Coughlin of Detroit and his legendary battles with the National Association of Broadcasters (to say nothing of President Roosevelt) are an essential part of the history of religious radio in the United States. James A. Brown's account of the imbroglio, "Selling Airtime for Controversy: NAB Self-Regulation and Father Coughlin" in *Journal of Broadcasting* (Spring 1980) concisely and articulately recounts the salient details. Shunned by the network after some early bad experiences, Father Coughlin displayed in the 1930s the broadcast minister's unerring gift for creating his own makeshift network. By the beginning of World War II Coughlin was broadcasting anti-Roosevelt and anti-Semitic commentary to a legion of adoring listeners. A fearful NAB, as frightened of external regulation as of Coughlin, adopted codes in response to Coughlin's vitriol. As in the biographies of McIntire and Schuler, Brown allows the power of Coughlin's personality and conviction to come through the piece as the energizing force in the controversy.

In addition to biographical information on famous radio ministers, religious radio attracts all manner of communication theorists and rhetoricians. William M. Clements's "The Rhetoric of the Radio Ministry" in *Journal of American Folklore* (October 1974) takes the delightful approach of analyzing rhetorical devices within radio ministry from the perspective of the oral historian. Arguing that the radio. ministry is often associated with America's folk churches (this is especially true in the South), he demonstrates that it also borrows some of its rhetorical traditions from the folk church. These borrowings range from sermon themes ("sinners must convert and saints must help them") to the role of the audience (audience reciprocity—an active role for the audience in both the radio ministry and the folk church) and delivery style (the chant, apparent in both forms but more subdued on the radio). Clements's tracing of the folk roots of radio ministry is more valuable for its larger conceptual framework than it is for its analysis of particulars. In general, the literature on radio religious broadcasting associates the radio ministry so closely with the sophistication of the broadcast medium that it overlooks its populist foundations. Clement's article provides an important measure of balance.

John H. Court's "Paralinguistic Cues in Religious Broadcasting" in *Journal of Psychological Theology* (Winter 1978) defines two levels of radio communication: verbal (speech) and paralinguistic (voice, quality, pitch, and range). Court emphasizes the paralinguistic dimension of religious broadcasting, grounding his argument in the literature of nonverbal communication rather than communications research in the field of radio. Among his more provocative conclusions are that religious broadcasting can be identified by the casual, "knob-twiddling" listener on vocal characteristics alone, so remarkably unique are they to the domain of the religious broadcaster; that radio ministers actually select a verbal style, often in response to other factors in the broadcast (such as choice of music); and that even experienced radio ministers sound like "media amateurs," and thus a self-imposed amateurism arises as a salient characteristic of the radio ministry. (This point is not unrelated to Clements's discussion of radio ministry and folklore, although Court does not cite Clements.)

Widespread interest in religion and broadcasting has produced several bibliographical sources worth mentioning (although, as is the case with most issues related to broadcasting and mass media, emphasis on television far outweighs the emphasis on radio.) Donald D. Dick published a superior bibliography on the subject of religious broadcasting between 1920 and 1965 in *Journal of Broadcasting* (Summer 1965). A follow-up bibliography is certainly needed. The *Religion Index,* published by the American Theological Library Association, serves as a reader's guide for all matter of publication on religion. Published annually, it contains a generous section on "Mass Media" with a separate (and inevitably smaller) section on radio. Although it is concerned with Mexican radio broadcasting, Gene Fowler and Bill Crawford's *Border Radio: Quacks, Yodelers, Pitchmen, Psychics, and Other Amazing Broadcasters of the American Airwaves* recounts tales of evangelists (as well as a myriad of radio oddballs) who were heard widely in the United States in the 1930s, 1940s and 1950s, owing to Mexican stations' joyous immunity to FCC regulation of wattage power.

ARMED FORCES RADIO

Perhaps the most interesting development of World War II, from radio's standpoint at least, was the creation of the Armed Forces Radio Service (AFRS), the first government-sponsored radio network and the direct ancestor of the Armed Forces network that still broadcasts on shortwave frequencies to American military personnel throughout the world. Not a great deal of information has been published about the AFRS; the only real history seems to be the unpublished dissertation "An Historical Study of the Armed Forces Radio Service to 1946" by Theodore S. Delay, Jr., done at the University of Southern California in 1951. The University of Southern California is the logical place for such a study. Hollywood was the headquarters for the programming and production of AFRS. There it could capitalize upon the wealth of experienced radio actors, writers, and executives who, by the early 1940s, had already begun to migrate to California, leaving New York to serve as the primary advertising and business capital of the industry while the creative and artistic talent enjoyed both the California sunshine and jobs with the movie studios. Information about the AFRS can be culled from a few sources, most notably Roger Burlingame's *Don't Let them Scare You: The Life and Times of Elmer Davis,* a fine biography of the respected news commentator who headed the Office of War Information under Roosevelt and Truman. However, much of what is to be known of this unusual network remains tucked away in moldy, hard-to-get copies of *ARFS Playback,* the weekly newsletter of the network.

BIBLIOGRAPHY FOR SHORT WAVES: MISCELLANEOUS SUBJECTS

Women in Radio

Abel, John D. "Female Ownership of Broadcast Stations." *Feedback* 25, no. 4 (Spring 1984): 15-18.

Berg, Gertrude. *Molly and Me.* New York: McGraw-Hill, 1961.

Dragonette, Jessica. *Faith Is a Song: The Odyssey of an American Artist.* New York: MacKay, 1951.

Heinz, Catharine. "Women Radio Pioneers." *Journal of Popular Culture* 12, no. 2 (Fall 1978): 304-13.

_____. "The Voice of Authority; or, Hurrah for Christine Craft." *Feedback* 25, no. 4 (Spring 1984): 3-6.

Karpf, Anne. "Women and Radio." *Women's Studies International Quarterly* 3 (1980): 41-54.

Mawer, Pat. "Ruth Crane: Early Days in Broadcasting." In *Women in Media: A Documentary Sourcebook,* edited by Maurine Beasley and Sheila Silver, 82-90. Washington, D.C.: Women's Institute for Freedom of the Press, 1977.

Shurick, E. P. J. *The First Quarter-Century of American Broadcasting.* Kansas City, Mo.: Midland Press, 1946.

Smith, Kate. *Living in a Great Big Way.* New York: Blue Ribbon Books, 1938.

Waller, Judith Cary. *Radio: The Fifth Estate.* Boston: Mifflin, 1946.

Radio Advertising

Archer, Gleason L. *Big Business and Radio.* 1939. Reprint. New York: Arno Press, 1971.

Barnouw, Erik. *The Sponsor.* New York: Oxford University Press, 1978.

Beville, Hugh Malcolm, Jr. *Audience Ratings: Radio, Television, and Cable.* Hillsdale, N.J.: Lawrence Erlbaum Associates, 1985.

Carroll, Carroll. *None of Your Business, or, My Life with J. Walter Thompson. (Confessions of a Renegade Radio Writer)* New York: Cowles, 1970.

Duncan, James, Jr. *American Radio.* Kalamazoo, Mich.: James Duncan, 1986.

_____. *Duncan's Radio Market Guide.* Kalamazoo, Mich.: James Duncan, Annual.

Dunlap, Orrin E., Jr. *Radio Advertising.* New York: Harper and Bros., 1931.

Havig, Alan. "Frederick Wakeman's *The Hucksters* and the Post-War Debate over Commercial Radio." *Journal of Broadcasting* 28, (Spring 1984): 187-99.

Heighton, Elizabeth, and Don Cunningham. *Advertising in the Broadcast Media.* Belmont, Calif.: Wadsworth Publishing Co., 1976.

Public Sentiment toward Wartime Advertising. New York: Association of National Advertisers, 1943.

Rorty, James. *Our Master's Voice.* New York: Day, 1934.

Schwartz, Tony. *The Responsive Chord.* Garden City, N.Y.: Anchor, 1973.

Smulyan, Susan Renee. "'And Now a Word from Our Sponsors . . . ': Commercialization of American Broadcast Radio." Ph.D. diss., Yale University, 1985.

Wakeman, Fred. *The Hucksters.* New York: Rinehart and Co., 1946.

Periodicals

Advertising Age, 1930-.
Broadcast Advertising, 1929-1932.
Broadcasting, 1931-.
Radio Broadcast, 1922-1930.
Sponsor, 1946-1968.

Religious Radio Broadcasting

Brown, James A. "Selling Airtime for Controversy: NAB Self-Regulation and Father Coughlin." *Journal of Broadcasting* 24 (Spring 1980): 189-97.

Cianci, William Howe. "Carl McIntire: A Study of His Philosophy and Use of the Mass Media." Ph.D. diss., Ohio State University, 1972.

Clements, William M. "The Rhetoric of the Radio Ministry." *Journal of American Folklore* 87 (October 1974): 318-27.

Court, John H. "Paralinguistic Cues in Religious Broadcasting." *Journal of Psychological Theology* 16 (Winter 1978): 40-45.

Dick, Donald D. "Religious Broadcasting, 1920-1965: A Bibliography." *Journal of Broadcasting* 9 (Summer 1965): 249-79.

Fowler, Gene and Bill Crawford. *Border Radio: Quacks, Yodelers, Pitchmen, Psychics, and Other Amazing Broadcasters of the American Airwaves.* Austin: Texas Monthly Press, 1987.

Mulholland, Robert Joseph. "Carl McIntire: The Early Radio Years (1932 to 1955)."
    Ph.D. diss., Bowling Green State University, 1984.
Orbinson, Charley. "Fighting Bob Schuler: Early Radio Crusader." *Journal of Broad-
    casting* 21 (Fall 1977): 459-72.
Religion Index. Chicago: American Theological Library Association, annual.

Armed Forces Radio

AFRS PLAYBACK, Los Angeles. Weekly, 1944-.
Burlingame, Rober. *Don't Let Them Scare You: The Life and Times of Elmer Davis.*
    Westport, Conn.: Greenwood Press, 1974.
Delay, Theodore, S., Jr. "An Historical Study of the Armed Forces Radio Service to
    1946." Ph.D. diss., University of Southern California, 1951.

8 ORGANIZATIONS, COLLECTIONS, JOURNALS, AND INDEXES

COLLECTIONS: PRINTED AND AUDIO MATERIALS

The number of public and private collections on radio materials is virtually countless. However, researchers in the field of radio should become familiar with some of the more well known and useful collections, which, not surprisingly, tend to be found on both coasts and the northern Midwest.

The Washington, D.C., area may be the single best home for major library and printed archival collections. The Broadcast Pioneers Library (BPL), located in the National Association of Broadcasters building, houses both extensive primary material (industry records and documents as well as a superior clipping file) and an abundance of secondary material. The small staff is highly knowledgeable and very responsive to scholars. Located right up the stairs from BPL is the National Association of Broadcasters, whose own library collection provides a very good overview of important radio sources: major books, publications, reports, and so on. The NAB's library holdings, which are principally concerned with the current state of the broadcast industry, are very strong, and the library staff is extremely helpful.

Another major Washington resource center is the National Museum of American History, whose radio holdings feature the Clark Collection in the museum's Archives Center. The Clark materials are largely technical and economic (company correspondence and memoranda, clippings, and so on) covering the earlier years of radio history.

The Motion Picture, Broadcasting, and Recorded Sound Division of the Library of Congress not only has a wealth of primary and secondary sources, but owing to its location in the new James Madison Building, it offers an environment for research and study that is far more amenable than the forbidding main library building across the street. The manuscript division of the Library of

Congress is also an important source that holds several good collections, most notably the papers of Eric Sevareid.

In nearby Fairfax, Virginia, George Mason University houses the Institute on the Federal Theatre Project and New Deal Culture—the legendary New Deal-era archival collection discovered in an airplane hangar in the early 1970s. Although most widely used by theater historians, it contains a huge collection of scripts and other materials from the Federal Theatre Project's very active radio branch.

In New York the New York Public Library Collection, housed in the Lincoln Center Performing Arts Research Center at Lincoln Center, has a substantial collection of books and periodicals covering all aspects of radioana. Although all three networks have their official libraries and archives located in New York, these are not public research centers in the conventional sense. Some scholars have made use of their sources. However, they are not widely known for providing full and easy access for researchers. One hour away from New York by train is the David Sarnoff Library in Princeton, New Jersey, which is a major source of information on the business aspects of early radio days.

In the Midwest the State Historical Society of Wisconsin's library in Madison is probably the best-known, most widely used, and most beloved resource for radio historians. It has hundreds of collections, small and large, on almost every aspect of radio. While holding some important collections (such as the papers of H. V. Kaltenborn and papers of the National Association of Broadcasters), the society is likely to have some resource material on virtually any subject imaginable in the area of radio as well as film, theater, and advertising.

On the West Coast, some of the larger universities have developed important archives and libraries in radio and related fields. UCLA holds the National Academy of Television Arts and Sciences Television Library, which includes a major Jack Benny collection. The Theater Arts Library at UCLA contains substantial book and periodical holdings related to radio as well as a significant collection of radio scripts.

The North American Radio Archives Library has holdings in Seattle, Washington and the Los Angeles area. Among its holdings are over 15,000 taped radio programs as well as slides, scripts, and books.

Collections of tapes abound throughout the country. Universities, museums, and private collectors have put together formidable collections of old-time radio broadcasts (as well as more current programs), whose popularity seems to be experiencing a promising revivial in the late 1980s. Chicago now boasts a new, major tape collection in the Museum of Broadcast Communications (MBC), which opened in 1987. MBC has thousands of taped radio programs dating from the golden era through more recent vintages that are available for public "hearing." It also contains substantial film and tape holdings for television.

New York houses the famous Museum of Broadcasting (MB), which opened in the 1980s to great and well-deserved fanfare. MB has a substantial Radio Collection of 10,000 cassette tape programs available for listening to the public (it also has 8,000 television programs). This material is not available for duplication or checking out. But MB is marvelous and worth both a scholarly and recreational visit by anyone interested in broadcasting. (MB also has a modest library that has yet to attain the status of a major resource center in and of itself. The museum's main purpose is to function as a public tape and film archive.)

Other institutions with important audio holdings include several already cited for their publication and document holdings (Broadcast Pioneers Library; Motion Picture, Broadcasting, and Recorded Sound Division of the Library of Congress; and the State Historical Society of Wisconsin). There are many other significant general and specialized institutional collections that can provide exceptionally good audio resources for researchers. The National Public Radio Archives in Washington, D.C., is the repository for NPR's program tapes (mostly talk and information) since NPR's 1971 incarnation. The Johnson Collection in the Hall of Records in Dover, Delaware, has a remarkable collection of disc recordings dating back to the 1920s and covering all manner of radio programming and memorabilia. The Pacifica Tape Library of the Pacifica Radio Network in Los Angeles has a collection of material on recent and contemporary issues, including the cold war, the Korean War, and the Vietnam War.

Many major universities with large communications programs have audio archival material. Among the major universities with strong holdings are the UCLA Radio Archives, which has a wide variety of tape holdings including the Jack Benny collection; USC library also has a substantial collection of radio material. The University of San Francisco, which specializes in programming from radio's golden age; the Yale Collection of Historical Sound Recordings, whose concentration in music crosses over into broadcast music; the George Foster Peabody Collection at the University of Georgia, which has particularly strong holdings in public affairs radio programming; Northern Michigan University whose Catalogue of Classical Radio Programs boasts a solid collection of drama and comedy tapes from the golden age; the Radio Program History Collection of Memphis State University, which offers at least one example from almost every program on radio; and the Oral History Collection at Columbia University, which has a selection of interviews with key figures in the history of radio.

ORGANIZATIONS

There are over 200 national and international organizations concerned with some aspect of radio and an even larger number concerned with the area of broadcasting. These include major national professional organizations, fan and hobby groups, unions, legal and political associations, ethnic broadcasting associations, and specialty groups of every conceivable type (and several inconceivable types). Some that have achieved particular stature within the radio field are worthy of special mention. First among unequals, of course, is the National Association of Broadcasters (NAB), the major membership organization of radio and television stations and networks, including producers of programs. Within the industry it is regarded as the most important umbrella organization. Outside of the radio and television industry it is probably best known for its strong lobbying and public relations efforts on behalf of its membership.

Other highly regarded organizations for professionals within the broadcasting field include one of America's most glamorous AFL-CIO labor unions, the American Federation of Television and Radio Artists (AFTRA, formerly the American Federation of Radio Artists), with 66,000 members and thirty-eight locals. AFTRA's periodic labor disputes with networks and producers always make national and international news. Of the several service and advocacy organizations for management, executives, production, and sales people in radio and television, the International Radio and Television Society is widely respected and probably the best known outside of the NAB.

Although its activities have attracted increasing attention in the last few years, American Women in Radio and Television has been representing professional women in the broadcast industry since 1951. It has been highly visible and effective in promoting the cause of women in the broadcast industry through its educational funding, publications, lobbying efforts, and prestigious awards to individuals and institutions.

Historians and scholars should be aware of the Broadcast Pioneers, which is composed of individuals who have served for twenty or more years in radio or television broadcasting. Scholars and teachers within the broadcasting field are represented by the Broadcast Education Association. Affiliated with the National Association of Broadcasters, it is made up of representatives of university and college broadcasting programs. Like most scholars' and teachers' associations, it is largely concerned with curriculum, teaching, and research matters. Scholars interested in radio in the context of popular culture should be familiar with the Popular Culture Association, whose scholarly journal and annual conferences often feature relevant scholarly material on radio.

Countless radio-fan and old-time radio-buff organizations are scattered throughout the North American continent. In their publications and meetings the overlay of nostalgia can be very thick. But as disseminators of valuable information and catalysts for stimulating and promoting interest in popular radio history, they provide a significant service to the field. To take a few examples, SPERDVAC (Society to Preserve and Encourage Radio, Drama, Variety, and Comedy) has a few more members and a little more notoriety than most. Its bouncy monthly newsletter is a potpourri of updates on tape collections and book holdings, schmoozy celebrity interviews, and fan news. Its regular meetings and annual convention succeed in drawing the kind of membership and stars that most fan organizations would find enviable. Somewhat less formally structured but no less enthusiastic is the membership of Friends of Old-Time Radio, which has been holding annual meetings of fans and enthusiasts of the genre since 1976.

JOURNALS AND PERIODICALS

Researchers in radio will find important information not only in the major scholarly publications in the field but also in key out-of-print radio trade journals that contain excellent primary source material. The *Journal of Broadcasting and Electronic Media* (formerly *Journal of Broadcasting*) covers all manner of broadcasting material, from straight historical pieces to survey data and communications theory pieces. It is arguably the premiere academic journal in the field of broadcasting. Other important scholarly journals include *Journalism Review*, whose heavy focus on broadcast journalism often lends itself to important radio journalism pieces, especially scholarly pieces on the history of journalism. The British journal, *Historical Journal of Film, Radio, and Television*, publishes scholarly articles regularly. The fact that it is British should not turn off the scholar interested in American culture; the journal pays close attention to the American scene. *Feedback*, a small academic journal, publishes pieces on various issues related to broadcasting history and education. Articles on radio and early broadcast history appear frequently. Its authors are usually academics writing in a style that is accessible to scholars, laymen, and professionals. *Communication Booknotes* is extremely useful. Begun in 1969 as *Broadcast Bibliophile's Booknotes*, it has continually provided excellent, brief reviews and summaries of broadcasting publications. The widely known *Journal of Popular Culture*, which carries occasional pieces on radio and culture, published a special radio edition in fall 1978 (whose articles have been cited at various points throughout this book). After ten years very little of the material is badly dated, and much holds up well. It is a terrific reader. Scholars should also be aware of the industry's primary trade publication *Broadcasting*, the monthly journal that is closest to being the industry's official voice. *Variety* still covers radio, but the medium competes for space with film, television, and music.

Out-of-print radio trade periodicals are important sources of historical information. Inasmuch as many older university and public libraries still have their original holdings of these publications, they should not be overlooked as potential research sources. In the early 1920s *Wireless Age* and *Radio Broadcast* kept tabs on both technical and industry developments during radio's most frenetic period of growth. *Radio Daily*, although probably harder to find than either *Wireless Age* or *Radio Broadcast*, chronicled the industry's comings and goings both behind the scenes and before the mike during its glory years, 1937-1966. Material related to advertising is abundant in the old issues of the bible of the broadcast advertisers, *Sponsor*, which was published from 1946 to 1968.

INDEXES AND MISCELLANEOUS REFERENCE SOURCES

Radio is a windfall for compilers, indexers, and listmakers, who have contributed a splendid array of reference works to the field. Important indexes and references that are relevant to the subjects of the previous chapters have been included within those discussions. Some additional helpful indexes and references serving specialized needs in the area of radio study are discussed here.

Eleanor Blum's *Basic Books in the Mass Media: An Annotated, Selected Booklist Covering General Communications, Book Publishing, Broadcasting, Editorial Journalism, Film, Magazines, and Advertising* is all that its expansive name implies. It contains a generous selection of entries on broadcasting, many of them dealing with radio exclusively. Blum's skillful annotations enhance the book's considerable quality. Oscar Rose's *Radio Broadcasting and Television: An Annotated Bibliography* concentrates on works produced during the 1930s and 1940s. There are some curious omissions (Rudolf Arnheim's *Radio*) and some whimsical inclusions (novels and plays with radio backgrounds), but the index and subject headings are very useful. William McCavitt's *Radio and Television: A Selected, Annotated Bibliography* is widely respected and justifiably so. His attention to radio material is generous, his selections are sensible, and his brief, thumbnail evaluations tend to be right on the mark.

Those seeking to obtain scripts and tapes might choose to contact collections or organizations mentioned in this chapter. However, there also exist some useful catalog sources for this kind of material. G. Howard Poteet's *Published Radio, Television, and Film Scripts* allots some 120 pages to radio dramas available in printed form, cataloged by title of the program that actually broadcast each play. Michael R. Pitts's *Radio Soundtracks: A Reference Guide,* second edition, updates his 1976 catalog of available audio reproductions of radio programs. Concentrating on the golden age, Pitts presents entries for over 1,000 radio programs plus helpful background on each program, such as cast and broadcast date. Pitts is a highly prolific writer in the area of popular culture and has a good sense of what readers and researchers will want to know. Marietta Chicorel, herself a legend in the index business, has produced a three-volume set entitled *Chicorel Index to the Spoken Arts on Discs, Tapes, and Cassettes.* Her main emphasis is on drama and oratory, but she does include a broad selection of radio programs. Hers is a complicated volume, but it is indispensable (and thus worth the effort required to use it) for students of poetry and drama on radio.

There are several industry directories, past and present, that researchers might find very helpful. *Broadcasting Yearbook* has been published by *Broadcasting* magazine since 1935. It contains various directories of radio stations as well as backgrounds on history of ownership and licensure. Donald G. Godfrey's *A Directory of Broadcast Archives* gives names, addresses, and brief descriptions of various audio collections throughout the country. Although it only appeared from 1937 to 1941, *Variety's Radio Directory* is a uniquely valuable if admittedly obscure source. It is a compendium of information, concerning itself especially with advertisers. What makes this important is that during these years the majority of commercially successful programs were produced entirely by advertising agencies, and thus advertising personnel information is potentially very valuable to students of 1930s radio.

Other major radio reference works include Harrison B. Summers's *A Thirty-Year History of Programs Carried on National Radio Networks in the United States, 1926-1956.* Cited elsewhere in this volume, it is the authoritative index of what shows played when during those crucial thirty radio seasons. Christopher H. Sterling's *Electronic Media: A Guide to Trends in Broadcasting and Newer Technologies, 1920-1983* is, like Summers's work, a compendium of crunched numbers. Sterling covers a wide range of technical and commercial issues, including employment figures in the industry, advertising rates, ownership information, and so on. (Some of the issues raised in this work are fleshed out in Sterling and Sidney W. Head's excellent *Broadcasting in America: A Survey of Electronic Media.*) Every year the National Association of Broadcasters publishes *Dimensions of Radio*, which analyzes station revenues, audience listening patterns, and other information useful to radio management. For those interested in marketing information, *Radio Programming Profile* has for the last twenty years cataloged hour-by-hour analyses of station programming in the top hundred markets. It is written for advertisers but yields a gold mine of hard data for scholars interested in radio audience research. Frank J. Kahn's *Documents of American Broadcasting* is a wonderful compendium of major letters, speeches, and laws that helped shape radio and broadcasting history. It contains the full text of such pivotal works as the Radio Acts of 1912 and 1927, the Biltmore Agreement, Sarnoff's "Radio Music Box" memo to his superiors at American Marconi, and the Fairness Doctrine.

COLLECTIONS AND ORGANIZATIONS: NAMES AND ADDRESSES

Collections

Broadcast Pioneers Library
1771 N St. NW
Washington, DC 20036
202/223-0088

Catalogue of Classical Radio Programs
Speech Department
Northern Michigan University
Marquette, MI 49855
906/227-2046

Clark Collection
National Museum of American History
14th St. and Constitution Ave.
Washington, DC 20560
202/357-3270

David Sarnoff Research Center
P.O. Box CN5300
Princeton, NJ 08543-5300
609/734-2000

George Foster Peabody Collection
School of Journalism and Mass Communications
University of Georgia
Athens, GA 30602
404/542-3785

Institute on the Federal Theatre Project and New Deal Culture
407A Humanities 1
George Mason University
Fairfax, VA 22030
703/323-2546

Johnson Collection
Division of Historical and Cultural Affairs
Bureau of Museums and Historic Sites
Hall of Records
Dover, 19901
302/736-5316

Library of Congress
Motion Picture, Broadcasting, and Recorded Sound Division
Thomas Jefferson Bldg., Room 1053
Second St. and Independence Ave. SE
Washington, DC 20540
202/287-5840

Lincoln Center Performing Arts Research Center
111 Amsterdam Ave.
New York, NY 10023
212/870-1630

Mass Media Studies Program
University of San Francisco
2130 Fulton St.
San Francisco, CA 94117
415/666-6206

Museum of Broadcast Communications
800 S. Wells St.
Chicago, IL 60607
312/987-1500

Museum of Broadcasting
One E. 53rd St.
New York, NY 10022
212/752-7684

National Association of Broadcasters
1771 N St. NW
Washington, DC 20036
202/429-5300

National Public Radio Library and Audio Archive
National Public Radio
2025 M St. NW
Washington, DC 20036
202/822-2060

North American Radio Archives
5510 Corteen Pl. #7
North Hollywood, CA 91607
Contact: Ronald Staley

Oral History Collection
Butler Library
Columbia University
New York, NY 10027
212/280-1754

Pacifica Tape Library
Pacifica Radio Network
5316 Venice Blvd.
Los Angeles, CA 90019
213/931-1625

Radio Program History Collection
Memphis State University
Department of Theatre & CMU Arts
Memphis, TN 38152
901/454-2001

State Historical Society of Wisconsin
816 State St.
Madison, WI 53706
608/262-3266

UCLA Radio Archives
1015 N. Cahuenga Blvd.
Hollywood, CA 90038
213/462-4921

University of Southern California Library
Archives of Performing Arts
Los Angeles, CA 90007
213/743-6058

Yale Collection of Historical Sound Recordings
Sterling Memorial Library
Box 1603A Yale Station
New Haven, CT 06520
203/432-1795

Donald G. Godfrey's *A Directory of Broadcast Archives* (Washington, D.C.: Broadcast Education Association, 1983) was very helpful in the preparation of the discussion and listing of collections. It is highly recommended for anyone seeking out audio collections and radio archives because it covers nicely institutional as well as individual collections.

Organizations

American Federation of Television and Radio Artists
260 Madison Ave.
New York, NY 10016
Contact: John C. Hall, Jr.

American Women in Radio and Television
1101 Connecticut Ave. NW, Suite 700
Washington, DC 20036
Contact; Carolyn M. Del Polito

Broadcast Education Association
1771 N St. NW
Washington, DC 20036
Contact: Harold Niven

Broadcast Pioneers
320 W. 57th St.
New York, NY 10019
Contact: Ed DeGray

Friends of Old Time Radio
P.O. Box 4321
Hamden, CT 06514
Contact: Jay Hickerson

International Radio and Television Society
420 Lexington Ave.
New York, NY 10170
Contact: Stephen Labunski

National Association of Broadcasters
1771 N St. NW
Washington, DC 20036
Contact: Edward O. Fritts

Popular Culture Association
Popular Culture Center
Bowling Green University
Bowling Green, OH 43403
Contact: Ray B. Browne

Society to Preserve and Encourage Radio Drama, Variety, and Comedy
P.O. Box 1587
Hollywood, CA 90078

The information on organizations is compiled in part from information available in the *Encyclopedia of Associations,* 22nd edition, 1988. Its comprehensive index of organizations by subject matter makes it indispensable for individuals looking for highly specialized organizations. It is a standard reference work, and an invaluable one, in public and university libraries.

BIBLIOGRAPHY FOR JOURNALS AND INDEXES

Journals and Periodicals

Broadcasting. Washington, D.C., 1931-.
Communication Booknotes. Washington, D.C., 1982-.
Feedback. Athens, Ga., 1960-.
Historical Journal of Film, Radio, and Television. Oxford, England, 1980-.
Journal of Broadcasting and Electronic Media (formerly *Journal of Broadcasting*).
    Washington, D.C., 1956-.
Journal of Popular Culture. Bowling Green, Ohio, 1966-.
Journalism Review. Missoula, Mont., 1958-.
Radio Broadcast. Garden City, N.Y., 1922-1930.
Radio Daily. New York, 1937-1966.
Sponsor. New York, 1946-1968.
Variety. New York, 1905-.
Wireless Age. New York, 1922-1928.

Indexes and Other References

Blum, Eleanor. *Basic Books in the Mass Media: An Annotated, Selected Booklist Covering
    General Communications, Book Publishing, Broadcasting, Editorial Journalism,
    Film, Magazines* and *Advertising.* Urbana: University of Illinois Press, 1980.
Broadcasting Yearbook. Washington, D.C.: Broadcasting Publications, annual.
Chicorel, Marietta, ed. *Chicorel Index to the Spoken Arts on Discs, Tapes, and Cassettes.*
    3 vols. Chicorel Index Series, vols. 7, 7a, and 7b. New York: Chicorel Library
    Publishing Corporation, 1973-1974.
Dimensions of Radio. Washington, D.C.: National Association of Broadcasters, annual.
Godfrey, Donald G. *A Directory of Broadcast Archives.* Washington, D.C.: Broadcast
    Education Association, 1983.
Head, Sydney W., and Christopher H. Sterling. *Broadcasting in America: A Survey of
    Electronic Media.* 5th ed. Boston: Houghton Mifflin, 1987.
Kahn, Frank J., ed. *Documents of American Broadcasting.* 3rd ed. Englewood Cliffs,
    N.J.: Prentice-Hall, 1978.
McCavitt, William. *Radio and Television: A Selected, Annotated Bibliography.*
    Metuchen, N.J.: Scarecrow Press, 1978.
Pitts, Michael R. *Radio Soundtracks: A Reference Guide.* 2nd ed. Metuchen, N.J.: Scare-
    crow Press, 1986.
Poteet, G. Howard. *Published Radio, Television, and Film Scripts.* Troy, N.Y.:
    Whitston, 1975.
Radio Directory. Edgar Grunwald, ed. Hollywood, Calif.: *Variety,* annual, 1937-1941.
Radio Programming Profile. Glen Head, N.Y.: BF Communications, annual, 1967-.
Rose, Oscar. *Radio Broadcasting and Television: An Annotated Bibliography.* New York:
    Wilson, 1947.
Sterling, Christopher H. *Electronic Media: A Guide to Trends in Broadcasting and Newer
    Technologies, 1920-1983.* Westport, Conn.: Praeger, 1984.
Summers, Harrison B. *A Thirty-Year History of Programs Carried on National Radio
    Networks in the United States, 1925-1956.* Columbus: Ohio State University Press,
    1958. Reprint. New York: Arno Press and the New York Times, 1971.

INDEX

About the Author

THOMAS ALLEN GREENFIELD is Professor of English and Dean of the College of Arts and Sciences at Bellarmine College, Louisville, Kentucky. He is a member of the national board of the Federation of State Humanities Councils. Greenfield's first book, *Work and the Work Ethic in American Drama, 1920-1970*, was published in 1982.